THE ROAD TAKEN

*How to Dream, Plan, and Live Your
Family Adventure Abroad*

MICHELLE DAMIANI

with contributions from

JOHN AHERN	JERRY JONES
ELIZABETH ANCELL	KIRSTY LARMOUR
ANDREA CAMEROTA	TANIA LANDIN
CANADA-TO-FRANCE TRAVEL BLOG	LEWIS FAMILY
HEATHER CARLSON	GABRIELLA LINDSAY
KRISTIN CLARENS	JENNIFER MASSARO
LISA COLE	NITSA OLIVADATI
KATE COLLIER	AMANDA PONZIO-MOUTTAKI
NICOLAS DAMIANI	ALLYSON SHAMES
ESTELLE DEL PORTO	ALLISON SHERMAN
JULIE DESPAIN	ALISHA STAMP
CHERYL FALCONER	M'KENZIE TILLOTSON
SARAH BRINGHURST FAMILIA	ASTRID VINJE
RACHEL GERSON	HEIDI WAGONER
NELL GODDIN	SARA WARDEN
MARIE FOX-EDGAR	NICA WATERS
SUSAN HARWOOD	MELISSA WIRINGI
NAOMI HATTAWAY	STEPHANIE YODER

RIALTO
PRESS

THE ROAD TAKEN

How to Dream, Plan, and Live
Your Family Adventure Abroad

To David, who gave me the idea.

*And for my mother, who taught me
that an idea is an opportunity.*

CONTENTS

LIVING

COMING HOME

I shall be telling this with a sigh

Somewhere ages and ages hence:

Two roads diverged in a wood, and I—

I took the one less traveled by,

And that has made all the difference.

— ROBERT FROST

.

INTRODUCTION

In the summer of 2012, my husband and I moved to an Italian hill town with our three children and two cats. That sentence reads like the beginning of a story, but absent are the chapters that prefaced that turning point in our lives. From nurturing the germ of the idea to deciding where to live to saving money to getting a visa, the prologue to our move was rife with confusion and obstacles.

I never considered that our prologue would be of interest to anyone, until I wrote a book about our year abroad and the questions started rolling in. How did we find Spello? How did we find an apartment? How did we choose a school? How did our kids learn the language? How did we meet those endearing locals?

It was a challenge to respond to readers because I couldn't in good conscience tell them how to mimic our experience. Our experience was special precisely because it was ours, and we made it from scratch. If we had followed someone else's blueprint, we would have built somebody else's house. I didn't want to dissuade anyone from reaching for a family adventure, but at the same time, I wanted people to see beyond the rosy streets of Spello to design their own dream.

Right around then, my mentor Dave told me I needed to write a how-to book about moving abroad. As I was telling him about how I wanted to help people figure out their own path, it dawned on me that if I wrote a book that included various voices, it might inspire readers to reach beyond my story, or any one story, and instead realize that the possibilities were endless. Maybe by breaking down the conceptions of what mainstream society expects of families, I could empower parents to write their own story.

The Road Taken was born.

Via social connections (virtual and actual), I sought out families from different countries who had different adventures for different amounts of time. Thus, in this book you will read about a family that settled in Morocco for seven years and another that currently lives there. You will read about families that use travel as their children's prime teacher by worldschooling, others that enrolled their children in International Schools, and some that utilized the local public or private schools. You will read about a cross-generational family that settled on Italy's eastern edge and a family with four teen daughters that backpacked around the world. You will read about families that sailed through oceans and families that RVed through Europe.

The Road Taken is divided into the sections *Dream, Plan, Live,* and *Coming Home.* Each section is further divided into chapters. For each chapter, I'll tell my story, then share a contributor essay on the topic, followed by passages from fellow travelers to flesh out the details and demonstrate the variety of possible approaches. For example, in the "Working Abroad" chapter of the *Planning* section, I offer information on how to create revenue while living overseas. Then Gabriella will share her experience with creating businesses that support her family's life in Mexico. After that, you'll read passages from contributors relaying their stories of funding their journeys. My goal here is to illustrate that there isn't one right way to go about this process, so you can give your own ideas wing.

If you are fascinated by a contributor's story, I encourage you to flip to the Appendix where I've included biographies of all our fellow adventurers. Some chose to be anonymous and use a pseudonym or their blog name in lieu of their actual name, but all of them have a blurb for you to learn more.

It's true, there are other books out there about how to move abroad. Most of them are specific to a particular destination and are not geared towards families. Those books presuppose that you already know what you want to do for your adventure. In *The Road Taken*, we welcome readers who crave ideas for possible adventures as well as those who already have their visa paperwork completed.

While we will offer you a wealth of practical information, our main goal is to give you the confidence you need to blaze your path. Through my career as a clinical psychologist working with families and children, I've developed a way of approaching both joy and suffering that I believe can be of help for families contemplating a leap. Because as exciting as that leap is, it will inevitably include its challenges. I want you armed with strategies for how to approach resistance, how to listen to your children without sagging under the weight of their fear, how to be mindful of the changes you can expect in your family, how to keep a sense of wonder and perspective.

The road lies open ahead, so put on your dreaming hat and buckle up. I can't wait to see where your adventure takes you.

PART ONE

DREAMING

1

DECIDING TO GO

How do you decide to make the leap into the arms of a family adventure? If you're waiting for an invitation from the universe, chances are you'll be waiting until you hit senility and can hallucinate that golden ticket. No, the decision to go seems to be equal parts desire, timing, openness, honesty, and daring. It's a kind of magic really, which explains why my favorite part of listening to expat stories is the retelling of this moment in time. Expats get a misty look in their eye, some details of that moment are oddly hazy, while others are in sharp relief.

When I asked contributors about the moment when flirting with dreaming became dancing with dreaming, they often spoke of a defining moment, but from those that went into greater detail, it's clear to me that the seeds for this adventure were sown long before.

The stirrings of my own desire to create a different life likely began *in utero*, as I was born in Panama to a French mother and a father who grew up on the US-Mexico border. But in more conscious terms, my wanderlove teed off with my taking a semester off of college to backpack through Europe. The trip was pivotal in all the ways one imagines—I lived on $20 USD per day, I became self-reliant, I practiced flexibility, and I met fascinating people.

When I was in the Cinque Terre (a totally different scene 30 years ago, before Rick Steves exposed its charm), I glommed on to a group of Australian women. In my eyes, they were Amazons. They told me that my country was going to hell in a hand basket, and I cheerfully agreed. They mocked me for my inability to use Celsius, and I chuckled warmly. They offered their Vegemite, and I convinced myself it was manna from heaven.

One day, we hiked to a secluded beach for the day. By the time the sun was thinking about setting, we looked up at the peachy clouds framing the hill we'd have to clamber back up and decided we wanted none of it. An abandoned train tunnel beckoned—nice and flat, and sure to lead where we were going. It was the kind of foolish decision that marks the youthful backpacking experience—like taking strangers up on their offer to go to a Peter Gabriel concert together because they seemed to enjoy the Black Forest cake in Salzburg as much as you do, or obligingly sharing your personal details and itinerary with a stranger in the train line in Paris who ends up sneaking into your compartment through a window, or yelling the few words of German you know at a drug peddler in Lisbon so that he stops following you while boasting about his wares in English (yes, these all happened to me).

In any case, we shrugged, somebody got out their "torch," and we plunged into pressing blackness. Suddenly unsure, we found ourselves whispering. Was there an end to this darkness? The track appeared unused, but could a train be even now hurling towards us? Our ears stretched, our eyes stretched. Suddenly, the woman behind me began to sing.

Not just some ditty or commercial jingle.

No, she sang an aria. An aria that filled the tunnel, redoubling the sweetness of her voice. We lifted our shoulders and strengthened our steps until we turned the corner and discovered light.

Turns out she was an opera singer in Sydney.

That evening, over a splurge of pasta slick with pesto and a crisp white wine, the Aussies told me that taking a year off of life is completely expected in Australia. Everyone goes on the "dole" at some point or another. The government essentially pays for people to take that time off. They were using it to travel.

Wow.

A country that valued widening horizons so much that people are allowed, nay, *encouraged* to pack their bags and stamp their passport.

The idea dropped and settled in my brain.

I thought, I'd really like to take a year to travel someday.

But then I went to graduate school and got married and had three children, and it sort of seemed like someone else's dream.

I spent years convincing myself that the desire to live abroad was a stupid one. I would flip through high school and college "where are they now" books (in the days before Facebook, if anyone can quite remember that) and search for people who had lived abroad. When I found stories of former classmates who had lived the life I'd once envisioned, I told myself that they probably had a rubbish time. They undoubtedly had medical horrors and divorces and no sense of identity.

As hard as I tried to bat the notion away, it kept flicking back to the edges of my consciousness—a sparkly ball the kitten in me desperately wanted permission to chase. My husband, Keith, and I would talk about moving abroad for a spell, then drop it and move on.

A few months after Gabe, our third child, was born, Keith and I celebrated our anniversary with an evening out. We toasted each other with glasses of *prosecco* and gazed out over the rolling Virginia hills. I bit my lip and asked if he remembered the dream we'd had years before of living abroad. He said yes. I'm not sure if I even uttered the next words aloud, but suddenly we were speaking the language of dreams. Tentatively at first, and then with increasing excitement and wonder. Could we do this? With children? Was it possible?

By the time we'd finished dinner and drained the last of the Italian red, we had a rough plan.

Five years.

We'd go in five years.

We'd live off Keith's income so we could put mine in savings. We'd save and save. We would do it. Gabe would be in kindergarten, Siena would be in fifth grade, and Nicolas in ninth, but with his September birthday he was on the young side for his grade, and we could likely opt to put him in his final year of middle school.

A lot happened between the time we strolled starry-eyed out of that restaurant and five years later when we stepped into our new home in Spello, Italy. I've lost track of the times I was sure Italy would never happen. Or the number of times I complained about our restricted lifestyle, and doubted it was worth it. And there were plenty of bleak moments when I convinced myself Italy was a pipe dream; growing up meant releasing pipe dreams and settling into lives of convenience meals and back-to-school nights.

But we did it.

You can, too. Here are stories of other families, just like you, and how they decided to take the plunge.

The Life of Franki

JOHN'S STORY

I t had always been a dream of mine to roam around Europe in an old VW combi. Time, marriage, job, and kids took over, and at some point, I gave up on that quest. Then one day, in a work meeting, it hit me like a face-slap. My health was shot, my work had become my social life, I was away for five months a year, and my kids had turned four and two and I'd barely noticed. Most of all, I wondered what happened to that guy who once rode on bus rooftops across Africa, stowed away on a cargo plane over the Amazon. What happened to the guy who once vowed to live a life of adventure, yet now was chained to its treadmill? As soon as that meeting was over, I raced home and sprang it on my wife that we should re-spark our travel dreams and take off, kids'n'all. We jumped on the idea before logic got in the way.

Our goal was to reconnect as a family by wandering through Europe. Our first step was purchasing a vehicle; after that, we'd work out the path as we went. The wine-induced day we pressed "send" on the computer to whiz twenty grand over the 'net to Holland to buy an old seven-berth Fiat Frankia motorhome was both terrifying and exulting. Affectionately dubbing our new home "Franki," we took off, aimlessly, with no real plan, eventually hacking our way through 30 countries. Through East and West Europe, to the Arctic Circle, Morocco, Turkey, and back, we rolled along for 40,000 kilometers.

The first four weeks were tough, like a breaking-in period. We'd gone from a big house where everyone had their own room to suddenly being wedged together in this rolling can on wheels where we all ate, slept, and peed. Personal space became a decadence from a previous era, and this took some serious adjustment. We got through by sheer perseverance, some selective time-out, plus the fact that we'd bought the machine and had no other choice. By week three, I would have gratefully pulled out. By week five, we discovered a whole new groove and the trip surged from there. For anyone who asks, I say, "Hang-in; it gets better!"

Our two kids were under five when we set off, so they were still waking in the night and keeping us alert with their not-so-endearing squeals. The upside of their young age was that they happily had no input into our itinerary. They were more interested in playgrounds, gelato, and their bunk bed "cubby-houses" than the great cities of Europe.

To make the voyage easier on the kids, we dedicated ourselves to slow travel. We had entire days of "nothing," in which they could chill. We routinely took long morning, afternoon, and tea breaks while on the road, and while we made the decision to slow travel for them, it became an unforeseen blessing for all of us, as we immersed ourselves in our experience.

The utter freedom of the road meant we were like cats chasing a light, bounding off to anywhere that seemed of interest, with no set plan, almost on a daily basis. We traveled old school, without Internet, carrying Europe-wide road maps, a Lonely Planet guide book, and a camping guide to get around. Whipping into tourist information offices soon after entering each country provided additional details on new sights and camping spots. East Europe and North Africa in particular were constantly evolving, and our guide books were out of date within six months.

It's funny how thoroughly we grew into our new life. Franki broke down in Croatia, and while she was being fixed, we moved into a cheap one-bedroom flat. On entering the apartment, after months in a camper, I instantly hugged the full-sized fridge as though it was a long-lost lover. We watched TV obsessively, cooked chicken in an oven because we could, and had multiple hot showers—all extravagances not available in the RV.

Partway through our apartment vacation, my son Callum approached my wife, Mandy, and asked, "Mummy, when are we going home?" Mandy and I were instantly terrified he was homesick for material stuff. Just as we thought our whole trip was about to crumble, he added, "When do we go home to Franki?"

For our kids, home was no longer a place of bricks and mortar and all the things we owned, but in our van, where we were together.

We met a lot of older people on the road, "grey nomads," who continually repeated a similar story: Their great regret was that they worked so hard during their kids' early years, often hardly seeing them, and now that they had the bounty of time, their kids were gone. If they could change one thing, they would have restructured their lives to spend time with their children.

This was my wife's and my greatest mutual takeaway from our journey, and it became our new challenge when we returned to the "real world." I never wanted to forget the feeling of lying in the sand of the Sahara Desert at night, my kids making sand angels beside me. In that moment,

I realized that I had once been an absent father and was now connected with my children beyond my wildest aspirations.

We returned with a committed vision to change how we lived together as a family—trying to harness the connectedness we had achieved in "the life of Franki." Putting that into action, however, was a challenge, when jobs and bills and schooling entered the equation. So, we did the only thing possible—we went on another road trip, this time to devise a plan for how we wanted to live our lives, and how jobs and kids would sit within that, not the other way around.

The radical changes we subsequently made wrenched us away from our previous life. We sold our house and downsized to wipe out our mortgage, ensuring we would no longer be chained to big jobs to survive. Our year in Franki taught us that simple living was achievable, if we were willing to fight for it. We bought our freedom from the rat race and haven't looked back.

When It's Time

CONTRIBUTORS' STORIES

HEATHER · LIVED IN ITALY FOR TWO YEARS

I grew up in the Midwest, dreaming of travel. I collected maps and read as many travelogues as I could get my hands on. I obsessed about walking through Florence, dreamed of living in Boston, imagined visiting the Rocky Mountains with my future family of eight. But my dad had his own business and money was always tight, so we never even took a family vacation until I was in college.

When I got married, my husband, Chris, and I discussed visiting

Europe. But with having kids and paying off school loans, we didn't make a plan, and the dream languished. Then, ten years ago, Chris flew to Belgium for work, and I tagged along so we could take a detour and finally get to Italy.

Over the years, we returned to Italy several times, our love for it growing with each visit. Back in Idaho, I was working for a radio station and getting burned out. I longed for a change. Then one day, Chris came home and asked me how I felt about moving to Milan for two to three years. I didn't even hesitate. It was an immediate HECK YES! He had waited until it was a sure thing before telling me since he realized that once I knew, I would be in planning mode 24/7. He was right.

CANADA-TO-FRANCE · LIVES IN FRANCE

We always dreamed of living abroad, probably a side effect of watching too many episodes of *House Hunters International*. My husband and I both work from home, so we can work from anywhere, but we assumed we couldn't follow our dream until our daughter went to University. Then Easter 2015, while enjoying a family vacation in Cuba, we met a family volunteering their way through the country. They had sold everything, put everything on hold to commit to a one-year journey with their 12-year-old daughter. Their story sparked our interest, and we told them about our idea of moving abroad. They vigorously encouraged us to do it NOW— forget about later, life is too short, and moving abroad would give our daughter an invaluable experience. Since we had time on our hands as we sipped mojitos at the pool bar, my husband and I toyed with possibilities. We had a busy life in Canada with a house in the suburbs and a cottage on a ski hill—could we give it up? We discussed how we could do it, and also where we could go. My husband suggested France. Since I am French and my daughter went to a French-speaking school, the language transition wouldn't be so difficult...and from there, we had a plan!

NICA · SAILED THE CARIBBEAN

On our fifteenth wedding anniversary, Jeremy and I went out for dinner. The conversation started with "Hey, let's get an air conditioner for Calypso since all we're doing with the boat is sleeping aboard at the dock, and summer on the Chesapeake is hot hot hot hot." By the time dinner was over, we were leaving for the Bahamas in nine months. We changed the wording from "Why should we?" to "Why NOT?" and that forced us to consider all the obstacles differently. House? Rent it. School? Homeschool. Jobs? Quit. We already had a boat, and already knew what would be required for an extended sail. I had recently told my boss I wasn't coming back the next year, so it was only a matter of Jeremy being confident he could reenter the workplace on our return. Really, it was more a matter of realizing that we were ready for a change, and the uncertainties of heading off were less scary than just staying put.

TANIA · ROAD-TRIPPING THROUGH EUROPE

We traveled with our three daughters quite a bit while my husband, Matt, was working in Europe for the US State Department. But we dreamed of someday taking an entire year to travel with our girls. After moving back to the States, we decided it was time to take that gap year. Matt needed a career change, and we were eager to start our own business.

We had decided to combine our passion for travel and our passion for storytelling to create a company that tells stories to teach kids about other cultures and countries. We called it *Around the World Stories*.

We started planning for the trip about a year before leaving. We turned our bedroom into a planning room, with maps hanging everywhere. We had huge sheets of paper with endless to-do lists hanging around the house—everything from destination ideas to notes about visas to picking the proper shoes for everyone. We knew we'd have to be pretty lean, which was not easy. To top everything off, we'd welcomed a dog into our family, and there was no way we were going without her.

We decided on thirteen countries to visit and then planned around various factors like weather, festivals, and seasonal activities like skiing in the Alps and biking along the Danube. Our general plan was to spend about one month in each country—homeschooling the kids and working at the same time. We wanted to grow closer as a family by experiencing travel and learning together.

We weren't ready in many ways, but I don't think one can ever be truly ready.

NELL · LIVED IN FRANCE FOR ONE YEAR

I grew up in Richmond, Virginia, which in the 60s was not the hip city it is now but a deeply provincial Southern backwater. In 1971, my mother took our family on a trip to France and Italy. I was eleven and had never tasted good bread before, never eaten a fresh cherry, never seen women with unshaved legs. The world opened up with a violent, ecstatic CRACK! and my relationship to my country (and myself) changed forever. In some deep way, I was home. I found myself returning to Europe again and again. I always ended a vacation vowing I'd one day live in Europe. I wanted to see if the connection I felt was a shallow one, just about the croissants. Or something bigger.

Once I had children, I was filled with a desire to give them the best of my own childhood. That trip to Europe I took as a child was tops on my list. So I started travel-scheming when they were newborns. We took two summer trips to France when they were toddlers (easier than it sounds!). Finally I decided it was time to take the leap.

I didn't bother about the *where* too much. I knew there were many right answers. I chose France over Italy simply because I kinda-sorta spoke French, and I had heard that French schools were better. But doubtless Italy would have been equally glorious—there are so many right places, and luck is certainly part of the equation.

ASTRID · PREPARING TO WORLDSCHOOL

We talked about slow-traveling for several years. Even so, the idea didn't evolve into an actual plan until we attended the Family Adventure Summit in Penticton, British Colombia in September 2017. At the summit, we met families that were actually doing long-term slow travel, and we decided to commit to making this lifestyle our reality. When we returned to Seattle, we picked July 2018 as our take off date.

We are planning to do a gap-year style trip, where we spend an extended amount of time in different locations, but eventually intend to return to the US. So far, we have plans to stay in Costa Rica, Mexico, and Indonesia. We plan to rent apartments and live like the locals. My husband will primarily be working, and I plan on doing some consulting work while we worldschool our kids.

NAOMI · LIVED IN INDIA AND SINGAPORE FOR FOUR YEARS

I was born in Nebraska and lived my early childhood days in a blip of a town surrounded by cornfields and rolling hills. Our idea of adventure was big and exciting, but it was always contained in the expanse of how far we could explore before being called home for dinner.

As adults, my husband and I moved to Ohio with our three children. I suffered quite a bit from the long winters, and grew increasingly depressed, unhappy, and lethargic. One day my husband came home and asked what I thought about moving to India for eight to ten years. It sounded the opposite from the gray and dreary Cleveland days, so I said, "Why not? I'm up for anything!"

My husband solidified his employment a few weeks later, and I immediately started planning. We brought home armfuls of library books, and I started researching life in India. For three months after he left, I solo-parented our 3-, 6-, and 14-year old children, while preparing to sell our home and move our entire existence across the ocean. In retrospect that to-do list seems crazy, but it shows it can be done!

SARA · LIVED IN MOROCCO FOR SEVEN YEARS

Pre-family, I was a professional dancer. I always loved the adventure of finding my way around new cities, discovering my new grocery store and gym, and experiencing what the city had to offer. When I was 23, I was hired by the Chinese Government to teach musical theatre dance in Beijing. I loved every moment of it.

Once I met my husband, traveling moved to the back burner as we headed into a direction of "responsibility" and "stability." We were buying an apartment and planting roots. Travel seemed frivolous. We had traveled to Europe when we got engaged and again for our honeymoon, and we always said, "Wouldn't it be great to live abroad?!" But we never knew how that would work out.

We didn't plan on turning our lives upside down. But when my husband received a job offer in Morocco, we went from digging into our careers to researching what language Moroccans speak. Two weeks after we accepted the offer, we had sold our apartment and most of our belongings and were living in Morocco with a toddler and baby.

Because we were open to the idea of living abroad, we recognized the open door and flung ourselves through it. Over time, I've watched friends get job offers that include travel and heard them explain how they couldn't accept them, often due to fears or notions of what determines the "right" job. We refused to limit ourselves in this way. Instead, we saw the opportunity like winning the lottery, a chance to turn everything we knew on its side and get a taste of the high we felt on our previous travels. We reasoned that the kids were young enough that there was no risk to their education. Even if it was terrible, we'd just move back to the States and it would still have been a life-changing experience. For that reason we had to do it.

2

YOUR CHILD'S RESPONSE

Kids will exhibit a variety of responses when you tell them the family is going to up sticks. It's important to remember that—like any aspect of childrearing—nothing lasts. Travel enthusiasm can wax and wane, so don't get wrapped up in having your children's opinion define your reality. Just because they are reluctant to go doesn't mean they have secret information that it's a bad idea. And just because they are enthusiastic doesn't mean it's going to be nonstop ponies and cupcakes with rainbow sprinkles.

In addition, if you'll allow me to put on my child psychologist hat for a moment, when you tell your children they are going to move abroad, that's a whole lot to process. Children just don't have what it takes to quickly assimilate such a big piece of news. So even if they react with joy or horror, they are likely to go right back to playing with their Legos. That doesn't mean they don't care or that they've experienced short-term memory loss. Rather, it means they are shelving the news to process in digestible chunks. The next day, when your son is in the bath, he may ask, apropos of nothing, "Who will be sleeping in my bed when I'm gone?" Or your daughter may pipe up from the backseat, "Will I get to eat Chinese food every day in China?"

There isn't a right way to process; each child will do it differently. Your job is to be matter-of-fact and treat all their questions, concerns, and anticipations as if they are important, while not getting attached to them as being prophetic or durable. So give them space to talk and feel. Don't tell them not to be nervous. Nobody ever changed his feelings on being commanded to. Those feelings just go underground. If they confess that they are scared to go to school with people who don't speak English, tell them, "Of course you are. It's a scary thing until you get used to it." If they say they can't possibly leave their best friend behind, assure them that leaving is always difficult. Don't cheerlead, or wheedle them with promises of daily gelato, or make it okay for them. They'll make it okay for themselves, given time and space to do so. Simply reassure them that their feelings are normal and a natural response to a big adjustment, that you are glad they are expressing themselves, and that you trust them to deal with the hard stuff, because they always do.

Listen, I'm not going to sugar-coat this for you: There will likely be times when the transition is hard on your children. They'll need you as a soft place to land. So starting now, be that. Hear them and acknowledge their feelings as valid. That way they'll go into the adventure knowing that when the chips are down, they can rely on you for support.

Now, you may not ask your kids for their opinion, but understand their limitations. It's important to not think of this as "obstructing your vision" but rather "opening your focus." I remember our first trip to Rome with two children. We were spending so much time on playgrounds, and I had the thought (a dangerous one, to be sure), "What would we be doing right now if we didn't have kids?" But quickly images of those leisurely strolls through museums became blurred with the certainty that this experience was not worse, just different, and in some ways richer. We were surrounded by Roman families, the tang of Italian was all around us, we traveled more slowly, more deliberately, we stopped to wonder at the most minor of rocks at the Forum. Children change the way we travel, children change the way we live, and that can be a good thing.

This is all to say, take your children's reactions to the idea of this adventure with a grain of salt. And a few rainbow sprinkles.

It's a Family Adventure

TANIA'S STORY

I n our pre-children lives, traveling abroad was relatively easy. We watched movies on the flight, read books on the beach, met locals in pubs, and spontaneously explored our surroundings. But eighteen years and three kids later, we knew things were going to be different. There would be a whole new set of priorities, considerations, and challenges, but also countless memories filled with more joy than we could have envisioned as young travelers.

Before we began planning the destinations for our road trip through Europe, we had to discuss what to pack. The girls' idea of what constituted a necessity was not the same as mine. My inner dictator wanted to decree what we were bringing and where we were going, but instead we opted for the democratic approach. For our adventure to be successful, the girls needed to feel that their opinions mattered, that they weren't held hostage to their parents' dream. So I stepped back and listened to my children, rather than educating them on what a "real traveler" packed. It was easier to let go once Matt and I realized that though we were old hands at moving, this was the first time our children would leave good friends, a house they considered home, and even our minivan that they'd lovingly named. Letting them choose what they carried was critical to easing their transition.

After deciding which toys, mementos, and stuffed animals were joining us, we moved straight to an important subject—birthdays. It seemed like a great starting place to activate their enthusiasm for the journey ahead. So we opened up the map and told them to choose where to celebrate their birthdays. We ordered them to think big. They enthusiastically considered their options. Our 14-year-old knew she wanted to do an adventure sport so chose skydiving outside Amsterdam. Our 11-year-old decided on Playmobil Fun Park outside Nuremberg, Germany. Our 8-year-old wanted to be surprised, so we chose a trip to Efteling, a theme park in the Netherlands complete with a fairy tale forest.

As we continued to plan together, we read H.C. Andersen's fairy tales, Pippi Longstocking, Paddington. We excitedly talked about what we'd do, the history there, the stories that belong to each city. We also turned Friday movie night into "trip research," watching movies like *The Sound of Music* for the Alps and Salzburg, *Ratatouille* and *A Cat in Paris* for France, and *The Secret Life of Walter Mitty*—a great family movie to inspire wanderlust.

Once we were on our journey, we ceded more decision power to the children, because they genuinely had great ideas. We never would have gone skiing in Andorra if our eldest hadn't suggested it. And we might never have gone to Cornwall if our other daughter hadn't wanted to make English-speaking friends. We explored caves, snorkeled, went paragliding, and visited Heidi's mountain in Switzerland, all because of our girls' suggestions.

We homeschooled the kids on the road, but our eldest asked to attend a school in Germany to improve her German and see what school there would be like. It's something that never would have occurred to me, and I was so proud of her for stepping out of her comfort zone. We found a Waldorf School in Hannover that was more than happy to take her for a month, and it was a memorable and wonderful experience.

Traveling, for us, is about experiencing new places together as a family. When we let our kids be part of it—to contribute, to explore, to learn—they grow in ways greater than we thought possible. In the end, taking the time to involve the kids throughout the process made our travels a true family adventure.

Involving Your Children

CONTRIBUTORS' STORIES

HEATHER · LIVED IN ITALY FOR TWO YEARS

When we told our kids that we were moving to Italy, they were immediately on board. They had never been to Europe and were so excited. That excitement lasted until about seventy-two hours after we arrived in Milan and reality set in.

NICA · SAILED THE CARIBBEAN

When we first told our children we going sailing for nine months in the Bahamas and Dominican Republic, they both let us know that they'd be staying home. Neither Jeremy nor I come from families where children are consulted in big decisions, so it never occurred to us to involve the kids other than telling them the plans. We did, however, incorporate their needs by, for instance, making sure we arranged our sailing schedule so that we could meet up with other family boats.

SUSAN · REMEMBERING MOVING TO SINGAPORE AS A CHILD

My father was posted to Singapore as part of his career. We had about three months' notice, just enough time to pack our belongings. I did NOT want to go. Brought up on a diet of Enid Blyton books, I pleaded to be left behind and allowed to go to boarding school. My parents insisted I was too young. As it happens, I was sent to boarding school at a later age and did not enjoy it at all.

CHERYL · RV-ING THROUGH EUROPE

My kids are too young to be involved in the planning, but they defi-nitely influence *how* we travel. At their age, backpacking would be too stressful and flying would be too expensive. So we settled on traveling in a motorhome; that way we don't spend money and time hunting for accom-modations. Plus, the kids still have the security of our "bit," a Scottish term for home.

MELISSA · PREPARING TO LEAVE FOR SPAIN

We've been prepping the kids for the past two years. I think they are a mix of nervous and excited. We have friends who moved to Germany, so I share stories of those kids learning German to reassure my kids that they can learn Spanish quickly. I homeschool my oldest, so there's no attach-ment to schooling for him, but my daughter, who is in traditional school, has a few reservations about leaving. But she's left a school before and survived, so hopefully she'll have that experience to give her confidence.

KIRSTY · ROAD-TRIPPED THROUGH NORTHERN AFRICA
AND CENTRAL ASIA FROM HER ADOPTED HOME IN ABU DHABI

The kids were six and eight when we set off and we involved them in making choices on what they wanted to see, where they wanted to go, booking accommodations, and finding places to visit. They enjoyed taking ownership of aspects of the planning. They were both quite opinionated about where to spend their birthdays—in the end we had three birthdays in Morocco and one in Iran.

LISA · BACKPACKING AROUND THE WORLD

We involved our four daughters in both the planning and the

execution of this global backpacking year. We figured they would be more willing travelers if they got a say in the process. They aren't always interested in the finer details, and that's okay. We hold frequent family round tables about destinations, experiences, as well as accommodations and flights (our eldest now loves researching flights). We trained our daughters to read maps, understand GPS systems, decipher weather forecasts, and investigate attractions. They have also learned how to research transportation—trains, buses, Uber, etc—by downloading apps, Googling sites, and reading reviews.

As our daughters mature, they ask us how we can afford 365 days of travel. After all, everyone back home assumes we had a windfall. Yes, it's expensive and can be a slog sometimes. But this journey together is worth every cent, every argument, every lonely moment. Just as a picture is worth a thousand words, our experience is worth everything with regards to connection, resilience, and understanding ourselves and others. Not to mention the exposure to different people and cultures.

Oh, and the answer to my daughter's question is this: This year was possible because we made sacrifices based on our priorities. When we focus on what we truly value, rather than what society or advertisers decide we should be valuing, we can realize our dreams. It's a lesson that I hope will be with them forever.

3

DEALING WITH OPINIONS

Your decision to take your family on the adventure of a lifetime is like everyone else's Rorschach test. That is, the way they react to it says a lot about them. Friends and family who cheer for you are probably living their own dream (whatever that looks like for them) and so are happy to support you in living yours. Those who grumble and judge are likely not as satisfied with their own choices. Those that point out the dangers are likely scared themselves. You get the idea.

It seems the universal reaction burgeoning expats receive when they announce an impending move is, "You are so brave, I could never do that." With or without a contemptuous glance.

That pronouncement will make you feel foolish and weak. After all, you know you aren't brave. It's just that the part of you that wants to change your life is bigger than the part of you that's fearful. In that moment, I want you to remember that just opening yourself to this possibility means that you *are* strong and brave and creative and in tune with yourself. And also, it's not crazy to consider changing your life for no real reason other than "I want to." People who don't get it are people whose craving for a paradigm shift is smaller than their need for stability or their fear of change.

That's okay.

I'm not saying you are on the side of the angels because there isn't one right way to do life. What I *am* saying is that other people's reactions are indicative of their own calculus, not yours. There are plenty of people who share your longing to feel the pinpricks of adventure around the corner. You have their stories here in the pages of this book. I hope you use that as a bulwark, to hold you up when other people's judgment threatens to drag you down.

Because you'll get it:

"You're taking your kids out of school? Won't that put them behind in math?"

"Don't you worry about how it'll impact their odds for college admission?"

"Won't they miss their friends?"

"Won't you be lonely?"

"Isn't it selfish to disrupt your kid's life?"

"Won't it take a chunk out of your retirement? Isn't that financially irresponsible?"

"But they aren't fluent in the language—what will they do at school? How will they make friends?"

Right now, I want you to go to the mirror and practice your Italian, "*Boh,*" the ubiquitous shrug that Italians do with their arms outstretched that means, "I don't know, and it will be fine." When I wrung my hands and worried aloud with Italians at our local bar about how hard public school would be for my children, they smiled and cocked their head and said, "*Boh. Piano, piano, e tutto bene.*" Slow, slow, and everything will be well, one step at a time. *Boh.* It's a good gesture to practice. The kind of thing I hate when my kids use it to answer my question of, "Did you bring home your math homework?" but an excellent response to a question or comment that has no real answer.

Even when loved ones meant to be kind, their responses often struck an odd chord with me. For instance, I felt prickly and weird when friends told me that they admired me. I'm a pleaser by nature, so I'd rather be liked than admired. I wish I could say I've outgrown this quirk now that I'm solidly veering towards 50-years-old, but it is still present. In fact, this time around, I've noticed that I avoid telling people that we're planning a year around the world (Oh, did I not tell you that? Looks like that avoidance runs deep). So when it comes up because we're discussing anything related to the year 2020, I'm distinctly uncomfortable.

With our year in Italy, I had plenty of friends laugh off the dream with an airy, "Oh, you guys. Always planning something. You'll never go through with it." Now that we've done it, people believe us, and yet I'm the one waving my own hand, "You never know what will happen. But that's the current plan."

I don't hedge because I'm afraid of losing face by not following through or because I cower in the face of disapproval. I hedge because I don't want anyone's admiration or awe, or really any of their thoughts and feelings about my plans. I assume people will have judgments about it, positive or negative, and I really don't care. I'm not interested in unpacking their baggage, so I have learned to put up the boundary. Not my circus, not my monkeys.

As you'll read in the contributors' stories, my experience of having to grapple with other people's reactions is universal. Everyone you know will have an opinion. That's okay. After all, you living your dream makes them confront their own lives, and they have to deal with that in their own way. It's not your job to make it easy for them, and it's not your job to force them to reflect authentically. More than once I was tempted to blurt out, "Isn't it possible you think it's a dumb idea because you are afraid of admitting your own dream?" It *is* your job to own your experience. So sing it from the rooftops, or keep it as private as the beginning of pregnancy, or anywhere in the middle. There's no right way to do it, as long as you are being honest with yourself.

I would add that, like telling your children, it's important to listen to people, without necessarily accepting their truth as universal truth. Friends and family may have important information that you had not considered, like about factoring in the cost of International School or about a recent outbreak in drug-related violence in the region you are considering. It makes sense to take in offered wisdom. But ultimately, you decide what's right for your family.

I trust you to do that. I hope your loved ones can do the same. And if they can't, I hope you can find the resolve to not let that butcher your fun.

Brushing Off Other People's Narratives

SARA'S STORY

People make so many assumptions about our experience living in Morocco. That I covered my hair (I didn't). That because Morocco is a developing country, we must have lived on a grand estate (our incomes were measly compared to the wealth we saw all around us). That I was brave. That last one is the most surprising to me. I'm not brave, I'm just me, and I always have faith that things will work out.

Our families never understood why we moved away for seven and a half years. They know we're free spirits, but they don't get why we'd choose to miss out on life in the United States. I never felt that way. I am so much richer for my life in Morocco.

Part of the richness was the nearness of other countries to explore. We took so many family trips that travel became routine, and we could jet off with just two small duffel bags. If my daughter had a book and my son found a stick, then everyone would be entertained even in the most arduous travel moments.

Somewhere around our fourth year in Morocco, I began to realize that when my husband was traveling for work, I didn't need to remain home with the kids. I began taking them to Europe on my own. We visited Paris (four times!), Ireland, London, and Edinburgh. At this point the kids were becoming more interested in history, so our adventures grew to include historical sites. By visiting the Tower of London, Versailles, and Edinburgh Castle, they experienced first hand the history they read about in books. This forever changed how they learn.

After all those solo trips with the kids, I began to wonder what it would be like to live in Bali for a few months. When I mentioned my idea to my husband, he encouraged me to pursue it. I had become a confident traveler, and my husband and I never wanted to stop each other from fulfilling dreams. If that meant that I traveled with the kids alone, so be it.

We fielded quite a few questions from people who wondered how I could travel without my husband. But we trusted our strength as a couple, and knew that society's notion of a good marriage had no bearing on our choices. After all, we had already picked up the kids and moved them to a developing country. What was one more disillusionment of the American cultural expectation of family?

Dealing with Judgment

CONTRIBUTORS' STORIES

NAOMI · LIVED IN INDIA AND SINGAPORE FOR FOUR YEARS

At the time we left the United States, I felt incredibly supported and, at the same time, incredibly misunderstood. Surface-level friends came out of nowhere clamoring for connection in the weeks before our departure. Looking back on it, I get that our moving to India would be the closest many of our acquaintance would come to a similar experience. It felt like

I was behind a glass wall, with many eyeballs peering in—waiting to see what happened next.

NICA · SAILED THE CARIBBEAN

Since we'd done sailing vacations pre-children, our family was supportive. For years, they have listened to us wax rhapsodic about sailing, and Jeremy's mom and dad had planned to set off on their own cruising adventure before his dad unexpectedly passed away. To be honest, I think our families were more surprised that we came back than that we left.

People did ask how we could possibly give up our jobs. They wondered how we'd manage on a small boat. The concept of sailing at night was impossible to fathom. They wanted to know if we'd be stopping anywhere, or if we were just going to be sailing all the time.

The hardest thing for people to grasp, other than the space limitations that we whole-heartedly embrace, is the speed with which we do *not* move through the world. A 60-mile day in the Intracoastal Waterway is a long day of boring (you hope) motoring, perhaps punctuated by dolphins. It's not an hour jaunt to Richmond undertaken flippantly. The level of planning we do as sailors in terms of weather, anchorages, and safety is hard for non-cruisers to comprehend.

CANADA-TO-FRANCE · LIVES IN FRANCE

People judged us for moving to France. We left Canada because we wanted to change our pace of life. We wanted to experience more time with each other and experience new adventures while traveling. Not everyone understands that wanderlust. Most people are so buried in their busy, over-scheduled, day-to-day lives that they cannot imagine leaving it all behind for a simpler existence. But I envisioned it and went after it, and am grateful.

JOHN · RV-ED THROUGH EUROPE

I'm glad we ignored everybody who told us that traveling in a camper with small kids would be terrible. In general, there was very little support from others for our quest. We had to deliberately avoid the "dreamstealers" as we had enough of our own doubts without adding their premonitions of doom. As it happens, the only thing I would do differently would be to worry *less* about the trip and how the kids would adjust. It was an awesome experience.

KIRSTY · ROAD-TRIPPED THROUGH NORTHERN AFRICA AND CENTRAL ASIA FROM HER ADOPTED HOME IN ABU DHABI

Travel of this nature is like Marmite—people love the idea or hate it. Some people were supportive, some thought us irresponsible, some were frankly jealous. Many voiced concern about our kids' education. They either erroneously worried that we were breaking the law, or declared that they could never do a trip like ours because *they* valued their kids' education. We also value our kids' education. We want them to become articulate, open-minded, well-rounded citizens of the world, so we choose to educate differently. So many other people told us they wished they had done an adventure like ours. Or they always wanted to, but now the kids were too big. Or that they never managed to afford it.

We weren't special. We just prioritized our dream over and above new cars or home renovations or technology upgrades. Most people who dream of traveling can do so if they really want to. If it's a big enough dream they will find a way.

4

CHOOSING YOUR ADVENTURE

T he alternative title for this chapter is: *The Therapy Hour.* You'll
see what I mean, as we discover together what you want for your
family adventure abroad.

But first things first, I'll tell you how Keith and I decided on a year in
Spello. From the get-go, we were clear that we wanted to learn a language,
so a solid year in one location was a must. Besides, we wanted connections
and a deep understanding of another community that one only gets from an
extended stay. We wanted market day to be ingrained in our weekly routine,
we wanted to see the same street in four seasons, and we wanted to create
friendships with people who grew up with an entirely different ethos.

We chose Italy because we wanted to live in a country that felt familiar
and knowable, and where a year of language learning would bear fruit. In
truth, it came down to where we could picture ourselves. We feel at home
in Italy, every time we go. It resonates—a feeling we realized we needed
to pay attention to.

Italy was unified in the latter 1800's, so the regions can still feel a
bit like different countries. It was important to us to settle into a region
we'd been to and enjoyed. Rome was out because we figured it was too
big to easily form connections. We hadn't been south of Rome, and the
north of Italy lacked a bit of spontaneity, so our search was limited to
Le Marche, Tuscany, and Umbria—in short, central Italy, where we figured northern Italian predictability would be blurred by southern Italian

warmth. Le Marche is gorgeous with its sunflower fields rolling down to gentle blue seas, but towns are spread out which we figured would require more driving than we wanted to do. We ruled out Tuscany because it's a region dubbed "Tuscanyshire" thanks to its lavish helping of expats. We wanted to rub shoulders with locals.

Our gaze turned to Umbria. We had visited two years before and melted at the landscape and food, found the people welcoming, and we also liked the idea that in Umbria we'd be two hours away from a celebrated city. Turns out, we rarely went to Florence or Rome because of school schedules. Anyway, we learned you'd be hard pressed to find a genuinely unappealing major Italian city—they all have their unique advantages, and frankly being farther from the tourist track would have been a bonus.

All that said, we have contributors who settled all over the Boot who had luscious experiences, so I'm very clear that we over-thought the issue. It is likely that we could have thrown a dart at a map of Italy and found a wonderful region to live.

We chose Spello because Keith and I made a scouting trip to Umbria, and it was just obvious that Spello was home. While I fully believe that there is a beauty in embracing the imperfect, and thus it's a gift to make any place home, I also think that determining whether or not a town fits your basic specifications is important. Here's what I mean—when we arrived in Italy for our scouting trip, I had already made up my mind about where I wanted to live. I'd found a perfect home in a perfect village in a perfect location and figured I could've canceled the scouting trip except my mom was already coming to babysit and how often could Keith and I go abroad without our three children? (*Answer*: just that once.)

So I had my list of five apartments in five towns with five school systems in my pocket, but the list was just for decoration. I was set.

Until we arrived in the first town, the one I'd so anticipated I was already warming up my lease-signing fingers.

It was dead, people.

It was so dead, we had to hush our voices to library levels.

It was so dead, we thought perhaps everyone was hiding.

We found out from the woman who let us into the much anticipated apartment that of the one hundred twenty kids in the elementary school, thirty-five were native English speakers. And they kept to themselves. This was the exact reason we'd avoided looking at Tuscany. Then again, this town was close to the Tuscany border. Could the expat influence be bleeding into Umbria?

This was not the experience we'd envisioned.

At all.

We suddenly realized that we had *thought* we wanted picturesque streets and views, but what we really craved was a sense of life. It hadn't occurred to us that there would be places in Italy that didn't have that. Maybe we hadn't noticed the variations in animation across towns when we were just bopping in and out as tourists, ready to be charmed.

That night, we drove to the neighboring town where we had an appointment a few days hence to see an apartment. Our hopes rose with the hills—this town would be it. This town would have some spark to it.

Nope.

Over dinner we strangled down our disappointment. Had we gone about the process all wrong? By looking at vacation rentals had we limited ourselves to towns with well-established tourist infrastructure rather than authentic life? Or was what we'd envisioned just not possible? Were we so late to the expat game that Italian towns were "full," and our best bet would be to embrace having an international experience rather than a quintessential Italian one? Maybe Italy had been "done," and we needed to look to a whole other country? Could we do that?

The next day we drove across the Umbrian plain to Spello. As we climbed out of the car, we looked at each other with huge stupid grins on our faces. We had found it.

Home.

There were people, ITALIAN PEOPLE, sitting in the *piazza*. There were Italian people walking by with gelato. Our prospective landlord, Loris, asked to take us and our translator, Doreen, to coffee before we saw the apartment and everyone in the bar was yammering and laughing. Doreen shepherded us into her friend Paola's shop while Loris paid for the coffee, and Paola was warm and friendly. We watched a line of children jostle their way down the street into the waiting army of little blue buses. In short, Spello is a living town.

We found out much later, when I was asked to the vice mayor's office at the end of our year, that Spello's burbling vitality has been intentionally protected. In many Italian towns, bars and restaurants and police stations and schools have moved beyond the ring road encircling the town. This makes it easier for people living in the outskirts to access those services, but leaves the center of town to flicker and die.

A scouting trip illustrates how closely a prospective town hews to your image in a way that blogs and websites cannot. Also, visiting helps you avoid pitfalls. One expat family discovered on a scouting trip that the house they had been hoping to rent had a sheer drop-off into a canyon. Not so good for their toddler.

So if you can—visit.

If you can't, you'll make it work. If we'd lived in that first village, I'm sure we would have had a wonderful, if different, year.

And now, the therapy portion of the chapter, the part where I guide you to dig deeper into who you are as a traveler and what kind of adventure will fill you...

I want you to slip a bookmark onto this page and invite your partner on a date. Take this book with you, and ask each other the questions I list below. Not in a game show kind of way, but the way you would if you had all the time and space to consider and play with and explore each question. Let ideas bubble up, half formed, until they knock you over with their shining clarity. Allow this process to give you a bigger and brighter window into each other. This is a launching pad for finding your dreaming dance, together.

When I do couples therapy, I ask couples to go out on a date and not talk about their children. They invariably look at me blankly. "What are we supposed to talk about?" I give them a list of topics not unlike this list of questions to reflect on who they have been, who they are, and who they want to be. I once had a couple suggest I turn questions like these into cards, called "the couple's deck of dreaming." Haven't done that yet, but a list will work just as well.

If you are a single parent planning for a solo trip with your kids, first of all—*bravo!* Invite your best friends over and light some candles and open a bottle of red and make these questions an opportunity to dive deeper into your friendships. Remember: No judgment, no comparisons. This is a space for all present to get clearer on what they value.

If you are a person of color, I'm sure I'm not telling you anything you don't already know when I say that as a white person who settled in Europe, I can only imagine the factors that will go into your decisions. When I was living in Italy, I had a reader write me about her experience being an African-American woman in Sicily, and it was so appalling that if she hadn't already fled home, I would've bolted across the ocean to buy her all the *arancini* in a ten-kilometer radius just to sit and connect with her. It may be worth it for you to consider living in a place that you've been and where you felt comfortable, rather than plunging into uncharted waters. As another thought, people of color often report that international cities are easier to settle into than more provincial towns, where newcomers are specimens, foreigners trebly so, and locals just don't know what to make of people of color. The very provinciality that can charm the stoniest expat can prove actively aversive to racial minorities, at least at first. In an international city like Paris or Brussels, you'll be more defined by your citizenship than your race, and for some that can actually be pretty freeing.

Another consideration is to settle into a place where you phenotypically match the skin tones of the residents. Suddenly not being a color minority can have a profound impact on families.

Now, before you begin this process, believe the following—there is no perfect place that is best for everybody, and in fact, there is no perfect and there is no best. You will not find a place that is glorious in every particular. *And that is good news.* If you expect a place to be perfect, you'll have unrealistic demands of place and of yourself in that place. Life should never be an unbroken stream of halcyon moments. There needs to be some darkness, there needs to be some work. In fact, I believe it's the very convenient nature of life in America that makes so many of us want to flee. Yes, it's nice to be able to park outside your house and get your mail picked up from your front door and have fifty million choices of dog food and prepackaged plastic boxes of cheese and crackers and ham with carrot coins. But all that convenience separates us from the stuff of life. We need to think, to engage, to get our hands dirty. It's only by falling, and then brushing off our knees and getting back up again that we feel any sense of ownership over our journey. So, please. Rid yourself of the notion of best, and instead allow yourself to feel transported by possibility.

LANGUAGE

* How much do you think about language—its role in culture, its passport to other peoples?

* Which languages fascinate you?

* If you could learn one language, as if by magic, which one would it be? Why?

* Which languages do you think you'd be able to learn in a year of immersion, based on what you already know and your knack for learning languages? Which seem impossible?

* How important is it for you and your children to learn a language by the end of your sojourn? Why?

* If you don't think you could learn a language to at least a functional level at the end of that time, would that rule out a country?

* How much do you want the language your children learn to be a language they can actively use later (for being able to learn other languages, for opening doors to other countries, for being able to communicate with immigrants in your own community, etc.)?

LIFESTYLE

* Without thinking too much about it, answer the following—are you a city person or a small town person or a rural person?

* What experiences in a city have you enjoyed, and why? What experiences in the country have you enjoyed, and why? What experiences in towns—both tiny and large—have you enjoyed and why?

* Ask yourself the above questions again, but think about what you didn't enjoy in the city, country, and town.

* When you travel, do you tend to gravitate towards cities or more rural locations? Where have your favorite vacations been? What made those vacations special?

* Think about where you live now—does it fit you like a glove, or do you want a different kind of experience for a year?

* How important is it to you to walk places?

✳   How important is it to you to have things to do—shows, shopping, a choice of bakeries?

✳   How important is it for you to breathe air that's not full of traffic and bustle? How important is the sight of green things? Are these important daily, or is getting a nature tune-up enough?

✳   Do you like the anonymity of cities, or does that bother you?

✳   Do you want to go car-free? Or do you value the freedom to jump in your car and drive?

✳   What are your favorite foods to eat? What are your favorite foods to make? What kind of cuisine have you always wanted to understand more fully? What foods do you reject and would hate being a cornerstone of your local cuisine?

✳   What cultures have always fascinated you? Why?

✳   What books have you read or movies have you seen that sparked a desire to visit a place?

YOU

✳   How anxious are you in new places? Is that something you are willing to work on?

✳   How uncomfortable does it make you to not be able to communicate? Is that something you are willing to work on?

✳   Do you like it when strangers pull you into their lives and their conversations, or do you want to be left well enough alone?

* What are the parts of you that you wish you could shrink or extend?

* Where have you traveled that you have felt the happiest? Why?

* Do you envision creating connections with locals, or are you more interested in creating connections with people from other countries, not necessarily the country you are landing in?

* Do you make friends easily?

* Would you describe yourself as an open person?

* Do you need to see the same people day after day to begin to feel like you know them and can reach out to communicate with them?

* How easily bored are you? Do you want to see as much as you can, experience as many cultures as you can during this time, or do you prefer the idea of digging deep into one or a handful?

* How much do you hate versus love packing and unpacking and hanging around train/plane terminals?

* When you think about spending an extended period of time in one place, how exciting is that thought? What place comes up for you?

* When you think about traveling as a lifestyle, which cultures call to you, what do you feel like you simply must see? Do you have a go-go-go personality or do you need time to recharge your batteries?

* How much do you value the freedom to change plans on a whim?

YOUR CHILDREN

* How do you feel about putting your children in a school where they don't know the language?

* How accessible are International Schools in the areas you are considering?

* What appeals to you or doesn't appeal to you about homeschooling?

* Do you want all of your children out of the house during the day (like at school), or do you want them home? Is your youngest child old enough to go to school? Would you consider a preschool?

* What do you want your children to get out of this experience?

* What are the dynamics between you and your children and between your children? Do you think an adventure abroad will change those? How?

* Do your children have learning differences or personalities such that you need to modify their experience?

NUTS AND BOLTS

* How important is access to medical care, and how important is it that your medical heath care providers speak English?

* Does someone in your family have health issues? Mobility issues? Mental health issues?

* If it is important to homeschool, which of your possible countries allow it?

* How important is reliable public transportation?

* Do you have ample cash reserves? Do you have an itch to do this on a shoestring?

* How important is the political stability of a country? Do you have the resources to flee if there is violent unrest?

* How comfortable or uncomfortable are you with bureaucracy and/or bribery?

* Do you have a pet you must bring with you?

* Do you have a boat or an RV or camper you can use? Does the idea of RVing, driving, or sailing appeal to you such that you are willing to consider purchasing an adequate vehicle and putting in the time to train yourself on it?

From these questions, skim the globe. Now that you are clearer on what's important to you and your spouse, let your fingers linger a little. Think about what would be your ideal time frame, and how you want the experience to feel. Think about your children and the kind of family experiences you crave. Think about what places on that globe sing to you. Sketch out ideas. Notice which ones make your heart skip a little.

Do all of this before you start to limit yourself to what you think is possible.

Only when you have your ideas laid out, only then, think about what you would need to make it work and what sacrifices you would have to accept to make it work. This part will take some mulling. Think about how you could draw an income, how you would downsize your current lifestyle to afford your dream, how you could shift your life to make it match what you need. The upcoming chapters will help you do that.

If what you want seems impossible, then start to play with the variables. What if you shortened your travel time? What if you went to a less-expensive country? What if you liquidated some assets (selling your home, for instance)? What if you found a way to make money overseas? What if you lived in the countryside rather than the city? What if you sent your kids to public school rather than the International School you had your eye on? What if you saved for a couple more years?

Pare the dream down to its essentials, to figure out how you can meet your desires.

Let it sink in.

Then practice saying your dream aloud, to your spouse, to the mirror, until you are ready to own it.

Off-beat Destinations

ALISHA'S STORY

Before having children, I went to college in Colorado and joined the military, which is where I met my husband. We traveled quite a bit when we were DINKs (Dual Income, No Kids). Three children later, my husband retired from the service after twenty years on active duty. With his pension we have been able to travel. First, we lived in Tanzania, where he taught at an International School. After two years there, and missing the seasons that are absent in equatorial Africa, we went back to the US to decide our next move.

After our experience in Tanzania, we had clearer ideas about what we wanted in a new location. Changing seasons for one, but we also wanted a life in the outdoors—reading, crafting, hiking, being with people. As homeschoolers, we had discovered that connecting with an International School is an excellent way to connect to other families, so we wanted not only the ability to homeschool, but also access to an International School for extracurricular activities, resources, and connections. At the same time, we wanted to avoid getting caught up in the "expat bubble" that can happen with an International School. Research on climate, landscape, International Schools, and cultures that value the outdoors, plus our interest in Central Asian history and culture led us to Kyrgyzstan.

We spent the bulk of our first year here in Kyrgyzstan learning Kyrgyz, the heart language, or mother tongue, of the people. It was harder than we anticipated to be so isolated, particularly for our children. My husband and I were required by our visa to attend a language school three times a week and that gave us a solid grammar foundation. But most of our family's Kyrgyz learning was thanks to a language helper who came to our home and utilized the Growing Participator Approach to learning language. I'll add that when we went back to the US earlier this year to visit family, our kids lost quite a bit of language ability, whereas my husband and I kept most everything we had learned. That was a surprise.

Increasing our connection with the International School was a gift in terms of alleviating our isolation. Even as homeschoolers, we meet other families and have found a happy balance of expat friends and local friends. We homeschool all the essential subjects and use the International School for the extras, like sports (it was rugby and swimming in Tanzania, here we haven't done sports at the school, though my boys are involved with *sambo*, a Russian martial art), drama productions (tryouts for *Fiddler on the Roof* are tomorrow), and standardized tests (like the PSAT a week ago). I stay active and involved by helping in the library—running book sales, helping to sort materials, prereading and reviewing books.

Our social lives are important to us, and we invite friends to dinner at least once a week. We meet people through the International School, but we also attend a local church and interact with neighbors.

It's not always easy. There is reliably a "honeymoon" period right after you arrive when everything is new and wonderful, but then come the dark days. Four to six months after we arrived in Kyrgyzstan, winter set in and everything got hard. Language learning was harder, school with the kids was harder, and there were days I struggled to leave our apartment because I didn't want to have to speak Kyrgyz just to get food. It got better, and it helped to just allow myself to be a hermit when I needed that.

Then there are moments of surpassing beauty. Last summer, we went on a horse trek in the Naryn region. We picked up our horses in the morning and rode up the side of a mountain, single file. On the way up we watched an eagle soar over our heads. Once I reached the crest of the mountain, a bit out of breath, the view back down to the village on the one side and then down to the lake on the other side made me so grateful to live here. I realized that even when I'm tired and my horse is being *tentek*, naughty, taking the time to see the beauty all around me makes the work totally worth it.

We made our way down to the lake and found a traditional yurt camp. The inside of the yurt, which is a conical tent, was covered in warm, felt carpets called *shyrdaks*, and we felt instantly at home as the family began making dinner preparations. Kyrgyz hospitality is well renowned; they give their best to strangers and guests. We sat and chatted while the kids ran and played in the *jailoo*, a high alpine meadow. We agreed, this is how kids should be raised—running and playing in the fields.

We have all changed these last few years, though whether that is from living overseas or just growing older, together, I can't say. I do know that when we go back to the US, we are so excited to see everyone and expect to fit together like we used to. But the cousins have grown up and can't relate to our experiences living abroad. Sometimes people are jealous of where we've been and what we've done and I can explain, yes, it's been wonderful, but there are days we are jealous of your stability and that your kids have a place to call home. There is no perfect answer. We are thrilled that our children have had an opportunity to experience life and meet people overseas. We have been able to travel in Africa, Europe, and now Asia, and I wouldn't trade that for anything, but there are days I think I would like the quiet life, on a farm, with animals, a homeschool co-op, and an attic full of memory boxes and old children's toys that have been saved for the grandkids.

Our family is tight, we are a team, we are each other's best friends (as we remind the kids when they get testy with each other). The memories we have made together have knit us closer than most families I know.

For that, I am grateful.

Creating a Journey

CONTRIBUTORS' STORIES

SARAH · LIVES IN THE NETHERLANDS AFTER YEARS OF WORLDSCHOOLING

We've done two basic types of experiences: Slow travel (a few months in each country) and moving to one place long-term. The slow travel was exciting and fun, but ultimately exhausting. It's difficult to figure out how to do everything from grocery shopping to getting Internet to making friends in a new country and language. And to do it repeatedly every few months is overwhelming. If I had it to do over again, I would pick one country as a base, and travel while there.

MELISSA · PREPARING TO MOVE TO SPAIN

We decided on Spain after reading travel blogs. The rents are reasonable compared to Sydney, which means we'll be able to do it on a budget.

The idea of bouncing from country to country each month or every few weeks isn't appealing at all. I'd rather be semi-settled and travel from a home base.

ASTRID · PREPARING TO WORLDSCHOOL

My aim is to give my kids a better understanding of where they fit in the world. As a family of color, our experience may be different from other traveling families. I'm curious to see how people in other countries see us.

In my own travels, I have noticed that the world often favors travelers who are white skinned—this could be subconscious remnants of colonialism, or it could be that people associate white skin with wealthy countries, and therefore assume the white travelers are the rich travelers and will spend more. But sometimes I find my darker skin color is an advantage, as I can more easily blend in compared to my companion lighter-skinned travelers. Being of Southeast Asian descent, I've often been mistaken for a local when I'm in India, Malaysia, Philippines, Thailand, and Cambodia. Even when I travel in Africa, I notice that I don't draw as much attention.

JULIE · WORLDSCHOOLING IN MEXICO AND BEYOND

We first drove to Mexico because the border is only five hours from our home in Houston. Plus, we wanted to keep our car. It's given us a lot of freedom to explore Mexico. Our first stop was in San Miguel de Allende for two months. It's a small, mountain city with a lot of culture and a lot of expats, a great place to transition into a traveling life. Then we moved to Oaxaca City for a month, after a five-day stopover in Mexico City. After Oaxaca, we spent a week driving to the Yucatan, stopping in San Cristobal de las Casas and Palenque before we arrived in Playa del Carmen. We're here in Playa for two months before heading back to the US to fly to Malaysia. Our goal is to spend a month or two in each destination, and visit a few other locations in between. We want to slow travel so we can really experience a country, but also see a lot in our one-year trip.

CHERYL · RV-ING THROUGH EUROPE

We chose to motorhome through Europe for a year, or more if we can stretch our finances, we may extend our trip. Europe is really set up for motorhome travel, with loads of free parking spots, electric hook-ups, toilet and shower facilities, and waste facilities to empty the motorhome cassette and grey water tanks. We bought a motorhome outright from the sale of our house, which also eliminated any monthly car payment.

So far, we are loving motorhome life. We have complete freedom to stay almost anywhere—big cities, small villages, beachside, lakes. Every place has been its own kind of special and all have been new experiences for us.

PART TWO

PLANNING

5

FINANCING YOUR ADVENTURE

PART ONE · THE BIG POTATOES

Yes, it's true. Giving your family the world ain't exactly cheap. Springing to another country with your children (and possibly pets—*ahem*), setting up housekeeping, paying your rent and possibly some of your mortgage back home, covering utilities, keeping up on bills like health insurance that you can't let lapse—that requires a hefty stockpile of cash. But even if settling in a flat along the Seine isn't in your financial cards, there are ways to create a family adventure that fit almost any budget, as long as you are willing to make some sacrifices. The level of sacrifice varies by where you land and how you live and how long you stay and if you'll work, but as you'll see from our contributors' stories, there are many routes towards having a family adventure abroad. Your job is to play with which scenarios fit your resources and decide if those scenarios sound appealing. And maybe none will be—maybe you'd do better to think of adventures closer-to-home, other ways to shake up your life and avoid complacency, or other ways to incorporate a multicultural experience into your family story. But don't close that door until you at least peek through and explore the possibilities.

So, let's figure out what your options are.

The amount you'll need to have nestled in the bank depends on your monthly expenses while you're gone, minus any revenue streams you can count on during that time.

How did we figure out how much to save for a year in Italy? Well, we spitballed mostly. We researched modest apartments in tenable Italian towns to get an idea of how much we could expect to pay for rent. We scanned expat forums to find people complaining about utilities and estimated double the cost of our current utilities bill and added that to the running list of monthly expenses. We added in our privately purchased health insurance; being self-employed, we can't count on employers to purchase this for us when we return (very much something to consider if you are an American, given the shifting approach to pre-existing conditions). For cost of living, we figured we'd spend roughly the same on food (the cost of food is far less in Italy, but we knew we'd be eating out more). We threw in a couple of thousand dollars for a car and a few thousand more for emergencies. Putting all that together, we calculated that we'd need about $60,000 USD for the year (since we wouldn't be working), provided we were able to get in rent for our house in Virginia what we paid for its mortgage.

Armed with numbers, we calculated that if we put aside my income as a part-time clinical psychologist for three years, and just lived on Keith's income as a self-employed graphic designer, we'd have a nest egg big enough to blow on a year-long adventure. Living solely on Keith's income meant tightening our belts. Keith gave up his office space downtown and built a studio in our backyard to save on rent. We only had one car (still do), which was possible because I work walking distance from the house, and now Keith works just steps away from our kitchen. We didn't go so far as to subsist on rice and beans, but we almost never ate out. We didn't hire people to do tasks we could do—clean, taxes, paperwork, home remodeling. We gave up our gym membership and bought some weights instead (which are now coated with a prodigious layer of dust that's proportional to my expanding waistline—not sure I'd advocate giving up the gym membership).

Once we practiced living on one income for two years and realized that it pinched but didn't bite, we told the children the plan. As an aside, I'll share that telling them was akin to flinging ourselves over a cliff. It made it real. Really real. Not just pretend real. This thing we'd only imagined in whispers when the kids were sleeping—we were committing to it. My mouth almost couldn't form the words.

Back to finances.

Our plans didn't pan out the way we anticipated. Nothing does, after all. A chunk of our savings went to hire people to complete the last of the home renovations we'd promised our renters we'd have done before they moved in and wound up taking far longer than expected. So Keith ended up keeping some American clients and working while we were in Italy. Thankfully, this didn't mean working his American hours which were roughly from 8 AM to midnight, daily. Instead, he worked when the kids were in school, about 8:30 AM to 1 PM. It kept him from having the long swaths of free time he'd been looking forward to, but it did allow us to travel. So we spent more than we had intended on vacations, and also more on gas for our car (gas is heavily taxed in Europe).

We spent less, though, on utilities. Yes, they are more expensive, but we hadn't considered that Italian apartments are far smaller than airy American homes. Plus, expensive electricity means that Europeans are very conscious about energy usage. Our apartment had energy-efficient windows and appliances, and lacked energy-sucking machines such as a clothes dryer and air conditioning. We over-budgeted for utilities, but we under-budgeted for gas and travel, so it worked out, particularly with Keith drawing in some income as a buffer.

Finding someone to rent our house for the year was the part that I was most sure wouldn't work. But it was actually the easiest and more surprisingly positive aspect of the planning. We'll talk more about this in the "What to Do with Your House" chapter.

From talking to other families who have done extended family adventures abroad, it seems like our ballpark of $60,000–$80,000 USD for a year is fairly standard. But there are ways to go with less.

The most obvious fact to remember is that some destinations are expensive to live in, and some are not. Industrialized nations are more expensive than developing ones, and cities tend to be more expensive than rural areas. However, tourist hot-spots throw those rules out the window as economic pressures jack rents up. Just as an example, there's a home in Paris where the *nightly* rent is almost as much as our *monthly* rent in Spello. But simply setting one's sites to a developing nation like Thailand won't necessarily drop the price tag. There are apartments in Bangkok that rent for not much less than ones in Paris. Deviate from the tourist trail, and prices drop precipitously. I found a home along Thailand's back roads that totaled $11 USD a day. With a scooter.

Remember, too, that daily expenses drop when you get away from the stream of tourists clutching their Fodor's guidebooks. An espresso in Rome is three times what you pay in Spello. Now, this rule of thumb isn't always reliable. When we traveled in Asia, for instance, we were shocked at how cheap it was to eat in Vietnam. An entire meal, including cokes and beer, for five of us, was routinely about $10 USD. Laos, though, was about as expensive as Europe. We discovered that Laos's infrastructure is so challenging, everything is shipped in, and those costs are passed along to consumers. So do your research, and don't make assumptions.

If you will be moving around a lot during your year, you'll be paying a premium because a discount is given to renters who stay for long periods. Plus, travel between locations adds up, particularly with each additional child in tow. Not only airfares and transfers, but tourist visas, which are required in some countries (more on visas later).

You could sum up these last few paragraphs by saying that it's cheaper to live in Jakarta for a year than to travel around Southeast Asia for the same time period, and both are less expensive than settling in Helsinki.

If rent, even in a low-cost country, gives you pause, there are some accommodations that will actually pay you to live there. These aren't a euro a dozen, and they often aren't for an entire year, but they are worth pursuing. For instance, some people who list their homes on house-sitting websites (see *Resources*) are willing to pay to have you, particularly if they have a home or a pet that requires some extra care. I saw one house-sitting offer in Ireland that paid a small stipend for the incoming family to take care of an aging goat. I stared at that listing for far too long.

Missionary work pays for a family to go abroad, though obviously the purpose of that work tends be less about "I have a bucket-list wish to taste every dessert in Austria" and more about a desire to provide ministry or do faith-based service work. But if you are oriented that way anyway, talk to the head of your place of worship about options and resources.

There are also farm stays and volunteer opportunities (see *Resources*) that will provide a modest place to stay and sometimes a small stipend. These most commonly last for a few months, but you can either dig harder to find a longer term option, or you can decide to hop from one of these to another as a way to have your family experience more than one culture and way of life.

Those are ways to decrease the costs of accommodations. But remember you can flip the financial calculus if you have a revenue stream. What it comes down to is this: The more money you have going into your adventure, the less you'll have to worry about generating an income while you are abroad. People do move abroad with little to no savings, armed with only job hopes or prospects, but I don't recommend it. You'll want at least some cushion for safety purposes.

So, if you can make roughly the same amount of money traveling as you did when you were home, the cost of life abroad becomes not much different than that at home and the amount you save ahead of time becomes that cushion. Now comes the important question—how do you create an income abroad? A logical first step is to find out if your current employer has oversees locations you can transfer to. If there are no over-seas options, take the bull by the horns and draft a proposal that outlines how you could work remotely and submit that to your employer with a bottle of Scotch. Be sure you take into account the time zone difference in your proposal—if you need to be available for Skype meetings, then traveling up and down the globe may be more appealing to your employer than skipping laterally across time zones.

If you can't continue to work at your current place of employment, it's time to look elsewhere. There are sites that will help you find employment abroad (see *Resources*), or you can dig deep and get creative and think of how you can make money on your own—either by using your existing skill set or switching gears entirely. More on this in the upcoming "Working" chapter.

There are many ways to see the world. Settling in a country or coun-tries is just one. Some contributors reduce costs by investing in their roving accommodations, such as RVing or sailing. Some families already own those vehicles or feel optimistic about purchasing them and then selling them at the end of their adventure, thus making the cost of their accommodations mostly just docking or parking fees.

If you are thinking of transversing the globe (rather than settling down) without taking a home with you, I've seen estimates for that vary from about $100 USD/day to $250 USD/day for a family of four (not including flights). That's a ballpark-figure. Make sure you research your specific requirements to make sure you don't wind up out of cash in Geneva. The amount varies by how many places you fly between, if you can secure discounts for long-term stays, how many meals you'll cook for yourselves, how expensive your destinations are, and how many paid attractions you'll visit. One-way tickets are generally more cost effective than the sexy sounding "round-the-world ticket," though you should check prior to your travel, remembering that regions often have low-cost airlines for jumping from point to point.

Some families discover that they'd rather keep their current home base (or a downsized version) and experience short-term adventures. For instance, they might accrue long swaths of vacation time and work on a farm for several months at a time, every few years. Perhaps the same one, so they get a sense of "home," perhaps new ones to show their children that the world is a wide place.

I find it fascinating to write this chapter as we have one year in Italy behind us and a global trip planned to launch summer of 2020. In the intervening years, we've become, for lack of a better word, spendy. We eat out once or twice a week, we renewed our gym membership, we still only have one car but we're looking at getting another, we buy skin care products in fancy bottles, we go out to movies, we buy clothes we don't need. Last night Keith and I were trying to figure out if we can make our trip around the world work, and I had this realization that though we earn more than we did pre-Italy, we are saving far, far less. Yes, granted we now have a kid in college, but it hit us like a slap of salt water that because we aren't saving "for" anything right now (other than retirement, look at us, we got a retirement account!), we just aren't saving. We're going through money like it's meaningless. It was a wake-up call. We've started going over our expenses to figure out how to once again be intentional. This is far easier when there's a vision for our future.

In summary, if your main goal is to have a family adventure but money is tight, get creative and practice flexibility. Consider options that reduce your costs or increase your revenue. It may mean not having a year munching croissants while pondering which Provençal red will best match your daily cheese selection. But truly, once you are on your adventure, you'll be much more enamored with the road in front of you than the one you left behind.

PART TWO · THE SMALLER POTATOES

This chapter is a bit of a junk drawer. It's where all extra keys and half-used lighters land. Here is where you'll find the little details you should start thinking about, even though they are relatively fine hairs in the bulky adventure rope. Because this chapter includes so many minute details, I'm organizing it in list form so you can easily check items off with a flourish. Every one of these chores puts you one step closer to living your dream. How's that for motivating?

PASSPORTS

* As soon as you decide where you are going and for how long, check your passports. Does every member of your family have a current one? Are there enough pages left for more stamps? Is the expiration date distant enough so that countries will admit you? (Some countries won't admit visitors whose passport expiration date is within six months of entry.)

* If the answer to any of the above questions is no, your first task is to get updated passports. Go to your home country's government agency that processes passports (in the USA, that's *travel.state.gov*) and be detail oriented as you complete your passport application. Contrary to popular belief, Americans are not required to apply for passports at the post office. The State Department website lists alternatives. We now get our passports renewed at a nearby circuit court. No lines, friendly people, it's turned the passport process from a reliable nightmare into a pleasant family outing.

PAYING WITH PLASTIC

* Get yourself a debit card (or two) that works internationally and that doesn't incur foreign transaction fees (check with your bank to see if your current card fits the bill).

* Use your debit cards to get money in foreign countries because ATMs are everywhere, and they offer the best possible exchange rates. If your current bank charges foreign transaction fees or high ATM fees, consider switching to an expat-friendly institution. Your access to different cards varies by how much you'll be depositing, but begin by looking at Capital One (no ATM fees or foreign transaction fees), Charles Schwab (interest bearing and pays rebates on fees), Citibank (offices around the world, waives international ATM fees).

* Don't use a credit card at an ATM since there is a cash advance fee, and you'll start accruing interest right away. But you'll still need a credit card. Make sure your current card is compliant for travel. Many countries use chip and PIN credit cards rather than chip and signature, as is common in the States, so talk to your credit card company about what the foreign transaction fees are and if you can get a chip and PIN card. Plan on this well in advance, as it can take awhile to get the PIN in the mail. If you decide your current credit card company isn't advantageous for your travels, look at Chase and Citibank. Both have cards that offer trip protections, no foreign transaction fees, and solid foreign currency exchange rates.

* Whether you stay with your current financial institutions or make a switch, make sure you let them all know about your plans and get the name and phone number/email address of a contact. When charges start ringing up in locations far from home, banks and credit card companies assume your card was stolen and freeze your account.

Even if you inform them ahead of time. Which is why you want contact information for a point person.

* Bring two photocopies of your debit and credit cards, and store them in a secure place.

DRIVING

* If you are planning to drive during your adventure, get an international driver's permit. These can be purchased at AAA if you live in the United States, NRMA if you live in Australia, and your international driver's permit-issuing post office if you live in the UK. Google will help you find an office. The fee is nominal, usually around $20 USD.

* Bring two photocopies of your local driver's license, as well as your international driver's permit, on your trip.

HEALTH

* Get a comprehensive physical well in advance of your trip so you can take care of any issues ahead of time.

* Ask to stock up on medications (keep them in original containers if you are going through security) or have them mailed to you.

* If you are planning to live in another country long-term, international health insurance will most likely be a prerequisite for applying for a residency visa. If you are an American, you'll be shocked at how much less international health insurance costs than your home insurance.

* Look for international health insurance online. After many hours

of investigating, we went with the Patriot Travel Medical Insurance plan through IMG (see *Resources*). The cost in 2012 was $100 USD per month, and we had a $2,500 deductible. We never actually needed that insurance beyond demonstrating we had it for our visa, since Italians are so used to everyone having health insurance they offer health care as easily as our dentist gives us a spare toothbrush. For you non-Americans who are recoiling at the idea of spending $100 per month on health insurance, let me hasten to add that I know American families of four that pay close to $3,000 per month.

✳ Consider immunizations. Check embassy websites for your intended destinations and/or call your doctor for a referral to a local travel clinic where you can chat with someone about what you'll need. Keith and I get our travel vaccinations at our local pharmacy, as it is far cheaper than going through a travel clinic or our doctor's office.

✳ Get two photocopies of your vaccination records and your insurance policies/cards. While you are at it, get two copies of your children's school transcripts, particularly if you are planning on enrolling them in school.

PHONES

✳ We moved to Italy in the age before smartphones were practically necessities, so we just bought cheap phones there. That can work if you'll be in one location, but not so good if you are in multiple places.

✳ Investigate the cost of an international plan. They tend to be expensive, though that fee is sometimes reimbursed if you work for a company that agrees to foot the bill. Contact your current carrier and find out how much their international plan is, and how to add it to your account. We used to have to go to the brick-and-mortar AT&T Store to enable an international plan, but it is now possible to do it online.

* Investigate the possibility of buying a local SIM card at your destination, and popping it into your phone for each cellular network you want to access. Your first step is to make sure your phone can receive a SIM card—you must either have a phone designated for use on GSM networks (the network used by most of the world), or a CDMA-network phone that has the designation of "world phone" and can accept a SIM card. Check with your carrier, who can provide you with details about your particular phone.

* If you want to go the SIM card route, your phone needs to have been "unlocked"; "locked" phones are only able to connect to the network of your domestic carrier. Whether your phone can be unlocked depends on the nature of your plan and how long you've had it; contact your carrier to see if your phone is eligible, and if it is, there is usually no charge to unlock it. If it is not eligible, you can purchase a used unlocked phone on sites like eBay or Swappa, or, if you are flush with cash, you can buy a new, contract-free phone directly from Apple or Samsung that is not tied to any particular carrier.

* Remember, you can get non-smartphones for your children if that makes sense for your family. If you are looking at this trip as an opportunity to have your kids take a break from Minecraft, you can certainly tell them they need to leave their devices at home because Wi-Fi doesn't work the same in Europe. I won't tell. But you may want to consider that if your children will be in school in a foreign country, the ability to communicate with new classmates in a low-stakes way can be a boon, so texting and communication apps like WhatsApp, Instagram, and Snapchat can actually be valuable.

* To save minutes and data, I advise using FaceTime or Skype or WhatsApp for keeping in touch with people back home.

HOUSEKEEPING

* Some people ask a friend to serve as property manager in their absence, and some prefer to pay someone. If you are in the latter camp, start exploring local companies that can serve in this capacity for you.

* Think about what do to with your mail. We forwarded our mail to a company that scanned it and sent us images (see *Resources*). You could also forward your mail to a friend's house and have them flag anything important and let you know. In this digital age when most mail is junk, all you really need flagged is the occasional summons for jury duty or notices from your community about taxes.

* Consider setting up auto-payment for your monthly bills such as your mortgage so you don't have to think about that while abroad.

In addition to these odds and ends, there will undoubtedly be expenses that arise specific to your situation. Which is why including a large slush fund is important when you create a budget.

The How of How to Do It

JULIE'S STORY

O
nce we decided that we were really (yes, really!) going to leave our lives in Texas and travel for a year, we sat down to plan. After countless hours of research, we came up with a list of what we needed. Then we got to work.

First on the list was downsizing. We gave away what we couldn't sell at yard sales or online. Downsizing was a year-long project that gratifyingly lifted the burden of possessions from our shoulders. Prioritizing what is most important and shedding everything else is a task I recommend to everyone, not just families preparing to travel.

The next item on our list was healthcare. I found an international healthcare plan that covers us anywhere in the world, except the United States. Surprisingly, it was much cheaper than what we were paying for our US plan.

Then we had to get the proper vaccinations. Jodee is already covered from his multiple world travels, and the kids had some of the vaccinations recommended, including Hep A and B. But I had to get the Hep A/B shots (three total, spread out over six months). Then there were the typhoid fever pills, which are recommended for some of the countries on our list. The typhoid pills are more effective and last longer than the shot. But none of my kids could swallow a pill. We practiced for a few weeks with Tic Tacs, and finally they could choke down typhoid pills. Whew!

We also had to get passports for the kids. We applied in April, two months before our trip. Normally passports take four to six weeks to process, which was fine for our boys (theirs actually came in two weeks). But Macie's was delayed because of a missing letter on her birth certificate. I had to scramble and get another birth certificate with that pesky missing letter. Luckily, we got her passport a few weeks later and we didn't have to leave her behind.

Then we had to decide if we should sell our home. Realizing that having a place to come back to was important, especially for the kids, we opted to keep the house. Talking to people led us to family friends who needed a home to rent for just a year. We were able to leave much of our furniture for them to use, and we stored the rest of our belongings in one of the bedrooms.

With the house taken care of, we considered our cars. We are keeping our van for the first six months, to drive through Mexico and Central America. Then we're planning to sell it. But our other car is a 4-year-old Hyundai Elantra. At first we tried to sell it, but after considering taxes and the cost to replace it, we opted to store it at a friend's house. My husband took charge of getting one vehicle ready for storage (fingers crossed it still runs in a year) and the other ready to take us to Mexico.

Along with finding people to take care of our house and car, we had to insure both. Our house went from owner-occupied to a rental, so we needed different (and more expensive) insurance. We found an agent to take care of this for us. As for the car, driving in Mexico requires Mexican car insurance, which is less expensive than our US plan.

As for phones, we needed to make sure our phones would work abroad. I've been using Project Fi for a few years now, and it gives me international data and texting for no additional cost. International calls are very cheap, and phone calls to the US using Wi-Fi are free. My bill is usually under $40 USD per month. You only pay for the data you use. My husband gets a SIM card for his phone in each country we visit, and that's been easy and cheap. Although not as easy as Project Fi.

Next came figuring out how to handle our money. Much of the world uses cash and not credit cards, so we needed easy (and free) access to ATMs. We were able to change our account with our bank to get debit cards with no foreign transactions fees and no ATM fees on either side.

Chase Bank also assigned a contact person, which is helpful because banks often put a stop on your card if it's being used in an unusual manner. It's useful to have someone at your bank to contact to prepare for changes or to quickly resolve errors. Another option we considered was getting a Charles Schwab debit card, which also has no ATM fees and no foreign transactions fees. But for us it was easier to just stay with Chase.

Along with handling our money, how did we afford this trip? It's a question we're often asked, and I'm sure many people secretly wonder. Here are a few factors which allowed us to afford this trip around the world.

1. We are tightwads. Seriously, we save a ton by rarely going out to eat, mowing our own lawn, cleaning the house ourselves, only buying things on sale, and constantly looking for deals.

2. We own our house. We bought our home at a good time when prices were relatively low, and we've worked hard to pay off our mortgage. Therefore, the monthly rental payment is a pure source of income.

3. We've lived in Houston for almost 16 years. This city—and our neighborhood particularly—is probably one of the least expensive places to live in the country. Cheap housing, food, gas, and activities translate to more money in the bank.

4. Jodee's job is a huge blessing. He was able to work remotely for the first few months of our trip, but now he is on a leave of absence for the rest of our year abroad. We are exploring other ways to make money, but for now we are living off of our savings, as well as the rental income from our house.

5. We're going to affordable countries (Mexico, Malaysia, Thailand, Cambodia, and Eastern Europe) and staying for a month or more to take advantage of extended stay discounts.

6. Flexibility in our plans helps us save money. We can look for the best deals and go when the prices are low. Not having work or school schedules (we're worldschooling) helps with that flexibility.

Quite honestly, planning to leave our home for a year was overwhelming. I spent more than one night lying awake, wondering what in the world we were doing. Stressful situations came up in the weeks before we left, but they all resolved and we pulled out of our driveway on time—nervous, excited, anxious, happy.

And ready to see the world.

How to Finance the Adventure of a Lifetime

CONTRIBUTORS' STORIES

NICA · SAILED THE CARIBBEAN

We cruised when we were in our 20s (same boat, same general cruising grounds) for $750 USD a month, so we upped that significantly for this family trip. Health insurance was required this time around because of preexisting conditions and not wanting to risk a hospitalization kicking our assets to the ground. We landed on a budget of $2,000 a month. We rented out our house, which covered the mortgage and insurance. So that $2,000 was for food, boat and health insurance, cruising fees, plus the work we did on the boat before we left. We tightened our belts a bit in the ten months leading up, notably adding to the cruising kitty by renting out our house for three months before we left and sleeping in a friend's basement apartment.

That $2,000 goes far on a boat. We do our own maintenance, cook our own food, and stock up on good deals. We know what's cheap to stockpile in the States (beer and paper towels) and what's better to stockpile in the Bahamas (flour and yeast and rum). We also anchored out almost every single night, which is a very cheap way to live. We buy food and hardware where the locals do. It helped that friends who were updating their kit passed down their old watermaker, so we didn't have to buy water. This allowed us to play for long periods of time in places where water is scarce.

HEATHER · LIVED IN ITALY FOR TWO YEARS

Our situation was pretty easy since our move was subsidized by my husband's employer. They gave us a budget for moving expenses and a housing allowance, and laid out all the details. We paid for our gas, food, household items, and travel. We did not have to save up, nor did we really have time, as this came up rather suddenly. If I could do it again, though, I would plan ahead and save. The extra cushion would have been helpful.

SARAH · LIVES IN THE NETHERLANDS, AFTER YEARS OF WORLDSCHOOLING

The easiest way to pinch pennies abroad is to choose an inexpensive location, whether that's a developing country or living in a cheap area outside a city. Rent on a furnished three-bedroom house two blocks from the beach in Tunisia was about $350 USD per month. Food was fresh and inexpensive, and we mostly walked or used public transport, occasionally renting a car when we wanted to do a day trip. Similarly, when we moved to Ireland we found an apartment for €400 in a small town called Mullingar, almost at the end of the train line from Dublin, where my husband was looking for a job. If we hadn't needed to be on the train line, we could have easily spent much less on one of many lovely, old-fashioned

Irish farmhouses. This is where working remotely or saving the money up before can be a huge help: You won't need to be close to a job, so you'll be able to find accommodation far from centers of commerce.

AMANDA · LIVES IN MOROCCO

We're lucky because we can live in my husband's family's home in Morocco, which saves money. Even so, we ended up spending more on the move than we expected. The conversion rate was terrible at the time of the move, so we lost a lot of money. Also, our shipping container cost twice the estimate. We also had to spend money to set up our apartment, which was completely unfurnished when we arrived. Luckily, we not only budgeted well, but worked during the move, which gave us more breathing room. My advice is to save double what you think you'll need as liquid assets.

I was working remotely before the move, so my employer allowed me to continue my job from Morocco. About six months in, we also started a food tour business in Marrakech, as we wanted to show English-speaking visitors to our city where Moroccans go to eat (navigating Marrakech is difficult if one doesn't speak French or Arabic, and finding great food can be equally tough). That brings in additional income.

Being location independent is ideal. If you don't have a ready way to do that before you go, I would certainly try to figure out a way to make it work once you land. People assume we had loads of cash set aside, and we really didn't. Our plan to make this work was to understand our budget and live within our means. So that's what we did.

It also helped that Morocco is relatively inexpensive. If we had moved to the UK, it would have been much harder.

CHERYL · RV-ING THROUGH EUROPE

To finance our trip, we sold almost everything. Our house was the main asset, netting us a £29,000 profit. By the time we had cleared our credit card debt and paid our taxes and insurance, we had £10,000 to spend on our motorhome. This left us £15,000 for the trip. We budgeted £1,000 per month which gives us fifteen months of travel. Apart from our first month in France we have stuck to our budget.

MELISSA · PREPARING TO MOVE TO SPAIN

We started out basing our budget on blogs of families that moved and now work abroad. We decided if they could make it work on $30,000 AUD, so could we. We stopped eating takeaways or at restaurants. I literally spent money only on necessities. I had enough clothes, so the kids' clothing was the only real expense, unless something broke. We didn't upgrade TVs or phones, and kept our phones on cheap plans we could abandon at any time.

KIRSTY · ROAD-TRIPPED THROUGH NORTHERN AFRICA AND CENTRAL ASIA FROM HER ADOPTED HOME IN ABU DHABI

My husband and I figured we needed to budget $100 USD per day for our road trip. It took us seven years to save what we needed, which we did by renting a small flat, driving an old car, living without amenities like a TV, and not hiring help for our house or children. We didn't eat out or indulge in big luxuries. Once we were on the road, it was considerably cheaper than living in Abu Dhabi—but of course we were paid less during that time too. Averaging out the year, we did keep to the $100-per-day budget.

ASTRID · PREPARING TO WORLDSCHOOL

I am currently putting together our budget for the trip. I'm taking into consideration the cost of airfares, lodging, food, local transportation, activities, travel insurance, Internet connectivity, phone, and other day-to-day expenses. Plus, our mortgage, student loans, and credit card payments. Since we'll both be working, I am factoring in business income and business costs. Additionally, we plan to rent out our house, so I'm also considering property management costs.

Right now these are all estimates, but as we go on our trip, I anticipate that I'll be able to have more accurate numbers. I use websites like Numbeo.com to determine the approximate cost of goods in different countries.

TANIA · ROAD-TRIPPING THROUGH EUROPE

We figured we'd need about $80,000 USD for the year. This estimate was based on other people's recommendations, which we found online. We saved for years for our trip. The $80,000 estimate was about right, but we ended up putting more money than we expected into our company, so that threw us off budget. It took six months for our business to turn a profit; then we were able to put that back into the trip. We had planned on working during the year so we didn't have to have the full $80,000 but since it was a new company, we also didn't know how much we would make that first year.

LISA · BACKPACKING AROUND THE WORLD

To plan what we'd need to save, we first researched and read about other long-term traveling families. We determined a daily spend figure of $250 AUD per day for our family of six which includes everything—flights, visas, accommodation, food, activities. So $250 multiplied by 365 days = $91,250. Steve planned to tally up the monthly expenses and check to see if we were on track, or if we needed to adjust. We expected the monthly spend figure would go up and down depending on where we were living and what we were doing. For example, rural India would cost us far less than we budgeted per month, where Spain would send us over (what with all the tapas and sangria). We needed to be mindful of our monthly goal, but also use that to aim travel to less expensive countries.

Our biggest backpacking expenses have been airfares and visas, accommodation, food, and activities. Steve takes an enormous amount of time finding cheap flights. Visas add up—India cost us $100 each per visa so there's $600 gone into that. As much as possible, we've limited our travel to countries that don't require a visa.

Accommodation expenses were reduced by extended stays in Airbnb accommodation as they discount heavily (usually between 30%-50%) for stays longer than twenty-eight days. Food was a matter of eating or shopping locally and cooking for ourselves. Activities, like hiring a car for weekend exploring or surfing lessons, were also factored into the expenses.

SARA · LIVED IN MOROCCO FOR SEVEN YEARS

I would advise people to focus not on the big ways of saving money. Sometimes that's too overwhelming. Instead, look at all the small ways, and you'll be amazed at what you can save. Our kids wear mostly hand-me-downs, and they don't care if their pants are a little short. We have never focused on material things, so they haven't either. I essentially ask myself if a new dress, something for the house, or a dinner out is worth more than a new adventure. Sometimes the answer is yes, but most of the time it's no. I'll take adventure over those little things any day.

There are people who won't travel unless they are in first class and at a hotel in the prime location. To them I say drop those ideals unless you want to spend your life dreaming instead of doing. We fly Europe's budget airlines whenever possible and are flexible with our travel dates. We scout out a late afternoon *prix fixe* lunch which offers more for less, so we only need a little snack for dinner. All it takes is creating a clear plan of what you want to accomplish, and it really is amazing how everything falls into place. Trust the process!

6

WHAT TO DO WITH YOUR HOME

I gave myself heart palpitations stressing about how in the world we'd find a renter for our house. Turns out, this was one of the easiest pieces of the expat puzzle. In fact, the rental fee we pulled for our house covered not only our mortgage, but also the rent on our Italian apartment. If you live in a community with a hot rental market, this may be possible for you as well.

How do you locate a renter for your home? The simplest way is to find a family coming to your town for a sabbatical that matches the length of time you'll be gone. There are websites you can explore for listing your house (see *Resources*), but what I believe is most important is to send your intention into the universe.

I don't mean this in a "*The Secret*/bring in luck by believing in it" sort of way, but more that you need to pull every thread in your social network. For instance, I mentioned our quest to a friend at a soccer game, not knowing that she was on the committee to recruit law school professors to the University of Virginia for sabbaticals (if your town has a law school, this is a great place to begin the search as it's customary for law professors to spend a year at other universities). Sure enough, she told us about a family coming to Charlottesville from Israel with three children. It couldn't have been more perfect. They arrived the day before we left, and they left Charlottesville just a few days before we returned. So I encourage you to not be shy. I have heard stories about families being denied visas and being forced to change their destination (more on that in *Visas*), but I have yet to hear of a family that wasn't able to rent their house for the lion's share of their time abroad. Persistence and optimism get the job done.

I should note here that if your house has a relatively high rental price tag, you may want to focus on leaving and returning in the summer. Your field of viable renters will be wider since you'll attract families coming to your community for an academic sabbatical. The one family I know who struggled to rent their house for the entirety of their year abroad attempted to do so from December to December. It's just harder.

You can also choose to use your house as a vacation rental in your absence. For this you'll need to find someone to act as your property manager—keeping track of the calendar, making sure the house is cleaned between guests, taking care of maintenance, stocking the house with supplies like shampoo and toilet paper. To determine if this is a viable option, look at your neighborhood on Airbnb (or VRBO, etc.). Zoom in on houses that are similar to yours, and see how much they rent for, then click over to their calendar and see how often they are rented (limit your search to homes that are exclusively rented, not the ones people live in and rent just when they are on vacation). Do some math to figure out how much they likely make, and then subtract Airbnb fees and local taxes on vacation rentals. In some markets, families only need to rent out their houses a weekend a month to make their mortgage, some need to stay rented most weekends. Ask around to find people who rent their houses on Airbnb and talk to them about their experiences. It would be prudent to try renting out your house a few times before you go, so you can decide how it feels for you and also land on a methodology that streamlines the process.

Another option is to list your house for a house swap (see *Resources*). This is literally what it sounds like—you and another family swap houses. The advantage of this is that you'll have a friendly relationship with both the family renting your house and your landlord. Because the arrangement is mutually beneficial, everyone tends to be on their best behavior. There are other perks, such as an easy avenue for leaving your pets behind, and oftentimes, families negotiate swapping cars as well. You can essentially slip into another life with some measure of ease, and fewer bureaucratic tangles. The downsides of house-swapping is that while you won't have to pay rent for your new home, you'll be paying your mortgage on your old one. Plus, of course, you'll have fewer options for where you'll live. Which can actually be an advantage for families who like the idea of going where the wind takes them, or are undecided and prefer constants to variables.

Of course, if you are currently renting, you won't have to worry about getting a mortgage paid, but then again, you won't have the possibility of gathering enough in rental income to subsidize your new pad. That's okay, we'll find you other ways to cut financial corners.

Exchanging a Home for a Travel-Ready Lifestyle

KATE'S STORY

P arents often homeschool because they are dissatisfied with the school system, but that wasn't the case for us. School and Oscar were a great match. It was attendance that was a problem. We returned from a trip to Africa, and the school essentially shook their finger at us, "You can't keep taking him out of school!" We had to choose between homeschooling or being a slave to the public school schedule that only allows eleven unexcused absences a year. We chose freedom.

Once we took Oscar out of school, our first trip was to South America for three months. We had just started homeschooling and were very rigid.

I insisted we school every day, for two and a half hours, to get through the planned curriculum. We homeschooled in the morning, when we would rather go out for breakfast and explore. This was hard on us. Oscar felt hemmed in, and like he was hemming *us* in. To make matters worse, this was before Eric and I divided the homeschooling, so he'd walk out of the house and I'd be irritated.

Now I see that I was nervous. Educating my child was a huge responsibility. What if he needed to go back to regular school one day? How would he have discipline unless we forced it now?

Over time, it dawned on me that I was replicating the exact structure I was trying to escape. Once we moved away from those expectations, we found the freedom we had been craving. Now we know that there are days where a kid's brain is in it and days when it's not. On those days when a kid's brain is not in it, it's a struggle. For everybody. It ruins the day. We don't fight that anymore. Instead, we throw on our coats and go for a walk.

Since that first trip, we've gone to Costa Rica, traveled all over the United States, explored parts of Canada. This year we have trips planned to Barbados and New Mexico. Oscar has discovered a love of go-karting, so every year we go to Spain for go-kart camp. He's raced in Dallas, and he has races coming up in Miami and Atlanta.

This life happened only because we made it happen. We not only sold most of our belongings, we sold our house. Needing a place to land, we built a little apartment in our storage warehouse. It's small, and sometimes uncomfortable, but the downsizing means that we can take off whenever we feel the call of travel.

Besides leaving behind a traditional home, the other important change we made was hiring a business coach. Eric and I own our specialty food shop, so the business was "us" from the beginning. We needed a way to keep quality consistent, even when we weren't on site.

Initially, we tried doing this on our own, reading books for ideas. But we realized we needed neutral support. We found a business coach through Emyth (see *Resources*), and worked with her by phone for eighteen months to put our values and vision on paper, through projects and workbooks. She helped us create systems and manuals and standards, and taught us how to communicate those and measure them from abroad. Working with her allowed us to nurture leadership that would continue to inspire, and a team that would continue to function as a team, even in our absence.

Our coach was particularly helpful because she specializes in working with couples that own a business together. This work is a unique combination of business coaching and couples counseling, that we found invaluable.

The phone-call approach worked well for us, and works for the coaches. They themselves can be location independent. Ours was living in Oregon, but could move or travel anywhere.

At the end of the eighteen months of working with our coach, we had a manual and a general manager for the first time. That worked until it didn't, which brought us back for a spell. We're looking for a new general manager, but in the meantime, that job is on us again.

We're toying with the idea of moving back to the American way of living—buying a house and settling down for a little while. The apartment in the warehouse is cramped, and we're thinking it's time to have an actual home again, maybe even with a yard. Being on the transient side for a few years does start to wear on us. Whenever we're home, we're always thinking, "Where's the next place I can be?" It makes it hard to be happy in our "here" life.

At the same time, we're considering a long trip to New Zealand and Australia. Settling down in a real way is difficult because as a family, we all have the wanderlust. When Oscar was five, he told us that he was happiest with backpack on, walking through an airport.

There are unexpected hard parts to intensive travel though. The freedom and joy I imagined often didn't measure up against the reality. I have learned that trusting myself and what I need is important to preserve that sense of freedom. For instance, during that first trip, we stayed in a series of tiny Brazilian Airbnbs. I don't know if women just need more privacy, but sometimes it felt like I would lose my mind if I had to sleep one more cramped night with all that breath.

Denying that feeling made me edgy. So, I started trusting what I need. Like sometimes I need a little luxury—a nice hotel with a comfy bed and room service. I began to accept that that's what I needed every once in awhile, which felt better.

Similarly, I remember coming back from that first three-month trip, and thinking, "That wasn't at all what I hoped it would be!" I had been so busy facilitating what my husband and son wanted to do, I hadn't acknowledged what *I* wanted. I was left out of my own experience, by my own difficulty owning what I needed. Since then, I make sure I'm clear, so that I can say to my family, "This is what I want to do. Do you guys want to do it with me?" And if they don't, it's okay to do things separately. It's okay if sometimes I don't want to ski, and instead want to curl up in the lodge and watch *The Crown*.

We've also worked at communicating about *how* we travel. I like to step outside in the morning with no plans beyond wandering and watching people. But Eric is a planner, he needs everything mapped out. Then there is my son who has his own specific needs. Over time, I've increased my ability to say, "You guys go do your stuff. I'll do what I want to do, and then we'll gather together later."

Once you clam up, it's sometimes hard to unclam. We've gotten better at it, but it's a work in progress. Eric and my 2018 resolution is to meet every day at 10:30 for at least 15 minutes. For the business, but also for each other. Which means we don't waste time wondering what the other person is thinking. And we meet while we have the energy, rather than hoping to find time at night when we're both tired.

I'm not sure what our next step will be, but for now, I like the financial freedom that comes from not carrying house payments and the societal freedom of homeschooling. I like our ability to travel on a whim. It's taught me so much about trust—trusting my child to take ownership of his part of the learning process, trusting my partner to create a life and work and home (such as it is) together, trusting myself that there's value in what I need. It's liberating.

Leaving Home Behind

CONTRIBUTORS' STORIES

NICA · SAILED THE CARIBBEAN

We found renters for our house on Craigslist, and we had a friend act as a property manager. Our experience was problematic. The renters panicked at the snowstorm of 2010 and were frantically emailing us that their power was out—there's a reason we specified they put the power in their own names. They wound up leaving a couple of months early, and we didn't fight them on the lease terms. It was easier to just let them go.

CANADA-TO-FRANCE · LIVES IN FRANCE

We chose to rent out our family home. We didn't know if this would be a permanent move, plus we've owned our home for 10 years and I was not ready to let it go. We found a renter who loves our home, which has made our experience so much better. My advice for renting out your home is to have a person check in once in a while, someone you can count on should an emergency arise. With all the rain we got this spring, our home flooded and our friend was instrumental in helping deal with the disaster.

AMANDA · LIVES IN MOROCCO

We were renting an apartment, so we moved to Morocco when our lease was up. We stored all of our belongings in a storage shed for a year. When we decided to stay longer, we sold off everything.

CHERYL · RV-ING THROUGH EUROPE

The hardest part about leaving was selling our home. It's *final*. We were really happy in that house, close to family and friends, with great neighbors. We decided to keep our rental property, which gives us security in that if we are forced to return home, we have a place to live.

NELL · LIVED IN FRANCE FOR ONE YEAR

We totally lucked out. All I did was try to get the word out that we needed a tenant for a year, someone who would take care of a dog and two cats. It turned out that our neighbor needed a place to live while his house underwent renovations, and the timing worked out perfectly. Obviously you can't summon luck with any reliability, but if we had not committed to going and begun making plans, it wouldn't have had the chance to fall into place.

7

VISAS: THE STICKY WICKET

T he lurching political landscape means that I can't tell you how to get a visa. In fact, you won't be able to base your visa process on anyone else's experience, unless that person is your brother who lives next door and he did it five minutes ago. You know what? Not even then. But there are some constants.

To start, you need to visit embassy websites for your destination country or countries to find out if you will need a visa (don't trust bloggers and authors on this one, because this changes). Those of you experienced with European travel may be surprised to learn that tourist visas are required even for short stays in many countries. Some countries allow you to apply ahead of time, and some have you apply once you land at the airport. Either way, you need to be very clear on the logistics so you are prepared. For instance, some visas-on-landing demand that you have passport-type photos for every member of your family as well as exact payment while some state that you must have an original birth certificate for each of your children.

Obtaining these tourist visas is a headache, but not particularly stressful if you do your research and stay organized. I've never heard of anyone being denied a tourist visa. It's the visas for *residing* in a country that are the real bruisers. Countries want to screen who will be living within their borders, and that screening process is known as applying for a residence visa. Once you arrive at your destination, you take that visa to the local authorities to procure your temporary residency. But the visa is the first step.

Now, each country has its own exciting brand of visa bureaucracy. For instance, Americans can stay in any European country for three months without fussing with a visa at all. It used to be that if you wanted to stay longer in Europe, all you had to do was go to a non-European country (Morocco was a popular option), get your passport stamped, and then you could return for another three months. It was popularly called the "toe out of the country" rule, and American travelers still sigh in wonder at the memory of those simpler times.

It's harder now. When we went on our gap year, an American could stay in the Schengen zone for only ninety days out of every one hundred eighty. The Schengen zone includes much, but not all, of Europe. The UK, for instance, is not included, so you could spend ninety days in the UK and then another ninety days in Spain, and then repeat. Enterprising want-to-be expats with towers of cash are known to fly to a Schengen country, stamp their passport, go back home for three months, and then return. Since the clock resets at one hundred eighty days after that first entry, they now get six months of residing in a European country.

We had no such towers of cash. Nor did we have an employer willing to take on the visa paperwork.

So we went the traditional route.

We applied for a residence visa ourselves.

The first step is to peruse the embassy website to research what kinds of visas are available. Most are typical work or study or marriage visas, but I've heard of visas for artists using the country as their muse, so it's worth considering each option as there may be some esoteric one that fits your purpose.

Your next step is to figure out what consulate manages your district. It's not obvious—most of Virginia is under the umbrella of the Italian consulate in Philadelphia, while parts of northern Virginia are serviced by the

Italian Embassy in Washington, D.C. It's worth researching what other would-be-expats experiences are like for different types of visas at your consulate, as different consulates apply visa requirements with different levels of rigor. For instance, at some consulates, it's a simple thing to get a self-employed visa. At others, it's a bit like finding a unicorn.

Think carefully and do your research to decide which visa you want to apply for. Some have restrictions that seriously impact your experience—for example, a student visa often means you have to leave for school holidays or you can't bring a family, whereas an elective residency visa often requires you to promise that you won't be working while you're abroad (though I've never heard of this being checked once you arrive). Dig deep to unearth information about why others were accepted or denied. If this sounds over-whelming, and you have the financial resources to make this possible, con-sider hiring a visa specialist. Google or ask your friends or Facebook groups (and look for candidate reviews on sites like Angie's List) to find people who are well versed in getting visas into the hands of travelers.

Further Internet digging can reveal how to maximize your chances. For instance, one Italian consulate accidentally let it slip that in order to grant an elective residency visa (the kind that's typically for retired people, so there may be plenty of raised eyebrows if you use this one to apply for a family), one needs proof of assets in excess of $50,000 USD per person. This is to make sure you don't wind up with your hand in the cookie jar of government handouts. Of course, this translates to $200,000 for a family of four, far more than a family needs to stay off social program rolls, and also far higher than the financial requirement to get any other listed visa. If you know this ahead of time, you can prepare your paperwork.

Getting a visa can be such a challenge that I know people who have resorted to chicanery to get the precious document affixed to their pass-port. I'm citing no names to protect the guilty, and while you may sneer in disdain at the flouting of regulations, remember this: In order to get a visa, one usually has to apply in person within three months of leaving with a signed rental contract, a plane ticket, and proof of health insurance, along with all the other documentation. This means that after you've notified your job that you're quitting, taken your kids out of school, and shelled out serious time and money, you still may well be turned away with a sarcastic eye roll six weeks before you are slated to leave. It's a difficult position, so I have empathy for people who bend the rules to their advantage. Keith would say it's good training for Italian bureaucracy.

For instance, some people just overstay their visas. There are penalties for this if you are caught, including fines and/or being barred from entering the country for a specific amount of time. I've heard rumors that some countries are less likely to check or prosecute, so you can fly in and out of those and then drive to your destination. There are other rumors that if you have a child, visa officials are unlikely to make a stink, because children are automatically afforded residency and parents are just hangers-on. Speaking for myself, the mental image of being dragged away from my children as they scream and bang on the plexiglass was enough to deter me from attempting this path with nothing but crossed fingers and optimism bordering on psychopathy. As an American, I now have contemporary images of this very scenario, some variant of which plays out on my newsfeed with alarming frequency. For me, it's not a compelling option.

I have heard of people moving so that their new address falls under the jurisdiction of a friendlier consulate. Even easier, some people borrow a friend's address, get a driver's license in that state or zone, to be granted access to another consulate. For instance, in Los Angeles it is notoriously difficult to get an Italian elective residency visa, while the San Francisco consulate is more generous. Some consulates offer helpful visa officers who answer the phone and talk you through the process or (gasp!) suggest an appointment to come and chat. Others ignore your calls, letters, tweets, and faxes, leaving you to wade through the process on your own. Or worse, I know of one Italian consulate that told a hopeful expat mom, "There's no way you are getting a visa because the visa is designed for retired people, so please don't even bother us with an application."

What's Italian for Debbie Downer?

Knowing that countries really like rich foreigners to come and pump up their economy, some people borrow money from friends and family to appear (on paper) so wealthy that the consulate falls over itself to roll out the welcome mat. You just need to have that money in your account when the bank prints out your financial statement and when you have your visa interview—a total of a few days.

Some people (like us) apply only for the parents. A couple is less likely to spark the furrowed eyebrows and thousand-yard stare than a family, especially for an elective residency visa. A family gap year is not a routine thing (yet), and if you are easier to peg into an expected box, you're more likely to get a visa. Bonus: Your assets are only for two people, which means the allotment per person is automatically higher when you divide your assets by two. This does create some uncomfortable ambiguity when you land and offer up two visas to gain residency for your whole family (more on this below). It helps to memorize the following, whether or not it's true: "That's what the consulate worker told me to do."

My main advice for your meeting with the consulate as your visa hangs in the balance is to be prepared. If you make extra work for your visa officer—either by being disorganized or trying to fit into a visa category that's not intended for you—they'll be less inclined to be accommodating. This doesn't mean smile and be gregarious (though one friend had good luck by bringing her consulate worker a plate of cookies). American friendliness is weird to non-Americans. Don't be weird. Just have all your documents ready, organized, and stamped with something shiny if possible (Italians, anyway, have a near feverish reverence for anything with a gold seal on it).

The most important piece of information you'll be bringing is your financials. You want to look stinking, filthy rich. So make sure you think hard. Include information about every single revenue stream you have. For instance, it wasn't until a few days before our meeting with the consulate that Keith realized we'd neglected to include the rent we'd be receiving from our house while we were away. This was a huge boon—having a source of income that flows in while you're abroad is excellent. Even better if you have a trust or retirement accounts to draw money off of in your absence (which we don't). But that rental income helped lift our financials to over $100,000, which divided by two is—*ta-da!* $50,000 each. The magic number. As soon as our visa officer got to those two numbers, he essentially stopped reading our application and not only welcomed us to Italy, but encouraged us to stay for longer than a year. When he realized what we thought was a signed lease was not what Italians consider a signed lease, he gave us his private contact information to fax the documentation and gently guided us through the rest of the process.

As I've alluded to, the process isn't quite finished with the visa. The visa allows you to apply for residency on arrival, but the rules for how and when to do that vary (once again) by country, and often by the week. In Italy, we had to apply for a residency appointment at the post office within a few weeks of our arrival, and then were sent a time to appear at the police station to complete the process. In our post office application, we couldn't see a place to note that we have children (this is unrelated to the fact that we didn't declare our kids, so to speak; the form we filled out is the same one any hopeful resident picks up), so we didn't, and found out later that our getting residency for them would have been easy had we completed that form differently. As it was, the residency officer huffed and shook his head and muttered something about birth certificates, at which point Keith used more than a bit of flourish to pull out the birth certificates, in triplicate, with their winking golden seals (official birth certificates, otherwise known as "apostilled," have such fancy designation). The officer's eyes widened, and he began the paperwork for the children. In the end, we parlayed two visas into five residencies just by feeling our way forward with optimism and tenacity.

I should add that the visa process is one of many spots where flexibility and creativity are key. Some people are so flexible that they design where they will live based on where it is easy to get a visa. After all, though some countries hoard visas possessively, some countries give visas out like Halloween candy. Energy might be well spent taking what's offered rather than arming for battle. This is an especially advantageous route for travelers who feel like they could live anywhere, so they might as well let the visa gods decide. It's astounding how your own attitude towards residing in a country can vary by how welcome you feel, which is a direct result of how turbulent and painful the process is. So if your heart isn't set on a specific destination, it may behoove you to consider the ease of acquiring a visa when deciding where to go. When you are doing research on easy-to-enter countries, bear in mind that this varies by country of origin. The United States has different arrangements with other countries than Australia or the UK does. So don't take this as gospel, but countries that are commonly considered to have less-stringent immigration policies are Uruguay, Mexico, Brazil, United Arab Emirates (UAE), Singapore, Ecuador, Israel (if you are Jewish), Belize, Panama, Paraguay, Dominican Republic, and Malaysia. I mention these not to create a dartboard to fling your expat dreams at, but rather to illustrate the wealth of possibilities.

If you are undecided on where to go, consider applying for citizenship in a country where you have ancestors. Think about it—you may well have some grandparent or great-grandparent who emigrated from Croatia or France or Argentina. It's worth a look to see if that country's requirements would allow you to apply for citizenship so you can skip the whole visa process. That can be a long road, but we discovered that if you are applying for citizenship in Italy, you are allowed to live in the country while your application is under review. It's a special kind of back-door way of living in the country visa-free. In fact, that's how I "met" Sarah, one of our contributors. She had blogged about her experience using the ancestry route for Italian residency, and she was extraordinarily kind when we reached out to her with follow-up questions.

Keith's great-grandfather emigrated from Abruzzo and didn't renounce his citizenship before Keith's grandfather was born, thus Keith, his grandfather, mother, and our children, are all technically Italian citizens, according to *jure sanguines*, law of the bloodline. Countries vary by how they determine citizenship, some by number of generations from home soil, some by gender of the ancestor, so the way to begin is to make a list of all of your countries of origin, even really far back. Would you be willing to live in any of those countries? If so, look into how to prove citizenship and if you can live in the country while you are applying.

Just a note: It's easier to apply for Italian citizenship while you are living in Italy rather than sending your application to the consulate and having them forward your application to Rome. Why? Because if you apply at your local *comune*, you can periodically check in on the process. Italians aren't known for calling if there's a problem. They're known for going out for a cup of *espresso* if there's a problem, so checking in can keep your application on course.

The bottom line is that you'll need a visa to set foot in some countries and to stay in others. You'll need to research not only what types of visas you qualify for, but also which visas are most likely at your assigned consulate. If your options are dim, you can opt either to resort to shenanigans to maximize your odds or change your itinerary to suit the reality of the visa process. I know it can feel unfair that other people can swan into their family adventure with nary a hiccup because of their mountains of cash or powerful translocation agents. But I also know that the kind of person who will pick up a book about moving their family abroad has the resourcefulness and adaptive skills to turn any negative obstacle into an opportunity for a more creative experience.

The Trouble with Visas

SARAH'S STORY

V isas and related immigration procedures can be a huge headache. I've spent many happy (ha!) hours collecting documents, stamps, and translations to placate various foreign governments. But some countries do make it uncommonly easy. In Tunisia, for example, Americans can stay for four months, and then after a short dash over the border (just an exit and reentry stamp, really) come back and stay for another four months. You can repeat this process indefinitely. The only catch is that the two countries bordering Tunisia are Algeria and Libya, neither of which constitutes a safe family destination. When it came time to break our eight-month stay in Tunisia, we took an overnight ferry to Sicily and enjoyed a week exploring Greek temple ruins.

It's worth checking the visa possibilities for several different countries of interest, since the requirements can be remarkably different, even in adjacent and otherwise similar countries. For example when we researched a one-year visa in Italy, we discovered that it required proof of an undisclosed but large sum of money in one's bank account (there were rumors of $500,000 USD for our particular consulate). In France, to get a similar visa we just needed to prove that we had enough money to support ourselves for the year. However, neither of these visas would allow us to work while in the country, not even freelance or for a company abroad.

In the Netherlands, on the other hand, the Dutch-American friendship allows US citizens to continue or set up their own business (including consulting, web development, dog sitting, or anything else you can imagine). Minimum investment required in the business? Just $4,500.

Acquiring Visas

CONTRIBUTORS' STORIES

NELL · LIVED IN FRANCE FOR ONE YEAR

Our family needed a *Carte de Séjour* for France. I remember being daunted by the hoops we would have to jump through. Since organization is not my strong suit, I wrote out the steps on a big piece of paper and taped it to the kitchen wall where I couldn't avoid seeing it every day, and with fanfare crossed items off as they were accomplished.

It wasn't so terrible, in retrospect. The process is scary because of the time pressure—you've rented the house, now what if the papers don't come through? ACK! But taking baby step after baby step finally got us to the end.

One of the last obstacles was an interview at the French consulate in Washington, D.C. I had read much about French attitudes towards Americans, and was determined to pass this interview with flying colors. We all dressed up like we were going to see the Pope, and the kids were harangued about proper manners until I nearly had a mutiny on my hands.

I had envisioned the four of us in a room with flags and a huge antique desk, trying to prove we would be respectful, indeed deferential, to French culture and able ambassadors of the United States. Instead, we pushed forms back and forth under a plexiglass window, the forms were stamped and signed, and we were free to go. I think we went out for ice cream afterwards.

HEATHER · LIVED IN ITALY FOR TWO YEARS

We had to go through all the steps, but didn't have to do the behind-the-scenes arranging since my husband's company took care of the visas.

His work visa came through quickly, but the kids and I didn't receive ours until thirty-six hours before we were set to leave Idaho. It was a nail biter.

SARA · LIVED IN MOROCCO FOR SEVEN YEARS

I quickly discovered that in Morocco, consulates and embassies are not there to support their citizens as much as they are there to support their government's interests. I think we all have this image from the movies that embassies are places that offer support. Not the case unless you're in a grave emergency. This being said, when it came to renewing passports the consulate in Casablanca was awesome. Once an appointment was made online, I could drop off our paperwork, and we'd have our new passports within a week! I once needed an emergency passport after realizing mine didn't have enough pages and I was leaving for a trip later that week, and they made me an emergency passport in twenty minutes.

Once I had to deal with the Indonesian Embassy in Morocco, and that was trying. They wouldn't give us extended-stay social visas until we had the plane tickets, but they also wouldn't guarantee that I'd get the visas from them (which I needed to have upon arrival to Bali) until after I bought the tickets. So, I had to risk buying the tickets and then not getting the visa. This involved a lot of paperwork, including bank statements and proof of residency in Morocco (even though I was an American). So word of note: When traveling, always have vital statements accessible in case you need to get a visa somewhere other than a consulate in the States.

GABRIELLA · LIVES IN MEXICO

Mexico has a very accessible tourist program. People holding US or Canadian passports are welcome for up to one hundred eighty days before having to exit or apply for a visa. Many people ("snowbirds" especially) will come for one hundred eighty days, leave the country and return when they're ready, with a new tourist card in hand. Due to the recent political change in the US, the Mexican immigration control has been targeting folks who border hop, requiring that they apply for temporary or permanent visas. These visas demand both proof of income and a lengthy paperwork process that begins in the country of origin.

I recommend arriving on a tourist card, setting yourself up, and then if you decide to stay, apply for a visa on your next stateside trip. It is a long, costly process, so be sure it's what you want before wasting time and money.

TANIA · ROAD-TRIPPING THROUGH EUROPE

We were able to get a French long-stay tourist visa that was valid for one year. It was relatively easy. We had to travel to San Francisco to get the visas, but we turned that into a fun family adventure. The main requirement to get the visas is proving that you have enough funds to support yourself. They don't want anyone taking a job in France. Getting a visa in Germany was not an option because homeschooling is illegal there. Although homeschooling is legal in most European countries, it's not popular and often frowned upon.

LISA · BACKPACKING AROUND THE WORLD

In some Southeast Asian countries you have to apply for a visa on arrival. Prior to landing in Vietnam I joined the local expat community Facebook page in Hoi'An to ask questions about the visa process and learned that many of those travel forms are online. While we were still in Cyprus, we arranged for our visas so that when we arrived in DaNang International Airport we did not have to wait at the visa area to fill out six visa application forms. Plus, we didn't have to have the cash all up front, as we were able to pay the airport fee on arrival and the visa at a later date.

CANADA-TO-FRANCE · LIVES IN FRANCE

Applying for visas is quite a process. They want to know everything about you from the beginning of time. We had to provide fingerprints, police and background checks, income verification, health insurance confirmations, bank statements for up to a year, and employment details. Being Canadians we were lucky—it was a pretty seamless process. Yes, there was mountains of paperwork, but it wasn't impossible. Just tedious. We demonstrated that we planned on continuing to work for our Canadian companies, we had health insurance and therefore didn't require French resources, and that pushed our visa through fairly quickly.

8

MAKING MONEY WHILE ABROAD

I'm a therapist, so my work isn't transferable. Even if I were fluent in another language, I can't imagine the hubris involved in counseling people in a country where I don't intrinsically understand their context. So keeping my job while abroad was a nonstarter and will forever be so, unless I work on a military base. Not happening.

Keith, however, as a self-employed graphic designer, easily transported his job. Unfortunately or fortunately, depending on how you look at it, the breather of our Spello year forced him to admit how much he loathed that job. Enjoying his life made him realize that happiness is actually pretty important (who knew?). Shortly after our return, he taught himself programming, with the goal of getting work as a developer. That's what he does now, which, as I like to remind him, is also a portable job. *Wink*!

He loves his work now, and plans to keep it when we travel the world in two years.

If your work isn't mobile, it's time to practice creativity. For instance, I can't in good conscience conduct therapy in another country, but I can use myself as a subject and write about that. Hence my idea for a book where I'd ask myself the same hard, important questions I ask of my clients. To acknowledge the stretching and growing endemic to living abroad, feel that discomfort, then document working through it. Every day, Keith and I would walk the kids to school, then stroll to Bar Bonci. I'd sip my *cappuccino* and wonder what to write about. Half-formed realizations leapt into fruition just by virtue of my allowing them space. I'd hustle back up the cobblestone streets, eager to get in front of my keyboard and write in a way that allowed me to really see—myself, my family, my new community, my new life. Then I'd select a photo from my rapidly increasing stockpile (photography was something I discovered I loved) to encapsulate the piece, hold my breath, and hit "publish now." By nightfall I'd find comments and questions from people reading my words all over the globe. Not only was I lucky enough to have not a single troll, but those strangers' words helped me through some tough times.

Once Spellani found out I was blogging (or *blobbing*, as my Italian teacher would sometimes call it), then the work took a turn.

I wasn't just documenting *my* experience, I was documenting theirs.

Spellani who could read in English or had the patience for Google Translate told me that my work made them rethink how they regarded their sleepy town. By seeing what I saw, the gleam of their lives became clearer.

This culminated in a book party in Spello the month after I published *Il Bel Centro*. Speakers from the Department of Culture, the former vice mayor, and my Italian teacher spoke about our family, how we became part of the community, and how the book captures what it means to live in Spello.

There can be no greater reward for me and my work than that afternoon in the shade of the Palazzo Comunale, holding back tears as I spoke my thanks to the people I had grown to love.

Now, it's true that in the topsy-turvy world of independent book publishing, it can't rightly be said that my writing constitutes a "job." In that it doesn't make actual "money." I mean, it keeps us in wine and cheese and the gym membership that I've decided is worth it to burn off that wine and cheese, but it's not a living in the strictest sense of the word. Then again, it could be if I wrote and marketed with more focus. One of our contributors, Nell, supports herself by self-publishing her books. Her most popular work is a cozy mystery series set in France. So you see how the experience abroad can shape our craft.

Since I can't do therapy abroad and my writing isn't lucrative enough to support a family, it was Keith's work that kept us afloat in Spello (though mine at home that provided the stockpile), and realistically it will be his work that joins us on our next year abroad. Being untethered to a brick-and-mortar office has advantages, so if travel is important to your lifestyle, it makes sense to consider careers that allow you to work from anywhere. If you plan far enough ahead, it may be possible to set your feet now on a path that will ultimately lead to that kind of freedom.

If location independence isn't possible in your current line of work, there are ways to monetize your present or future experience. For instance, you can create a business. Tania, one of our contributors, worked with her husband to combine their love of travel and storytelling into a company called Around the World Stories. The company launched about a month before their departure, and as you follow her through these chapters, you'll see that though it was hard work, it was satisfying and allowed them to continue traveling. She says, "Part of the beauty of our trip was that we were able to create authentic audio stories based on the actual places we visited and people we met. We ended up writing fifty-two stories covering thirteen countries. Even though the stories are fiction, many of our actual experiences inspired characters, settings, and plot lines."

Another option for generating revenue in a foreign country is to buy an investment property. Granted, this is only possible if you have the funds up front. If you do, you can purchase a property and rent out part or all of it to subsidize your life abroad. This can take a bit of time to set up, so this is only a viable option for people who have a lot of lead time or a stocked bank account, as these projects often entail some amount of renovation. I know one family that moved from England to Italy and worked remotely for a bit of time until they saved enough for land in the wine hills above Milan. Pondering the market and how they could muscle into a niche, they created a website about the attractions of the area as they designed and built a vacation rental geared to large groups.

Several of our contributors work remotely as consultants or coaches. Gabriella and Melissa both generate revenue by helping people with their lives or businesses. Life and business coaches are often location independent (remember Kate told us about how she hired a location-independent business coach in order to gain independence from her own family business?), so if you are interested in that work, research organizations that offer you training to make you comfortable hanging a shingle that says you are open for business.

Those dreamers who have lived vicariously through travel blogs know there are families that subsidize their life abroad by blogging. One of our contributors, the Wagoner family, does a wonderful job reporting not only on the financial costs of living abroad, but also how they make their income, which includes blogging. Websites abound to guide you in monetizing a blog, a simple search of "how to monetize your blog" will turn up loads of clear information. The moral of that story is: Build a website with interesting content that people want to share and link to, and get ads on your site that pay you for the right to appear on your space, while working on search engine optimization to increase traffic to your site and thus to those ads. AdSense and Mediavine (once you have great traffic) plop ads onto your website, or you can get specific sellers like Amazon and Booking to kick you some change every time someone buys something via your website.

A hot tip is to run a Google keywords search to discover what content people are searching for, and then write articles to address that subject. A website with a specific subject (for instance, your specific corner of Turkey, rather than all Turkey; or backpacking versus just general travel) is more likely to generate reliable traffic. Therefore, many travelers find it useful to host more than one website to showcase the different aspects of their knowledge base. Multiple websites mean more possible ad revenue and also more legitimacy for you if you decide to seek out consulting work.

You can further dig into this task of becoming an expert on your travels by creating books that address aspects as diverse as getting a visa for a specific country to driving in that country (even micro-books to sell digitally on your website or in online bookstores). Now that Amazon has made self-publishing a virtual breeze, this is a low-risk way to play with revenue generation. Having books to your name means you increase your odds of gaining income through consulting or contributing content to other people. Once you've established yourself as an expert, you can even teach courses on subjects like how to travel your way or how to monetize a travel blog.

It would behoove you to sit down and really think about what knowledge, training, skills, or passions you have that you can monetize. Can you consult? Can you create a website where people can find what you offer and then network to drive traffic to that website? The outlay of initial cash to experiment with these endeavors is relatively low, and you can begin while you are still in the dreaming stages.

If your current experience or skill set is just not an option in terms of thinking about employment, there are multiple avenues towards making money. Teaching English is a common avenue (online or at a language school, see *Resources*), as is multilevel marketing. You can also look for jobs doing translation or data entry or editing or coding or marketing (again, see *Resources* for websites that can help you find work abroad). A quick scan of Facebook groups that cater to traveling families will show you that with some creativity and tenacity, creating gainful employment where you want to live is absolutely possible. This is particularly true if your adventure involves shrinking your budget (via living in an inexpensive country, going without a car, etc.) such that you can make less than you currently do.

How We Afford Our Life in Mexico

GABRIELLA'S STORY

Eight years ago, my husband and I had a destination wedding in Mazatlán. As we were flying home, I said to him, "Wouldn't it be amazing to live here someday?" He agreed, but of course, life happens. Fast forward six years and three children, after the unexpected passing of my mother, we finally decided to take the leap to live in another country.

Choosing Mazatlán was easy. I had vacationed there so often it already felt familiar. It's a coastal city with a great deal of colonial charm mixed with modern amenities. Mexico as a whole is a very family-friendly culture. It's warm year round, making it easy to continue with the fitness regimens that are important to both of us (and luckily, we live close to an oceanfront running path). In addition, we hoped that the lower cost of living would translate into a healthy work-life balance, in a location where we could expose our children to a new way of living and a new language.

While we were still stateside, my husband and I began using our off-work hours to develop lifestyle ventures to fund our life in Mexico. I was already a blogger and health coach, but with the change in our lives, I decided to add coaching women in relocation support, business development, and eventually mindset enhancement. I love my work giving women concrete strategies for creating multiple revenue streams while transitioning to a lifestyle of full-time travel and adventure.

Vernon works as a writer. He is a featured author on a few blogs like Entrepreneur and The Good Men Project. His focus is also primarily personal development, but he also writes about critical race theory as well as diversity and inclusion. He travels stateside occasionally for speaking engagements, making Mexico an excellent location for us.

Neither of us has any specific training for our businesses, but we are both degreed (I have an M.Ed. in elementary education and Vernon has a Ph.D. in policy studies and urban education). Those degrees help with our perceived legitimacy, but they aren't required to do the work we do. We've learned what we need to from extensive reading, and get most of our clients via social media and word of mouth.

As our work continually changes, I'm learning the importance of flexibility. With everything. Especially as an entrepreneur, because the flow of money is inconsistent (especially at the beginning). Having savings to fall back on is vital in those lean months, but having a flexible plan that allows for change is essential to entrepreneurship, living abroad, and parenting. Flexibility really is important for everything!

Our businesses aren't lucrative, *per se*, but given the cost of living in Mexico, we are able to maintain a similar lifestyle to what we had before, but with far fewer hours sitting at a desk or in traffic. Our expenses here run about $3,000 USD less per month than our life in the States, thanks in part to the fact that now that we live in a walkable city; we sold both of our cars and save on car payments, gas, insurance, and maintenance. The lower cost of living gives us the flexibility (that word again!) to experiment with new revenue streams. Having multiple routes to making money is critical, as relying on one program, product, or job is just too risky. So not only do I juggle my lifestyle businesses, but I also do freelance writing. I wrote a book about fitness and developing healthy habits, which nets me a little money, in addition to the few online courses that I teach. Plus, I am partnered with a multilevel marketing company (Herbalife), from which I receive occasional residual checks.

It's a lot to juggle, but we enjoy our lives now. Could we make more, and would we want to? Sure, but we see increases each quarter and are just grateful for what we have here. Mexico has a slower and friendlier pace of life than in the United States. Rather than walking into stores demanding things, we greet store owners, ask them how they are, and make conversation. Smiles and greetings in the street are common. Neighbors help one another and are happy to play with our children.

As Black American travelers, I'm amazed at the 180° change in attitude my husband experiences from police and people of power here in Mexico. On our first day here, a police officer not only stopped his car, and traffic, to allow our family to cross, but he greeted my husband as sir, and waved. This is how my husband should be treated. With dignity and respect. I no longer worry about his safety, "Driving While Black" or otherwise. It's a huge weight off of my shoulders.

It's true that our experience is probably different from other Black Americans' in Mexico. There is definitely an element of colorism still present here, but our family kind of blends in. People assume we are Brazilian or Panamanian. If not those, the next guess is that we're Jamaican or Mexicans from Mexico City. American is usually the LAST guess, even when we're speaking English clearly. I think that phenotypically we fit in somehow, and we are then treated more inclusively. Now that the kids are so close to fluent, this inclusivity has only increased.

Nowadays, I'm the happiest when I hear my children speaking Spanish with their friends, without a care in the world. It comes so naturally, and that is precisely what I wanted for them. Isn't this what all parents want? To have their children be accepted and loved? In this life that Vernon and I have created, this is exactly what I see.

Generating Revenue

CONTRIBUTORS' STORIES

SARAH · LIVES IN THE NETHERLANDS AFTER YEARS OF WORLDSCHOOLING

Over the years, we have done a combination of running our own online business, working remotely for an American company, and finding jobs in country. If you can get your company to sponsor your overseas move, excellent! That's the easiest and least stressful solution. However, there are definitely other options. While working for an American company, I convinced my boss to let me work remotely from Amsterdam. As a trial, I worked from home a day a week to show him that it was feasible, and to get him comfortable with the tools we'd need to communicate. The company already did regular conference calls with offices around the country, so remote communication was an easy sell. I agreed to work from 1 PM to 10 PM Amsterdam time (starting and ending two hours earlier than my east coast counterparts). I will say that working remotely from another time zone means I can't do weeknight activities and my husband has to take care of dinner and bedtime. The schedule makes it hard to make friends and integrate. Plus, part of my brain is in Florida, so there's a disconnect between my working life and the rest of my life. But it has been worth it to make our overseas dream a reality.

LISA · BACKPACKING AROUND THE WORLD

We've funded our year of travel by careful saving. But now that we've had a taste of being a wandering backpacking family, Steve and I plan to transform our work-dependent roles into a location-independent digital-nomad lifestyle. My goal is to digitalize our family travel blog—*SixBackpacks.com*—from its current state as a chronicle of our journey into an online travel business. I hope the site will inspire and assist other families who are itching to explore the world together.

This process of transforming the site and perhaps creating a book will be a huge developmental learning curve, as I have no idea how to do either. But I'm excited to expand my knowledge base with the help of online research and other traveling families who have successfully created something similar.

MELISSA · PREPARING TO SETTLE IN SPAIN

I started my business in January 2017. At first my plan was to help people with lifestyle development. Because I needed support, I joined a mentor program, the Entrepreneur School. This helped me refine my direction and get me up and running. Around May, I decided to focus on business coaching (which meant overcoming a lot of self-limiting beliefs, as I had yet to own a business). I took on three practice clients for free, and service swapped with my Social Media Manager to build my skills. Now, I help people develop businesses and assist them with strategy and automation. I love documenting systems and processes, which is the key to setting up a business that you can run with minimal hours.

It's taken some time to build up my reputation, but with multiple glowing reviews, things are picking up. So I'd say to anyone with a passion to help people, you can make money online. Life coaching is another very lucrative online service that people pay a lot of money for. Again, you can expect it to take four to 12 months to become profitable, but it can work and I've heard of many life coaches who go full time within a year of becoming qualified.

KIRSTY · ROAD-TRIPPED THROUGH NORTHERN AFRICA
AND CENTRAL ASIA FROM HER ADOPTED HOME IN ABU DHABI

I have my own business as a photographer and so I photographed families as we traveled and also submitted photographs to a stock agency. In addition, I mentor other photographers, especially those who want to travel with their families and need to learn how to juggle everything. In order to keep our visas in United Arab Emirates we had to return mid-journey, so I also did photo shoots then.

ASTRID · PREPARING TO WORLDSCHOOL

We plan to work while we're on the road, and still need to figure out exactly what that will look like. My husband is trying to scale up his freelance web development business. For me, I currently work for an international nonprofit organization, but tax/HR issues may prohibit me from continuing that work while I am traveling. As such, I'm planning on starting a consulting business and marketing myself as a consultant to international nonprofits.

SARA · LIVED IN MOROCCO FOR SEVEN YEARS

Unlike many other traveling families, a job is what brought us into traveling. I also worked for five of the seven years we were there, but ultimately quit for the freedom to travel with the kids and give them more attention. We were fortunate to be financially set while living abroad, but I will say this—I'm incredibly inspired by my countless friends who figured out ways to support their travels. I've met people who taught English in schools or privately, or found jobs as a company's primary English speaker, or created their own companies, or made pop-up clinics if they were health or wellness coaches, or contacted charitable organizations and offered their skills in exchange for room and board, or of course, the digital nomads. Many of those who found the jobs once in the country found them from word of mouth and from personally seeking out the companies; these are not jobs that were ever posted on a search engine. Some of these companies didn't even know they needed this foreigner to work for them until the foreigner suggested how he or she could be useful. These travelers all thought outside the box and figured out what was unique to them that could be utilized by their host country. Once someone stops thinking within the lines of what stability should look like, they can find countless opportunities. I also think the differences in cost of living need to be taken into account. One does not need to make nearly as much in a developing country as in a developed country. So, before you brush aside a job because of what looks like a low salary, take into account the cost of living.

9

HOW TO FIND A SPOT TO UNPACK

I f you'll be seeking long-term accommodations, you have two house-hunting avenues. One is to peruse a vacation rental site like VRBO or HomeAway or Airbnb or Booking.com, and the other is to seek out local landlords or property managers. Using a vacation rental site is ideal when your exact location isn't fixed. Scrolling through websites with a cup of American joe in one hand, imagining that you could live there! Or there! Or *there!* can help you narrow your search criteria. We scanned all around central Italy and found possible apartments in a handful of towns. Digging into the options clarified our priorities: a three-bedroom apartment in the center of town, with elementary and middle schools in walking distance.

The boon of vacation rentals is that they are likely bedecked with plates and sheets and nightstands. However, they tend to be more expensive, so some travelers find that renting through a local agent and then furnishing through IKEA or thrift markets is more feasible. This depends on how long you plan to stay put, and how much you want to expend setting up housekeeping. Brooms and glasses may be cheap, but they do add up.

If you are exploring vacation rentals, the likely monthly rent of a year-long lease may be as low as the posted weekly rate or as high as double the posted weekly rate. Why so low? Owners often reduce rates in order to avoid a house standing empty in the low season. This is more likely in less-touristed areas that aren't booked year round, but don't be shy about asking potential landlords if they would consider a long-term rental, and what the cost would be. Some won't consider it because they make so much money in the summer or because they like to keep the house available for family, but it's worth asking.

A word of warning: Vacation rental sites can function like a weird travel porn/dating app hybrid—so many homes for you to imagine your family in, your children in drawing at the kitchen table after a stimulating visit to the local Dali exhibit. It fairly tickles the dreaming bone and can be addictive to the point where it drives you bananas rather than serves a purpose. There's also an inherent level of frustration when, for instance, a landlord of the perfect house doesn't return your email or won't rent for a year.

We inadvertently used a combination of the two methods. We scoured vacation rental sites to locate homes and then asked potential landlords about renting for a year. We formed relationships with a few of those landlords, even though they weren't able to host us, because they were interested in our story. For instance, Gina, at Casa Spello, couldn't rent to us for the year, but put us in touch with the man who became our landlord. His apartment wasn't listed anywhere.

Another way to combine the methods is to use a site like Booking (my preference because of its advanced search filters) for a month or so, and spend that month hunting for a home via word of mouth or a local agent. That's a bit riskier in a town like Spello, as apartments for what's considered a large family like ours are in short supply. But in a town chockablock with choices, this can be a viable option. I don't think I could handle that amount of uncertainty, but plenty of people do, to the delight of their pocketbook.

You have extra options if your chosen destination is a major city. Popular, high-density locations like Madrid often have throngs of people advertising their relocation services. A Google search, or query in a Facebook group, should turn up at least a handful. These folks (often expats themselves) will help you find a home in your price range, and can also serve as resources when researching schools for your child. This isn't a budget option, but you can see if it would be worth it for you, particularly if you have needs not easily addressed by web searching. The amount you save by not going the vacation rental route may make the hire vastly worth it, and anyway, many of these agents are paid by the landlords, meaning the financial calculus is all in your favor. Again, it's worth at least a peek.

Housing is going to be your biggest expense, so be mindful. If your budget is tight, don't bother looking at that castle, no matter how romantic it seems with those dramatic gardens. Instead, adjust the "price" toggle to meet your budget. Striking out? Your options are:

* Join Facebook groups for your chosen area to get leads.

* Look a bit outside your chosen area (for instance, suburbs are often cheaper than cities, and some neighborhoods within a city can be less expensive).

* Look to a different town in the same country. Smaller towns or less famous ones or ones with less tourism will be cheaper, sometimes exponentially so. For example, our budget was €1,000/month. Which is impossible in Florence where low rents on Airbnb run about €2,500 per month. Our budget turned up plenty of reasonable apartments in Umbria. But (and I'm totally not joking here), we found a former Ducal Palace in Le Marche that rented for €900/month. Five stories, a garden with olive trees and views to the ocean to the left and the snow capped Apennine mountains to the right, a cavernous wine cellar, pool table, five bedrooms, a fireplace big enough to stand in, multiple cozy living spaces. In a word, unbelievable. We ultimately decided against the palace because the town's remoteness meant we felt uncomfortably conspicuous, plus our daughter's carsickness made the amount of required driving a non-starter. Did we choose correctly? Who knows?

I can tell you that sending that email declining the Ducal Palace was physically painful. Luckily our apartment in Spello was even cheaper, which softened the blow.

* Go back to the *Where to Go* chapter. Get clear on why you want that destination. Could you get those needs met by a whole different country?

* Explore the notion of other ways of traveling. For instance, RVing or volunteering or house-sitting.

Finding a place to live is one of those myriad tasks that calls for ingenuity, flexibility, and tenacity. Think of this as an opportunity to cultivate adaptive perspective-taking. Every negative has a flip side. I know one expat who commented that the town she landed in was less attractive than she had hoped. But then she realized this meant that it wasn't touristed, which leads to a more authentic experience.

I suggest that you abandon any notion that "things always happen for a reason" and instead practice saying, "I can make any situation work for me."

And then do just that.

Creating a Cross-Generational Home in Le Marche

A fter years of expat life, my husband and I were enjoying our retirement in Switzerland. We had painstakingly renovated a home among vineyards, with a view over glittering Lake Geneva and up to towering Mont Blanc. We socialized with a small group of mostly expatriate friends. It was nice. Quite nice. And yet I felt an itch for change. Charles and I started to realize we needed more exercise than our car-based existence afforded us, and we craved more "life" in our lives. Some expatriates like us who have moved continuously sometimes just have to get up and go once they've "completed the mission."

Around the time our restlessness was ramping up, we planned a trip to Bologna, an Italian city I love, as well as Le Marche on the Adriatic coast, a region we'd never explored. Craving the stirrings of a new venture, and also realizing that taxes on retirees were going up in Switzerland, we decided that perhaps we would investigate homes in Bologna. Just to see what was available.

In advance of our vacation, I scrolled real estate listings. A photo of a blue kitchen popped up. Something about it caught my eye, even though it was in Le Marche, not Bologna. The kitchen was part of a wine and olive oil property, just ten miles from the sea. It spoke to me. "In another life, of course," I muttered to myself. Yet, I couldn't help sending the listing to Charles with the note, "We're too old for this, and it's not in Bologna, but boy is it pretty!"

Our real estate search in Bologna was a bust. We enjoyed our visit nonetheless and continued onto Le Marche. Our new son-in-law, Chris, a chef at the Waldorf Astoria in New York City, suggested we visit a seaside restaurant where he had once worked. After that meal, we planned to visit two wineries that had supplied the wine for Chris and Marjorie's wedding. Those wineries were closed, and having nothing to do on a lazy Sunday afternoon, when *everything* is closed, I said to Charles, "You know, that wine property with the blue kitchen, it's just right around here. We could go have a look..." We did, and Charles immediately thought of Chris and Marjorie, how much they would love it.

A long story short, Chris and Marjorie are the new owners of that blue kitchen, and Charles and I are new grandparents of their beautiful daughter. We have settled in Ancona, the provincial capital on the Adriatic sea, fifty minutes from Tenuta Marino di Monterado, Chris and Marjorie's wine-and-olive producing property. There is not a more impractical kitchen anywhere, I hate to say, than that blue kitchen that changed our lives.

As blissful as a cross-generational move to Italy may seem, there are hardships. Moving three generations just four months after a birth was complicated. Plus the house renovation, settling in two places fifty minutes apart in a new country, and starting a fledgling business. As my chef kids agree, this isn't just a recipe for stress, it's a complete cookbook.

I've moved enough to know that settling in a new land is a bit like a military campaign. There are triumphs, large and small, as well as setbacks and defeats. There are retreats, advances, and quagmires. There is scouting and setting up camp, and you may require special reinforcements. One day though, you will plant the flag of victory and relish that day together.

I remember early on, I had a horrible week that made me wonder if this move was a gigantic mistake. We were stymied in each and every attempt to get a bank account, a mobile phone, utilities. Italians felt no urgency to process the paperwork required for the smallest of tasks. Erratic afternoon and midday closings compounded this, and our progress was screamingly slow. Meanwhile, our car broke down. And we discovered that the previous owners of the vineyard left a cat who we began to realize, little by little, was pregnant and oops! having kittens. While ferociously attacking our gentle dog. If only the Internet installer could multi-task like this.

Searching for a kitten pound (*gattile*, by the way, should that ever come in handy) taxed our language skills. The elevator broke down in our apartment building in Ancona. We live on the fifth floor and it was 95°, and the doggie must be walked four times a day. The electricity clicked off every morning at 9:30 for no reason. The meter is in the basement (remember, the elevator was broken, and they couldn't find the right piece for at least six days). I became paranoid, sure that this problem was manufactured by the electric company. That makes no sense, of course, but at a time when nothing made sense, that felt par for the course.

When I sent a text message to complain about the daily cut offs, the answer was, "Come down here to the office, *signora*, we have a whole room of people like you, and our phone will not be installed for another three days." Wait, the electric company hasn't got a working phone? Welcome to Italy. Again.

Renovations dragged on at the winery house, forcing parents, baby, and the pit bull to move into our overheated Ancona apartment. Squished together, in three bedrooms with common walls, as an infant cried, and her parents tried, and we tried, to make this home.

In this first part of our "campaign," we learned that we all have a different stress tolerance. On Tuesday, one person cracks and needs support; on Wednesday it's somebody else. If you have had your "crack-up day," you empathize when somebody else has theirs, even if their triggers are not your triggers.

Luckily there are moments of reprieve. The sea breezes, the early morning coffee overlooking the water. Breathtaking sunsets and the delights that come with something being new and different every day. We walk more and see regular people going about their business with a smile and a wave.

My thoughts and feelings catch me off guard. For instance, I have this pride of *accomplishment* for being here. And I experience the wonder of connection when I hear the church bells call for devotees to pray at 6 PM, reflecting on all the generations that have stopped to listen and return home upon hearing those bells.

The wonderful surprise has been the *normalness* (for lack of a better word) of people here—unembarrassed elderly women in "can't help how I look" swimsuits, trips to the beach as part of a daily routine, grandmas pushing strollers and stopping to chat. I see young people having their fun and cigarettes in a group, not noisy or rowdy. They talk to me, a senior! Everyone loving on our grandbaby. People stopping to pet our dog. It's a regular life that I had forgotten, and if I had remembered, would not have dreamed still possible.

A culture shift in our family is that the evening meal has become an important daily event. When the baby DOES sleep, we eat outside and enjoy sea breezes. Our family closeness is a haven against the outside craziness, as everyone rants about the day, or shares moments of revelation, or plans for upcoming food festivals. My husband has started a new game, "Guess the Wine," and brings a bottle wrapped in a dish towel every evening. No matter what kind of day it's been, our family dinner, with that mystery wine, lightens our mood.

The food itself buffers us from the adjustment hardships. We shop as the locals do, daily. The grocery stores are practically like farmers markets. It's an odd thing to say, but food has flavor. For instance, chicken. It is fresh, flavorful, and juicy, so however we prepare it, it's a treat. When did you last say that about *chicken*?

Then there is a local farmer, René, who supplies us with goat, chicken, and rabbit. He invited us to sup with him, his wife, and his aging mother-in-law, who did much of the meal preparation and serving. When I heard that she tends the garden that's about a quarter of a football field, I asked, "It must get really hot, no?" This not-so-frail little woman answered, "No, I get out there by 6 AM and get it done!"

Their kitchen is a converted garage, with the table outside for summer meals. This is very common—a summer kitchen on a ground or lower floor with a table outside. At René's table we feasted on homemade bread and pasta and wine, garden vegetables, farm-raised kid, and René's own limoncello. This was a *wow* moment for us, all this spectacular food, everything right from René's land. We left laden down with new potatoes and onions.

It's good that we have these ways to sustain us. Because while it is true that "nothing is permanent but change," changes come at fire hose speed in a foreign country. This is especially unsettling when you have mistakenly imagined that you would be sending relatives and friends an unending stream of photos and descriptions of your adventures, aperitifs, and outings. Ha!

The hard parts in a new country are not funny flavors on your tongue, or missing street signs. You can be the ultimate overachiever in your quest for residency, health insurance, banking, all the time feebly trying to understand what these meanies behind the glass window are saying. Yet after all your hours and efforts, you will have successfully taken three steps further back. All the while, you, as the matriarch, will either be trying to pep up your family's current "Straggler-of-the-Month" or worse, you'll win the prize this month, having caught a virus that sucks away your energy, as the Christmas clock with all its demands ticks away.

But time and viruses pass, and if the behind-the-glass people are not worried about those papers, then maybe we can relax about them, too.

Before I know it, it's Spring. Well, not really. As I write this postscript, it's the end of January. But on an early morning walk through Ancona on the Adriatic Sea, spring is in the air. Our scorching summer is gone, the *spumante*, wine, and olive oil are bottled. Much learning has also been corked over these months. Winter has been calm, giving Chris more time for cooking and feeding his sourdough starters. Meanwhile, "Merlot," the one kitten we kept (known to baby Chloe as "keekat"), peeks in at the windows to watch. Everything at the vineyard is inching towards spring. Pruning has started at Tenuta Marino and over meals Chris and Marjorie decide to go organic.

This morning I was late to my 8:30 hair appointment, and moved at a fast trot having overshot my cross street by two blocks. I came out at Piazza del Papa, which was Ancona's main *piazza* in the medieval age. I paused and caught my breath, realizing no Italian in her right mind would be on time to an 8:30 appointment. I have learned the benefit of that Italian slowness that once enraged me.

So I slowed to enjoy that faint spring smell and slight warmth of late winter days. I notice the bar owners on the *piazza* have added more outside seats, the comfy "stay-awhile-it's-warm-now" types. They must also sense spring in the air. I climb a sort of "stairway to heaven," the central steps on this inclined *piazza*, arriving at the statue of Pope Clement XII. He is about five times the size of a real Pope, sporting an enormous three-tiered papal tiara. He is a bit like me, I decide, because he could have been situated elsewhere. He was supposed to be on an arch overlooking the sea, but the arch couldn't support him (no comparisons here, please), so the townspeople shifted the statue to the *piazza* to wait while they reinforced the arch. Only once the refashioned arch could hold him, the people didn't want him to leave the *piazza*.

If I could reach Pope Clement's outstretched hand I'd likely shake it as a newcomer, and tell him I like it here in my new life. I would add that while new places are fun and interesting of course, it is our family connections in this new adventure that provide everyone—young, medium, and less young—the uphill momentum after the roller coaster ride of our arrival. Spring is coming, and summer will bring a brand new family member, a second grandchild.

It is going to be a great harvest!

Picking a Home Base

CONTRIBUTORS' STORIES

NELL · LIVED IN FRANCE FOR ONE YEAR

Once we settled on France as a destination, the question was *where*. I wanted to go to a new area for me, somewhere I'd never been. I can't stand wind so that canceled out the south with its mistral. A friend happened to mention that the Dordogne was lovely, I looked around online and found a house I loved, and that was it. I didn't mess around with a lot of searching. I never once regretted our choice of village or of house—they were imperfect, of course, but perfection wasn't on our list of goals.

HEATHER · MOVED TO ITALY FOR TWO YEARS

Chris's company gave us a budget for housing, plus arranged a scouting trip to house hunt and tour International Schools. In total, we looked at twelve houses. It was exciting and fun, but took its toll as renting in Italy is complicated. Just because you like an "available" house does not mean you will get it. In fact, all three houses we tried to rent fell through. Of course, I had mentally moved into all three of those houses. I never learned. We wound up renting a house sight unseen.

CANADA-TO-FRANCE · LIVING IN FRANCE

Research led us to Annecy, France. The rental prices were too expensive, so I expanded my search. That's when I found Aix-les-Bains. With a beautiful lake and many ski hills close by, it was perfect. Rental prices were reasonable, and it was only twenty minutes to Annecy, forty minutes to Grenoble, and one hour to Lyon. Searching for an apartment from Canada was hard, for sure. People didn't always respond to my emails, and calling was close to impossible. It took quite a bit of diligence and patience to find a few places for us to visit in advance of our scouting trip. We used that trip to settle on an apartment and get our daughter registered for school.

NICA · SAILED THE CARIBBEAN

Our home was a sailboat, so deciding where to live was simple. For us the corollary was how did we choose where to spend each night? For instance, weather is the ultimate priority when deciding where to over-night. We also considered the right holding ground for the anchor and what activities we'd like to do. Did we need to be close to a store? Were we in the mood for company? There are helpful cruising guides and charts, and any time we met up with another boat we swapped information about destinations.

ESTELLE · CROSS-GENERATIONAL LIVING IN ITALY

In Italy, and I imagine in other countries as well, there are advantages to looking at small cities of about 100,000 people or so. Towns of this size often boast a claim to fame that unites the local people or region—opera, summer theater festival, walking groups, etc. It's a way to get involved, or at the very least, entertaining to observe. If you want a lakeside or seaside town, that certainly can add something to your daily life.

On the other hand, locals in a smaller and quieter town are more likely to take an interest in your family. There can be more opportunity for daily interactions, so you'll likely learn language faster.

NAOMI · LIVED IN INDIA AND SINGAPORE FOR FOUR YEARS

Each and every time it's possible and feasible to do a scouting trip, I would say go for it! Not only do you get the lay of the land, but you can also potentially meet individuals for future friendships, or gain valuable information going into the move.

JULIE · WORLDSCHOOLING IN MEXICO AND BEYOND

I have done hours of online research, including joining Facebook groups for upcoming home bases. I've found accommodations using those groups, as well as Airbnb and VRBO.

How long in advance to book depends on the city, the time of year, and how long you'll be there. For a long (over a month) stay in Playa, I'd recommend booking just a week and then finding a place when you get there. You can find lots of rentals in Playa just by walking around and looking at signs. But this might not have worked for San Miguel de Allende because there are fewer rentals available, especially for a larger family. It also may be harder to find a place in the winter, which is high season for many cities in Mexico.

SARAH · LIVES IN THE NETHERLANDS AFTER YEARS OF WORLDSCHOOLING

Because of our tight budget, we never had the luxury of a scouting trip. But we developed a talent for scoping out neighborhoods using Google Maps street view. I always checked proximity to a park (but beware that not all park-like areas are public; I was shocked at how many of the green spaces on Google Maps in Florence were actually private gardens, probably dating back to the Medici). Other important landmarks were grocery stores, produce stands, bakeries, a pharmacy, and public transport.

Sites like Homelidays, Airbnb, and Villas were good places to look for short-term rentals (and in some countries anything shorter than four years is considered short-term), as well as sometimes Craigslist. Italy had its own version of Craigslist called subito.it, for anything from house rentals to home accessories. In Ireland the place to go to rent an apartment was daft.ie. In the Netherlands, apartment hunting tends to be done via Facebook groups. In general, online forums and expat Facebook groups specifically targeting your country of interest can give you the lay of the land and where to find the best deals on housing.

On sites like Airbnb, even when the posted cost per night or week is prohibitive, the owners are often receptive to a far lower monthly rate for a long-term stay, particularly if it extends over the winter months, when they're unlikely to fill the property. So it is worth sending a message to ask, even if longer term rates are not posted. These houses also have the advantage of being furnished. It's always important to clarify what "unfurnished" or "furnished" mean. Unfurnished could mean completely empty, and in need of flooring, window coverings, and an entire kitchen, from stove and refrigerator to cabinets and counters—everything *including* the kitchen sink. Furnished could mean basic furniture, or it could include things like linens, pans, and dishes.

10

WHEN TO GO

Ask any expat family when you should set off on your adventure, and they'll likely give you a description that closely parallels what they chose to do.

Why?

Because it doesn't matter. There are pros and cons to any timing.

For instance, going when your children are small is challenging because early parenting is a lot of work. That work can be overwhelming on home soil, let alone in a country where you aren't exactly sure how to procure Tylenol. Also, your kids will need you to moderate their experience while older children will form a relationship to their experience on their own terms, without you having to be the conduit. That means there will be less "exploring who you are in another country" and more "exploring who you are as a parent in another country."

A point I never considered until my kids mentioned it on our last trip to Spello—if we'd done the year abroad before they were all born and cognizant, the family narrative wouldn't be shared by all of us. It's not something to base your decision on (after all, I'm a better parent after living in Italy, I bet another child could have benefited from my increase in gratitude and patience!), but an interesting thought.

On the flip side, little kids are cute. Adorable even. Children with cheeks still in need of squeezing can serve as a passport into a community. I doubt that Spellani would have folded us into their hearts if there were no Gabe for the old ladies to coo over. It's why we called him our mascot. Also, if your young children attend school, they will be learning reading and math alongside their peers, so they won't be academically behind, a factor that challenges high schoolers. Moreover, they are more resilient and open than older kids because they don't know better, and since you are their main playmate, they will suffer less from the social isolation that older kids invariably feel.

Here's what it comes down to. I did *not* want to live abroad while my kids were in arms, because I wanted the freedom to do my own thing for at least part of the day. So going with small children would not have been right *for me*. If you *want* to go when your kids are small, then obviously you or your family situation is different and you should practice ignoring people's opinions by starting with ignoring my personal preferences.

It's like having children, right? The moment when the abhorrence of midnight feedings is eclipsed by images of holding a new little life in your arms is the moment you are ready. So if you feel ready and able, I believe you are. And since there is no way to read the tea leaves about what the optimal timing is for a particular child, think more about how it will be for *you*. While you should consider your children (particularly if they have learning or health or other needs that I'm not addressing here), not being able to predict with any surety what their reaction will be means that it's more useful to focus on what timeframe would make *you* feel strong and steady. After all, strong and steady parents make for bulwarks children can lean on in a storm. Besides, I've now sifted through more expat stories than I can count, and while there are definitely some kids who never stopped demanding to go home, they are an infinitesimal minority.

Along with the issue of age, you also want to consider the calendar. You'll find that many families go abroad from summer to summer. That fits with the academic year, and avoids the pain of landing into a foreign school midyear, plus returning to course work and social lives already in progress. Summers are transitional times for families, so it's easier to insert another transition in there.

At bottom, if you have an opportunity to leap abroad right now, DO NOT PASS IT UP, no matter if you think your children may be too young or too old. Just go, you'll make it work. Luck isn't always given out like party favors. Take it while the universe is smiling.

Remembering a Childhood Year in Brussels

ALLYSON'S STORY

We arrived in Brussels on June 12, 1981. My father had been commuting from Connecticut since November, flying home every three weeks for the weekend. The move, to my 9-year-old self, was full of mixed feelings. I had little understanding of Europe or what overseas travel, much less living, meant. I was mostly worried about missing my friends, but I did want my family together again.

The realities of life abroad crashed in almost immediately, just in time for my tenth birthday. Things that mattered marginally at home suddenly mattered a lot in the transition to being elsewhere—things as small as an overwhelming desire for a homemade birthday cake. I remember my mother tearing open moving box after moving box looking for a cake pan, only to discover not only that she could not find anything resembling American cake flour in Brussels, they also didn't carry anything resembling a cake mix. That was the first time I remember sitting in my new room in tears. Throughout the year, the upsets were over those small things that seemed so big: frustration that the next book in a series I was reading couldn't be obtained without waiting for international post; frustration at my mother's inability to find American-style hamburger at the grocery store; horror at ordering chicken in the grocery store only to have the butcher raise a cleaver in front of us, asking "with head or without?"; wanting a favorite TV show, a new pair of sneakers, breakfast cereal that wasn't Weetabix.

Since we arrived in early summer, my brother (seven that year) and I spent the summer at summer school run by our new school, the International School of Brussels (ISB). It was a toss-into-the-deep-end, hair-first immersion into international culture, and it was one of the best decisions my parents made. So much was different. The kids came from a dozen different countries, including places I'd never heard of. There is a lot of mobility in International Schools, so there were many new students. I made friends quickly; my tight group of summer friends became a tight group of school-year friends. We were two Americans, a Swede, a girl from Lebanon, and one from Greece.

So much at school was different. Math was all based on the metric system, which was new to me. French was full immersion; my brother was near-fluent within months. The entire summer school stopped on the day of Charles and Diana's wedding, which we watched in real time; in this magical world of centuries-old churches on the corner, a royal wedding didn't feel so distant. School was less academic, more about experience and exposure. Cultures were celebrated, and we gained tolerance and appreciation without realizing it.

Outside of school, I adjusted to life in Europe quickly, and I almost immediately realized there were significant benefits to being one of the only people in my family who could speak workable French. In the bakery, I could order extra croissants, and my parents didn't know until we got home. It was my job to speak to the clerks in the store as my mother struggled with even basic communication, in spite of months of French lessons before our move. I had more freedom that year in Brussels than I had again until college, not only because of my language skills, but also because of the general culture of how children are treated. It was common for 10-year-olds to take the city bus with friends. I'd go to a friend's house after school, and we'd walk on a Napoleon-era road to get to the small shop that sold the best *frites* (with mayonnaise; ketchup was an American oddity), then take our toy horses into the forest where we'd play unsupervised for hours. The expectation that children were responsible and independent extended to school as well; in May, the entire fifth grade traveled by bus to Cologne, Germany, for four days. We stayed at a hostel and were each handed an itinerary and a city map, told where to show up and when. We visited Roman baths and ruins and met for meals, but were largely on our own. My parents, to their credit, let us follow the lead of what the school and broader culture expected of children. Whether an entire afternoon with friends when they didn't know exactly where I was, or on the school trip, they let me be part of the culture rather than imposing the same rules they would have at home.

We traveled a lot. We skied in Switzerland, my mother took cooking classes in Paris, we'd drive up to Amsterdam to go to the children's museum, we went to Spain for spring break. Friends from the States were eager to visit and join us on trips, and we were always happy to have them—in part because they would bring things that we couldn't get in Brussels at the time—such as peanut butter and American sneakers.

The original plan was to stay in Brussels for three to five years, but a change in my father's company meant that we were only there for one. In retrospect, our French would have been far better had we attended the local schools, but attending the International School gave us a window into dozens of cultures that the Belgian school wouldn't have provided. The downside of the International School was that my French never got to the point where I could talk to the neighbors; there were other kids on my street, but we only eyed each other, interacting little to none. Every choice, of course, has its trade-offs.

We moved back home on June 13, 1982. I left for seven weeks of overnight camp on June 29. Again, that was a smart decision—it slowed my transition home, and camp became my second home, and the closest thing to the time abroad that I'd get again until college.

The most difficult part of the transition back to the US was the loss of the independence I'd experienced while overseas. I think I expected to slide back in with old friends, and that didn't happen. I'd envisioned them standing still while I'd had my time abroad—like time-traveling where the traveler comes home and the clock hasn't moved. Instead, friendships had morphed, and I found we didn't have much in common. I chafed at boundaries and the social cliques that seemed based on rules that had been established while I was gone. That part never improved. My world had grown, and I had trouble once it shrunk again.

We weren't abroad long, but it was long enough to get a crash course in empathy and understanding and interest in those who were in some way different. I went on to teach children with learning and behavioral difficulties in some tough, urban schools. I like to think that my time abroad helped me connect with them, even though many of my students had never left their own neighborhoods, much less the country.

For a child, a move abroad is a balance sheet between the new and the familiar. I rode horses, just as I did at home. I went to school, just as I did at home. I spent time with friends, just as I did at home. In Brussels, I rode at a stable that was once a Napoleonic fort, went to school with peers from a dozen countries who had traveled to dozens more, and spent time roaming the city, eating after-school snacks prepared by a Swedish nanny or at the local Godiva shop. The details were different, but the framework was the same. I imagine it took tremendous work on my mother's part to build and maintain that balance, not to mention trust and leaps of faith.

A year abroad is eye opening, wonder building, difficult, and life changing. Look out for the small stuff, and know there is another side, even when the other side means tear-filled laughing at a flat, mealy attempt at a homemade birthday cake.

Timing Travels

CONTRIBUTORS' STORIES

ELIZABETH · LIVES IN ITALY

My eldest was only 2-years-old when we moved to southern Italy, so we thought that he would manage the transition relatively easily. But he initially suffered quite a bit. Not only did he move house and country, but he had just become a brother, was toilet training, and about to start nursery. Far too much for one little guy. We had to backpedal and support him a lot. Meanwhile, our baby took to Italy with ease, loving the attention his Scottish blonde hair and blue eyes got him. Plus, he loves the beach.

For me, the experience has not been what I expected. The reality of sleepless nights with young children and new-mum worries overtook a lot of the initial excitement, and my adjustment was slow.

But living in Italy is giving us more family time. My husband and I aren't rushing about, taking turns to do sports, see friends, etc. We know we will do all that when we return to Scotland when the children are older, so we don't miss it just now.

LEWIS FAMILY · LIVED IN MALAYSIA FOR TWO YEARS

As the two elder girls were already at university, the major impact was on our son, Richard. Richard was not convinced that relocating to Malaysia was a good idea. I had a great deal of angst about moving him away from all his friends and the area where he had lived all his life. Luckily his two older sisters thought it was a marvelous opportunity and told their brother to stop being such a wimp. The resettlement company provided us with advice and guidance about education possibilities, and Richard and I went to Malaysia in July to visit the school and the house where we would be living. That certainly helped, particularly when my son realized there was a swimming pool in the garden of the house—a luxury we do not have in London. He still wanted to spend the summer holidays with his friends, so we negotiated with my husband, Henry, that he would be our advance team to Kuala Lumpur, and I would stay in London with Richard. The two of us joined Henry at the end of August 2006, in time for the new school term.

JULIE · WORLDSCHOOLING IN MEXICO AND BEYOND

Our kids had mixed feelings about the trip. Our oldest did not want to miss her sophomore year of high school and her friends. Our boys were also sad to leave friends, but didn't mind going. They have adapted thoroughly to our new life, and though our daughter does still miss her friends, she is enjoying our adventure. We try to incorporate activities that the kids will enjoy—horseback riding, zip-lining, and living by the beach.

AMANDA · LIVES IN MOROCCO

We told our children we were moving to Morocco for a year, and then as we stayed longer, we included them in more of our discussions. Our kids fought the move a bit, even as they were a little excited. They were six and eight, and it probably would have been easier if they were younger. But we knew in the long run this would be something that would benefit them.

11

SHOULD YOU TAKE YOUR PET?

When I tell people we brought our cats to Italy, they are gobsmacked. Doesn't this reek of cat prejudice? If we brought two Pomeranians, people would be curious, but their mouths wouldn't drop open. To which I say—you don't know our cats. Juno sleeps curled around my head like a crown. Even so, I wasn't keen to bring them. I knew the journey would be far more complicated with two cat carriers. Plus, I wanted to travel while we lived in Italy, how would we find pet sitters? We didn't know anyone!

Keith maintained the cats were part of the family, so we had to bring them, even if it was complicated. We used Quaker decision-making principles to make the call. We all sat around the table and shared our opinions, and then we voted. In the Quaker way, all decisions must be unanimous. So we discussed until we agreed. Now, everyone doesn't have to be gung ho to have it be unanimous, some can "stand aside" indicating, "I want my concerns recognized, but for the good of the group, I'll go along with the majority." It's a workable system for us because no one is railroaded and everyone is heard.

When we went around the table, Siena said, "Everything is going to feel different. Everything. I want something to feel the same."

I found that compelling, as did Nicolas. So though we still believed the journey would be a wreck, we stood aside. For the record, the journey was indeed a wreck. Both cats caterwauled the entire three hours to

Baltimore airport (the only airport within driving distance with an airline that allowed pets), one cat vomited, and worse, the other cat "expressed." I'm sure you are wondering what expressing is in this context. It's like peeing, but, umm, muskier? I've tried to forget.

Then again, the wreck began long before we lured our beasts out from under the bed and into their carriers. I'm going to share the process, not to give you a recipe, but rather so you'll have an idea of the hurdles involved. Your vet may offer you information, but that may be just as outdated, so check the regulations posted on the websites for your airline, your country of origin, and your destination country (plus any country you are changing planes in).

Before our cats could board the plane, they needed rabies shots, International Health Certificates, and microchips implanted in their necks. Also, they each needed to weigh less than 11 pounds, as our airline required that any on-board pet weigh no more than 13 pounds (including the carrier), and the lightest carrier weighed two pounds. Animals that ride cargo aren't subject to the same weight restrictions, as we discovered when the airline accidentally canceled our pet tickets a few days prior to our departure. A desperate scramble procured us one pet ticket for the cargo hold, one for under the seat. Since Juno wheezes alarmingly when she is stressed, Freja was the lucky winner of the cargo hold.

A month before our departure date, I took the cats to the vet to fulfill the airline requirements. Juno howled the whole time. The vet was forced to shout her questions over Juno's complaining. And then this cat of mine, who has yet to learn what her name is, figured out how to unzip the carrier and pop on out. Meanwhile, Freja looked bored and a little annoyed, like she was missing her favorite program.

Juno weighed in at 10.5 pounds, so the fat-cat food we'd put them on after we read the weight restrictions worked. Success! Freja, however, had actually *gained* weight on her fat-cat diet. Fail. At 11.5 pounds, she was too heavy, according to Condor airlines.

Sweating at the image of being turned away from the gate because our cat was too fat (this was before we knew she'd be riding cargo anyway, so it wouldn't matter), I plunked down a small fortune for the super expensive fat-cat food our vet recommended for weight loss.

Juno and Freja resisted being microchipped, even though I told them that their swanky hardware made them like a box of crackers—I could swipe them across a check-out counter and get their barcode. This did not amuse.

But they were nonchalant at the worst news of all. News that struck fear into my already shivering heart. The vet found—a flea.

Yes, a flea!

Weird that a small insect could wreak such havoc. The vet would *not* give Juno a clean bill of health for the US health certificate (it hadn't occurred to us that the United States would require documentation to release the cats, so we hadn't researched that piece). At this point in the appointment, I was scrambling. Too much information: the filling out of the International Health Certificate, the instructions on how to use the flea medication, the microchip registration forms for both the vet and the company that houses the information, and now the US health certificate. The vet added that the cats must pass the physical for the health certificate within ten days of our departure, and then I must take that form to the US Department of Agriculture in Richmond to get it certified. With which time? I had no time. The vet cheerfully declared that neither cat had flea dirt, a testament to their excellent grooming habits. This was small consolation. And why in the world does the USDA have jurisdiction over my taking two tabbies out of the country?

The only vet in our practice who is licensed to complete official health certificates doesn't work Fridays, so I had to cut short our goodbye beach trip with friends for a Thursday appointment to leave enough time to get the form to Richmond and back within the 10 day window. I was grimly determined that neither cat would have fleas at the time of that appointment.

Luckily, somewhere in there, I realized I could FedEx the forms to Richmond (with a FedEx envelope for the return), rather than drive. Unluckily, our vet used black ink on the application—a major *faux pax!*— so our cats were rejected by the USDA. Luckily, the USDA representative begrudgingly accepted the email photos of the new documents my vet hurriedly filled out (no faxing! Faxing wouldn't show that all important *blue* ink!). Unluckily, not one person ever weighed our cats or looked at one bit of our paperwork, so it kinda, sorta feels like that three-week period of panic attacks was for nothing.

If you are considering bringing your pets, be advised that I've personally heard other stories just like mine (though none worse, none that included loss of a pet or other trauma). Before we returned to Virginia, I told Keith that getting the cats home was on him. At least half my gray hairs were from that process, and I was done. As it happens, getting them back was a breeze. The Italian vet happily dated our paperwork to whatever he thought would get us out easily (no extra appointments) and charged us a fraction of the cost of our US vet. Oh, and for the record, we found it easier to find friends to take care of our cats in Italy than at home. The only issue was that they fed the cats multiple times a day instead of the once we asked for, as they insisted this was better for the cats' digestion.

Even with all this hassle, you should know that within a few days of arriving in Spello, once the cats no longer stank from their experiments in "expressing," I couldn't believe we'd ever contemplated leaving them behind.

Moving our Dogs to Italy

HEATHER'S STORY

I n 2013, we moved our dogs to Milan. They are a huge part of our family, and because we were moving for possibly three years, we knew we couldn't live without them. We had never flown with pets, and found the process of figuring it out overwhelming. After reading horror stories online (not advisable) and getting thoroughly lost in the bureaucracy of dog travel, I found a company that specializes in moving pets around the world. We hired them to help with the process (see *Resources*).

The company figured out the best route to Milan, and discovered that our dogs were too large to fly out of Boise as we had planned. So the day before we left the United States, we rented two cars (since we had already sold our vehicles) to drive nine hours to Seattle, where we all departed for Italy. We required one vehicle for the dogs and their giant custom crates. The other vehicle was full of luggage and kids. So our "exit day" actually stretched over several exhausting days. Thank goodness we were living on giddiness at that point, or the sight of the dogs being carted away by forklift would have done me in. As it was, I was a crying mess.

We all flew out of Seattle on the same Lufthansa flight, but the dogs had an overnight layover in Frankfurt, which has a "Pet Lounge" for the dogs to recuperate from the long flight and get loved on before continuing. This worked for us, because we were able to sleep off the jet lag at a hotel in Milan.

Our Italian car was too small for our custom crate and forklift-needing beasts. We arranged for a local pet relocation service to pick the dogs up at the Milan airport, go through customs with them, and bring them directly to our rental house. The whole thing went very smoothly, and we were able to hire the same local company when we did the move in reverse a few years later.

The dogs did some traveling with us in Italy, but we also found a wonderful pet sitter through the Milan expat community. She stayed at the house with the dogs when we traveled, allowing us the freedom we wanted.

The return to the US in 2015 was more involved than bringing them over to Italy because of the paperwork needed and the "Italian-ness" of the whole thing, which included being told many different requirements by many different people. Only certain vets are certified to sign the papers, and only available on certain days at specific times and you couldn't make an appointment. It didn't help that my husband was out of the country during this period. It was tricky and I thought I was going to lose my mind.

My husband definitely made up for his absence during the leave-taking vet chaos. He flew back to the US with the dogs the month before we moved home, then drove from Seattle back to Boise to get them home before it got too hot for them to fly.

Taking (or Leaving) Your Pet

CONTRIBUTORS' STORIES

NELL · LIVED IN FRANCE FOR A YEAR

I missed my dog terribly, but would probably leave her behind again. It was hard enough managing all the moving parts of the trip without adding a dog to the mix. Plus, I would not want to give up the freedom to travel on a whim. Perhaps if we had a little dog we could take on planes and to cafés, but our ninety pound Australian Shepherd was not meant for traveling and cities.

CHERYL · RV-ING THROUGH EUROPE

Since we are from Scotland, we had to obtain Pet Passports which are required for pet travel within Europe. This was easy, we just needed to get rabies vaccinations at least twenty-one days before leaving the country. We now travel full time with Poppy and Angus. Before we left, we got Poppy neutered to avoid the risk of six pug-collie crosses on our motor-home journey. For the most part, the dogs have been fine, and honestly we wouldn't have wanted to come without them as they are a part of our family. Would it be easier traveling like we do without them? Yes, 100%. But it's an extra challenge that we are up for. On days when Angus runs about all day playing with the kids while Poppy snuggles up at our feet, well, we wouldn't change a thing.

NAOMI · LIVED IN INDIA AND SINGAPORE FOR FOUR YEARS

We did not bring our dog with us to India. We found him a home, and the new owners sent us photos for the first six months. That was helpful as our children missed him terribly. While in India, we adopted a *desi* dog (local street puppy), and he moved with us to Singapore and back to the United States. When we go overseas again, we will not take pets. It's a lot of stress on an animal to travel, and any quarantine regulations can increase the chaos and upset during what is already a very stressful situation.

SARA · LIVED IN MOROCCO FOR SEVEN YEARS

We decided not to bring our dear dog with us and I think it was for the best. After reading about the typical Moroccan attitude towards dogs, we decided she'd live with my mom instead. It was excruciating saying goodbye to her, but I'm so relieved we didn't bring her. In Morocco, it's common to see dog owners take their dogs out for walks with sticks in their hands to beat off stray dogs. I also knew of several people who lost their dogs to poison-filled meatballs placed in the street. In general, the Moroccan people are very frightened of dogs, even the cutest and smallest ones, and it was normal to see an adult running and screaming at the sight of an approaching dog.

TANIA · ROAD-TRIPPING THROUGH EUROPE

We brought our three-year-old Labradoodle. Europe is very dog friendly. The exception is France, where dogs are not allowed on buses or in most restaurants. In Germany and Austria our dog went into restaurants with us and had no problem just lying down under the table. Hotels are usually dog friendly, and there are plenty of Airbnbs that accept pets. For the most part, it's been easier than we'd expected, and we certainly would make the same choice again. Our pup has been the reason we've found countless beautiful hikes and befriended other families with dogs.

12

HOW TO EDUCATE YOUR CHILD
WHILE ABROAD

You have options when it comes to educating your child. Some families choose homeschooling (or worldschooling as it's called if you are globe-trotting and using the world as your favorite teacher), some choose an International School, some choose the local private or parochial school, and some choose public school. Based on your destination, there may be limits imposed on your options. For instance, homeschooling is illegal in some countries, and International Schools and private schools may be in short supply where you choose to live.

You have no doubt noticed by now that every choice you make in this process has a natural upside and downside, and your job is to figure out which ups and downs fit your family. Don't bother asking a forum or Facebook group what you should do, they will tell you what would fit *their* family, not yours.

Here was our calculus. It was critical for us that our children walk away from our year in Italy with a working knowledge of Italian. Without it, we doubted they would really experience an Italian year. Beyond that, we wanted them to make friends with local children, to give our children an understanding of how Spellani approach the world—their values, perspectives, habits, manners, and choice of snacks. We were also limited by cash, in that we had no spare change for private education. Finally, I craved alone time to explore this nascent freedom of having all school-age children; thus homeschooling was nowhere on my radar. Public school was a given for us from the first moment of considering our trip.

The downsides were real though, and not to be ignored. We had to be okay with the fact that our kids would fail every subject save English. This turned out not to be the case (Nicolas was top of his class at Italian grammar by the end of the year, Siena rocked history, and Gabe discovered a love of math, though, unlike the other two, he didn't have to completely relearn how to do long division). They slipped back into US schools at the level they would have been if they had never left, essentially skipping a year of American school (Note: Other states' and countries' educational systems can be stricter, and therefore harder to duck out of for a spell; Nicolas's middle school luckily gave high school credit for a handful of his classes, which allowed him to graduate on time). This caused Gabe and Siena nary a hiccup—they were wheels down without incident. But missing his freshman year was hard on Nicolas, and he stumbled that dismount. His friends had spent a year learning how to jump the high school hoops while managing academic pressures when he was lounging around reading Italian comic books. It worked out fine, but it was sticky enough there for awhile that Siena is adamant that she will complete her high school experience in four years with feet firmly on Virginia soil, thank you very much.

Beyond academics, there were times when Italian public school was just hard. Harder than I had predicted. Before we landed, fears of hostile children ostracizing my brood nauseated me. This was 100% unjustified, but the effusive friendliness that was a boon for the boys made Siena feel like she was under a microscope. A feeling she has yet to relish. Even with the unexpected welcome the children received by their peers, they often felt excluded just by nature of not knowing what anyone was saying. It was hard to feel different and confused, though it sure has given all of them a sense of empathy for marginalized people.

Those struggles weren't constant. There were good days and awful days, and the proportion shifted throughout the year. By the end of our stay, all three kids felt like regular Italian children. They had friends, they were successful (enough) at school, they hung out at the park, they bought pizza for snack. Just like anyone else. But I will confess it was sometimes an emotional slog.

I had an inkling it would be hard for my kids, but I had no idea that navigating their school would be challenging for me in ways beyond empathizing with them. What I neglected to consider was how much I rely on the effortless communication inherent in American schools. Not having a way to contact teachers, not having someone to talk to when Gabe was spanked by his math teacher, not having a class roster to facilitate contact with other parents, not knowing when the class play was and therefore missing it—those were hardships that I didn't count on.

Bear in mind that you can combine educational methods. For instance, if it is important that your child not fall behind in math, you can homeschool just math. Or, if you like the idea of homeschooling, but not the isolation, remember Alisha's story of homeschooling while utilizing their local International School's resources in Kyrgyzstan. You don't have to be boxed in. In fact, your school choice can even change once you've arrived, as you'll read in Sara's story.

Another factor to consider, school day structure isn't universal. When we arrived in Spello, we discovered that the school system was still debating whether to have five-or six-day weeks (with school days running until 1 PM). The day before school started, they decided to split the difference and alternate weeks. Since we left, it has changed to a five-day week with one long day, when the kids stay until 4 PM. Depending on your country, you may find that your school doesn't have school on Wednesday, or that school runs later than you are used to but has an extended lunch period that functions almost like another class, or Saturday school is the norm.

Our contributors used every educational method while abroad, and you'll see that there are variations in the educational pathways I've laid out (for instance, Sarah will talk about a bilingual Dutch-English public school). Read their stories and see what resonates for you. Talk to your local homeschool community, and scroll through Facebook groups for worldschoolers to get an idea of what homeschooling life is like (bearing in mind that for every one hundred families, there are one hundred ways to homeschool—from unschooling to adhering to an accelerated curriculum, and everything in between).

As you are mulling over what school situation would work best not just for your children, but also for your family, ask yourself the following questions:

* Is it important that your children don't fall behind their peers at home? Is that true for all subjects or just one or two?

* What do you want your children to learn this year? Answer this aspirationally but also practically.

* Do your children have learning challenges that would mean a lot of contact with the school or requirements for the school?

* Do you enjoy teaching your children yourself? Not just in the abstract, I mean, do you actively seek out ways to explore learning together with your children? How receptive are your children to your guidance? How much could you teach them just by following their curiosity? Bear in mind their ages, both for thinking about the process and content of teaching, and also to consider how many hours you would spend teaching based on if you can combine ages into learning groups.

* Do you have interests that you're hoping to pursue while abroad, and how much time do you envision needing in a day to pursue those?

Can you arrange schooling or childcare with your spouse to give you that time?

* Is it important to you that your child learns the local language? Why?

* Is it important that your child form local connections? If they don't go to public school, are there alternatives for making those connections, like community programs?

* Do you crave global connections for yourself and your child, even if you will be staying put?

* Do you want the freedom to travel at will, which would require you to take your children out of school?

Do a little Internet research to see what options are available in your chosen area, though be advised that many schools won't have a website, or it will be wildly out of date. If they do have one, contact the school for more information. This should be straightforward with an International School. With a public or private school, craft a polite email saying that you are considering settling in their community and have some questions about their school, might they have someone who speaks English (like the English teacher, if there is one) who could contact you? Your local language school or a translator you can find online or in your community will be helpful in constructing that paragraph. I don't recommend using Google Translate for this important first step, as different cultures have different values on manners and politeness, and you will want to use the proper honorifics and authority-based vocabulary to create the best possible impression of you. Plus, Google Translate is often wrong.

Anyway, it's not a bad idea to cultivate a relationship with someone fluent in the language of the country you are landing in. I'm sure you'll find loads of uses for proper communication in your host country's language.

In fact, I just contacted my go-to Italian expert (who tutored Nicolas for the Italian Advanced Placement Test, and who translated my memoir into Italian) to find out the word for "summer camp" in Italian. Gabe wants to go to one this summer when we are in Spello, but we want just a basic half-day, kicking a soccer ball and making a lanyard kind of camp. I didn't want to use the wrong word and get shuttled to sleep away camps, niche camps, or labor camps. *Campo estivo* is the phrase for a standard summer camp, in case you are interested, and they are just €35,00 a week.

The World is Our Classroom

ALLISON'S STORY

I n 2014 we moved to Panama. We wanted to expose our daughters to a different way of life and broaden their horizons. Plus, we felt that Spanish fluency could open future doors for them. Our plan was to live in Panama for two years, then return to our life in Gilbert, Arizona.

That's not what happened.

It wasn't long after arriving in Panama that we began wondering why we needed to go back at all. If we're able to work while traveling, which is possible due to my husband's online business, why not just keep traveling? We decided that Panama was really interesting, but there was also a big, wide world out there and we wanted to see it. A LOT of it. So after a year in Panama, we renamed our blog from *Panama Pause* to *Let's Just Travel*, we downsized our suitcases (from thirteen suitcases down to four), and we began exploring the world.

It's been over three years now since we left the USA. We've been to seventeen countries, living in five of them for longer than four months.

This allows us to get to know more of a culture and is a lot more sane than moving at a tourist pace.

We've learned so much about the world, but more importantly about ourselves. We've learned how much we LOVE to spend time with our daughters, how we value being their main role models right now, rather than a bunch of unknown kids at public school that may or may not be making good choices. We learned how much more the girls engage when we are out doing things, not just reading books, and how we also need down time to do nothing and zone out on YouTube in order to allow all the "newness" to sink in. We've learned that a lot of times you have to FSO ("Figure Sh!t Out"), and we show the girls that life is not always perfect, or comfortable, or fair, but you figure it out anyway. The #1 benefit to this lifestyle is how much time we spend together as a family. It can drive us crazy, of course, but the time we have right now with our daughters is something we can never get back and we are so grateful for the opportunity.

We plan to travel for a few more years before resuming our stateside lifestyle, only less so. We've learned that we need a lot LESS STUFF to be happy, but we also miss our family and friends, and our younger daughter has asked for a traditional high school experience starting in 2020. After six years on the road, we are all wondering how she'll enjoy that experience, but we have promised to give it to her regardless.

Our approach to schooling started with a structured format of homeschooling, using a curriculum, a lot of workbooks, learning goals, and rubrics. That didn't last long. We now have a teen who unschools and directs her own education, we take a few online classes in the areas that interest the kids, we take a lot of excursions and workshops, and we do some math. We like to watch documentaries, and we use Google to satisfy our curiosity. That's the extent of our homeschool, but it works. Simply from our travels we make connections daily; certain countries remind us of other countries and we compare the foods, history, and language. We layer on the new info on top of the old, and it all settles into one great big education.

Worldschooling is a broad term that can mean a lot of different things. For us it means learning from the world around us and using it as our teacher. In our opinion it's the best way to prepare our kids for the future.

Choosing an Educational Path

CONTRIBUTORS' STORIES

HEATHER · LIVED IN ITALY FOR TWO YEARS

The International School in Milan was initially overwhelming and wonderful at the same time. The kids went from a tiny Idaho school to a school with over fifty nationalities represented. They came home that first day telling me all the friends they had met and where they were from. It made our world in the USA seem so very small.

There were some adjustment issues. In fact, I never knew what to expect when I picked them up from the bus stop. That said, there were real advantages to the International School experience. For instance, expat kids understand what it's like to be the new kid. They introduced themselves and escorted my kids to meet other students. It expanded not just my kids' world view, but our whole family's. Interacting with people of all nationalities, religions, and languages blew my mind. Also, because teachers are tuned into what expat kids are going through, they are uniquely situated to support them. The faculty at our school bent over backwards to help our son when he had a rough time.

The curriculum was challenging, but my kids learned so much. I credit their current success in high school to the experience they had in Italy.

CANADA-TO-FRANCE · LIVES IN FRANCE

Since our daughter already spoke French, sending her to a public school was the natural choice. We chose a school we liked, then clarified with the principal what zone we'd have to live in to attend. Then we picked an apartment in that zone. We're happy with the public school. Our daughter has learned so much more French, her knowledge of European history flourished, she made many French friends, and we like that she's surrounded by locals.

SUSAN · REMEMBERING SETTLING IN SINGAPORE AS A CHILD

Because I went to a military school all the other students came from military families so sadly there was no interaction with the local Chinese and Malay families.

SARAH · LIVES IN THE NETHERLANDS AFTER YEARS OF WORLDSCHOOLING

We homeschooled as we moved back and forth from home to abroad. I loved the flexibility of taking the kids to so many amazing places without having to worry about school timetables. My main requirement for them when they were small was that they spend several hours outside every day, weather permitting. My daughter became an expert at catching frogs in Ireland, crabs in Tunisia, snakes in Florida, and lizards in Italy. I saw the flora and fauna of each new place through their eyes, and it was magical. Even the dirt in each location was different.

For more formal curriculum, we used sources available on the Internet, including audiobooks, ebooks, and educational websites like Khan Academy. Kindles were a must. Sometimes we would also order books online. The Book Depository ships worldwide, and Amazon.co.uk can be great for accessing English language books within Europe. I made a point of reading fairy tales, literature, and history from each place where we lived. When we lived in Tunisia, we read the Aeneid for children and learned about the Carthaginians. On a road trip to Spain, we read a children's version of Don Quixote. Ancient history came alive as we walked Roman roads and visited faraway lands together.

The only downside of homeschooling was that it encouraged us to rely almost completely on our own family unit, resisting integration with the local culture. If I had it to do over, I would probably still homeschool, but I might seek out more opportunities for my children to make local friends and learn the language.

When we stopped moving around and landed in Amsterdam, we were ready to plant roots and integrate. We put the children, then ten and eight, in a bilingual public Dutch school. I was worried that they would have a hard time going from the light structure and relative freedom of homeschooling to a school setting, especially combined with jet lag in a new country and language. However, it was a surprisingly easy transition for them. I think it helped that we were in a big city, in an internationally minded school with many children from around the world. For them, something between an international and local school was perfect.

KRISTIN · LIVED IN COSTA RICA, THE NETHERLANDS, AND ARGENTINA FOR ONE YEAR

We took three different approaches in our three different locales, which we considered acceptable given the very young age of our children (first grade, pre-K, and a baby).

First, we homeschooled in Costa Rica for two months. I loved homeschooling in theory, as did my kids. I loved finding interesting things to relate to our location and the activities we were doing. I didn't always love the experience in practice, probably also given my kids' young age.

We found schools in the Netherlands and Argentina, and these schools helped us connect to the community in ways that we wouldn't have had without kids. In the Netherlands, we put our children in the International Baccalaureate program. It was an opportunity for my kids to meet children from around the world. The education was pretty good in some ways, although the varied English ability of the students made it hard for the school to do any math the first semester we were there. But it was a great community, comfortable with having foreigners pop in and out. As a huge plus, the school gave us a home in a town that doesn't have a big expat community.

In Argentina, we enrolled our children at a local *jardin*, a lower elementary school. We chose not to go to the American/International Schools in Mendoza because we wanted our kids to speak Spanish. It was a *very* local school, and the community was not used to foreigners coming in and out. We didn't "get" things and they didn't explain them to us so it wasn't a great fit, and we were never really welcomed into the community. We realized in retrospect this affected our satisfaction with the experience. Moreover, the educational system was so 1950s. My daughter was literally copying arithmetic into a folder without any comprehension and it did a little damage to both of my children by dulling their school enthusiasm. However, it was a great learning experience for my husband and me.

AMANDA · LIVES IN MOROCCO

We chose a Moroccan private school because we couldn't afford an International School, we wanted our children to become fluent in Arabic, and Moroccan public schools aren't that great. It took some work to find a place that would accept our children because they were older and had no foundation in the language. Overall, it was a difficult adjustment for our kids. If I could do it again, I would have moved to Morocco when they were younger, but we're happy we did it. Today they are fluent in Arabic and French, which was our goal. The immersion experience was hard, but they learned so much faster than they would have if they could have fallen back on English.

KIRSTY · ROAD-TRIPPED THROUGH NORTHERN AFRICA AND CENTRAL ASIA FROM HER ADOPTED HOME IN ABU DHABI

Before we went on the road, we lived in Abu Dhabi where the law dictates that expat kids attend private school (not public or homeschool). Our kids attended a great multinational, multicultural school featuring play-based learning, which works well for them. Because it wasn't a formalized learning experience, the leap to homeschooling was fairly smooth. Homeschooling was more difficult for us parents as we had so many things to juggle, from driving, finding accommodations, cooking, etc. Studying often happened in the car. After all, it was hard to be disciplined enough to make time for schooling when there was a big wide world out there to explore.

LEWIS FAMILY · LIVED IN MALAYSIA FOR TWO YEARS

Richard had just completed his GCSEs, the examinations taken at age sixteen in the UK education system. We therefore wanted to find an International School that offered the two-year A-level courses in line with that UK system. This meant he could seamlessly take the subjects he had already chosen in the UK, and the curriculum would be familiar. The relocation company helped us find the right school. It was forty-five minutes away, but Richard very quickly learned to sleepwalk to the school bus and sleep the rest of the way. The school offered excellent facilities, and we were pleased with the support and education.

I do think that when you are taking children abroad it is important to research the schools, particularly if they are planning to take school examinations. If Richard had not been happy at the school, that would have seriously impacted our family and our time abroad.

LISA · BACKPACKING AROUND THE WORLD

Neither my husband nor I have a background in education or teaching, so we were nervous about homeschooling four teenagers. Also, I didn't want the pressure of having to be parent, teacher, and traveler. We chose a form of online schooling called Distance Education, which follows the curriculum of schools in Melbourne. Teachers deliver modules of school work and grade that work weekly. The girls can arrange to chat with their teachers over email or Skype. This means that our children will be able to return to a traditional school after this year away and move into their next year levels.

The program is great, but it can be difficult learning a new content management system, not to mention having all subjects delivered online. We have gotten really good at finding photocopiers so we can print English and maths modules, allowing the girls a break from working in front of a screen. We also lug a briefcase of books and materials with us as we travel.

My eldest daughter is studying her second-to-last year of high school (Year 11 in Australia), and many teachers advised against attempting to travel while distance studying. Yes, it's been tough at times, but she has actually performed better this year than any other year. Our 13-year-old was so good at managing her work that she completed all of her Year 7 online work early, and she has the entire final term off. This certainly says something about focused learning for only a few hours a day.

TANIA · ROAD-TRIPPING THROUGH EUROPE

We had homeschooled for three years before the trip, so transitioning to schooling on the road was easy. We spent time learning about explorers in Portugal, musicians in Austria, food in Italy, artists in France, authors in England, and so much more. We learned about the history and culture of the cities we'd visit, and the kids loved learning about things because they were surrounded by it in real life—not reading about it in a book. We've had incredible discussions about communism, classical music, art, and World War II, thanks to our travels.

At one point our oldest attended a Waldorf school for one month in Germany. She had been wanting to improve her German and was curious about Waldorf. I give credit to the school for allowing us to do something like that and also to my daughter for wanting to try it. It was a great experience.

My advice to worldschooling parents is to allow the learning to happen organically. I advocate for not getting bogged down with "keeping up" with what your kids' peers would be doing in school. Let your schedule and plans lead the experience. If you're in Barcelona, go to the Picasso museum and talk about his life. If you're in Berlin, talk about World War II. If you're in Poland or the Czech Republic, talk about communism. Take advantage of festivals and events to teach them about other cultures and traditions. This is a once-in-a-lifetime opportunity for both you as a parent and them as a child. I wouldn't waste it doing math problems all day.

13

PACKING YOUR BAGS

It's almost time. A year before your launch date, you probably looked at the promise of today and the image had a *sfumato* glow—full of wonder and excitement, with your family scrubbed and grinning and facing the horizon, hand-in-hand.

The reality is unquestioningly less glamorous. Even if you don't step on the plane covered in paint and cat effluvia and boasting ten ripped nails, as I did.

You will be frantic.

You will be frenzied.

You will think you are surely losing your mind.

You will forget the most basic of information, such as where your children are.

Your friends will regard your increasingly tangled hairdo with barely concealed panic.

And yet, I promise you—you will get through it.

It might not be pretty, but you will get through it.

So, while we have a moment, let's talk about what to pack. Right now, while you still have the energy and focus to take notes and underline and problem solve. The night before you leave you will have no such wherewithal.

You'll need to pack for two steps. The easier packing is for the airplane. The harder is for the time that you'll be abroad.

Let's begin with what's easiest—launch day. Even if you have traveled extensively, the day you move to another country you will be so scattered that it doesn't hurt to run through the essentials. For the airplane ride, dress comfortably for sleep, and I recommend putting your children in bright colors, so you can easily spot them in the airport. As for yourself, you don't want to land feeling like a complete wreck, so try to make that comfortable outfit one of at least moderate attractiveness. Particularly if you won't have an opportunity to change before you meet your new land-lord. Who will most likely *not* be covered in cat effluvia.

Neck pillows and masks and even new cozy socks can set the stage for sleep. I advocate for instituting some variant of your bedtime routine, as there will be so much stimulation (especially if your children have a zil-lion movie options six inches from their faces), and there will be so many ramped emotions, you'll need a way to signal to you and your children's bodies that it's time to slow down those brain waves. Be clear that your children don't have to sleep, but they do have to rest. If sleep is the goal, they may well doze for a few minutes and then pop right back up to watch another Sponge Bob episode.

You'll get differing opinions about sleep aids, and I advise you to talk to your doctor. Remember that melatonin is helpful for falling asleep, but the instant the flight attendant announces that the fasten seat belt sign's status is changing, that melatonin won't help anyone get back to sleep. I give my kids Dramamine, to keep vomit to a minimum and hasten sleep. As for me, I take an Advil PM to sink me into sleep and also to ward off the exhaustion headache I'm sure to wake up with.

Make sure any snacks you pack won't run you afoul with customs, for instance beef jerky (or just finish or toss it before you go through cus-toms). Bring empty bottles of water that you can keep refilling to maintain hydration levels. And hopefully you had a spare moment to oversee your children's packing of their carry-on backpacks. Children are notoriously bad judges of what they'll find entertaining. I've had to remove enormous board books that can be read in twenty seconds (rendering them useless for plane travel), Monopoly (with missing pieces so it couldn't be played, even if they liked it, which none of them do), flashlights, and handfuls of coins. Consider instead a stocked Kindle, a Ziplock bag of Legos, and a sketchbook with a tin of fresh drawing implements. These are useful for flight delays, at restaurants, and while you are unpacking. In fact, we never go anywhere without drawing supplies.

Now, for the harder part—packing up your life.

When you are packing, remember to keep it simple and that your children will grow. Bring basic clothes, a few special outfits, swimsuits, sporty clothes, and only enough toiletries to last you the first few days. Part of the fun is trying new shampoo and toothpaste, so don't bother with those. I do recommend a high-quality electric toothbrush. Why? It will be a while until your next dentist visit. Keeping tartar down will be key.

You'll also need to bring adapters so that you can plug your devices into their new outlets (don't forget charging cords!). We brought a few games (like Bananagrams and cards), art supplies, journals, and that was about it. The rest will depend on your lifestyle. Think about what you buy for yourselves or your children periodically, and if you need to keep that up, and how you'll be able to get that need met. For instance, one contributor realized that on her year traveling around the world, she wouldn't be able to dye her hair. Given how many photographs she knew would be taken, and how uncomfortable she feels with gray hair, she opted to bring along powdered dye that she could apply once in awhile.

Some people choose to ship their clothes to their new home. We just paid for extra luggage on our flight. Shipping has the advantage of having less to schlep, bringing it on the airplane means you can unpack when you arrive and settle in, but more than that, it tends to be much less expensive. Get quotes from a shipping company and from the airline to make your choice. Pay attention to weight restrictions for items you are taking on the plane.

If you are bringing your possessions on the airplane rather than shipping, you'll need to decide if you want to take traditional giant wheeled suitcases or lightweight enormous duffle bags. The former are far more expensive to purchase, and will also require storage space in your new home. The latter are harder to lug in the airport (those few times that you won't have access to a cart), but collapse to nothing. If you go lightweight, it makes sense to bring one carry-on suitcase of the rolling variety per person. A carry-on is free to bring aboard and makes local travel a breeze.

Consider how much you are taking to the airport. You may want to rent a minivan or hire a van to drive you, depending on the distance.

No matter how well you pack, you'll forget something. That's okay, don't beat yourself up about it, leaving is hard! I myself forgot all of Siena's winter clothes. Hopefully our fellow adventurers will give you some good ideas to add to your list, depending on what kind of journey is ahead of you and getting closer.

Boxing Up My Life

KENZIE'S STORY

I'm boxing up my life. The life I've collected for the past nine years. Some of the time it feels freeing. Like I am decluttering and untangling from so much. Some of it is hard to put behind me. From either too much love or too little love.

This house nurtured key parts of me and ignored other parts of me. As I pack up the love along with the hurt, it all mixes together. The love, though, always pushes the sadness, anxiety, and misunderstanding aside. Can I let it all go with calmness? With love? With gratitude? Some of the best and worst times in my marriage happened in this home. But I feel like it protected us and brought us back to each other time and again.

As I tell my sons, Porter and Beckett, that it is our last night here we share our favorite memories in this house. When the conversation starts to wind down, Porter says, "Mom I'll probably cry when we leave this house." I answer, "Me too." Then we both start to cry and hug each other.

We kiss our walls. Tonight, together, change feels impossibly hard. I am giving up predictability to better feel life. "Not knowing" is our home now.

I tuck the boys for the last time in these bedrooms. I look around at the scattered toys and metal bed frame, and the years feel as though they have slipped away. It seems endless when I think of the nights we brushed teeth and told bedtime stories. How many nights I closed this bedroom door and let out a big sigh, exhausted from the day.

You can never remember the beginning of things, but you always remember the end. Tonight it's not goodbye, but simply good night.

What to Bring

CONTRIBUTORS' STORIES

NELL · LIVED IN FRANCE FOR ONE YEAR

Rentals are not known for their quality cooking equipment, and ours was no different. So early on we bought a good chef's knife. When winter came I missed having hot water bottles, and I wound up ordering them from the UK. I am very fond of taking baths with Epsom salts, but apparently this is unheard of in France. I couldn't find them in any pharmacy or supermarket. So I ended up going to a big gardening center, buying a fifty pound bag of *sulphate de magnésie*, and I was good to go. I told the clerk why I was buying it, and she thought I was nuts. Maybe because I was so jubilant.

But I do want to say that the experience of not having all the stuff was part of the magic of the year abroad. The house was never cluttered. The things we did have (games, toys, new chef's knife) were valued more. It was wonderful to feel so unburdened by things, and if I had it to do over again, I would take *less* stuff rather than more.

HEATHER · LIVED IN ITALY FOR TWO YEARS

I recommend bringing cold medication, pain relievers, antiperspirant, and sunscreen with good SPF, as these are all are expensive and/or hard to find in Italy. I'm really glad we brought comfort items like music and our favorite books.

JOHN · RV-ED THROUGH EUROPE

In hindsight, a GPS in the camper would have been handy.

KRISTIN · LIVED IN COSTA RICA, THE NETHERLANDS, AND ARGENTINA FOR ONE YEAR

Things that were worth the weight: a giant bag full of Legos, photographs of our dogs, picture books and cards from our friends, and stuffed animal talismans. We also brought this magic potion that's supposed to bring good luck that we buy every year from a Cuban store. That was great to have.

AMANDA · LIVES IN MOROCCO

I was very glad I brought good kitchen knives, a Kindle, and my favorite pillow. There were a lot of things I thought I wanted but in the end I don't miss.

ALISHA · LIVES IN KYRGYZSTAN

I have naturally curly hair and live in Asia (where women usually have very straight hair). I brought my own hair products from home because there just aren't products for my kind of hair here. Chocolate chips are a truly American thing, so I bring bags of those in our luggage along with some favorite spices that are hard to find, and pure vanilla extract, buffalo wing sauce, and root beer extract, too.

CHERYL · RV-ING THROUGH EUROPE

Three items that we couldn't live without are our bedding and pillows, the dogs, and the kids' iPads! They don't use them often, but they are our secret weapon on long journeys. We whip them out before they start getting bored to avert mayhem.

LISA · BACKPACKING AROUND THE WORLD

Shoes are vital. I literally live in my Keens. They can be worn in all climates and conditions, and they're extremely lightweight. Plus, they clean and dry easily. They also don't rub my skin or slip on tiles, and are easily taken on and off, which is great in Asian countries.

My husband would be lost without his lightweight travel shirts that dry quickly. He has three as it works like a cycle: one to wear, one to wash, and one that's drying.

I use a camera bag as my carry-on luggage, which holds my Mac laptop, mirrorless DLSR camera, a couple of interchangeable lenses, and spare batteries. I use my Mac most days as I'm a blogger, so it's necessary to have a lightweight and strong laptop case. Same with the camera.

KIRSTY · ROAD-TRIPPED THROUGH NORTHERN AFRICA AND CENTRAL ASIA FROM HER ADOPTED HOME IN ABU DHABI

We brought Marmite because Brits always need their Marmite!

LEWIS FAMILY · LIVED IN MALAYSIA FOR TWO YEARS

I wish I had brought my Christmas decorations. Luckily I was able to source some in Kuala Lumpur. I do wish I had brought more clothes in my size. I am a standard UK size 14, and this is off the scale in Asia. I also would have loved to have had my cake decorating kit. Sometimes it's comforting to pursue familiar hobbies, even while away.

SARA · LIVED IN MOROCCO FOR SEVEN YEARS

My most treasured items were cranberry sauce for Thanksgiving, peanut butter, and coconut oil. I became an expert at food substitutions. Who needs baking powder or Worcestershire sauce when you've got my subs?

GABRIELLA · LIVES IN MEXICO

I brought our high-powered Ninja blender. Small appliances and electronics are considerably more expensive here. Additionally, before departing we upgraded our phones and computers (we're a Mac and iPhone family) which was necessary as there are few Mac products, much less the brand-new ones, and we need them for work. Lastly, hair products for Black people are difficult to find here in Mazatlán. I brought an ample supply, and when my husband travels back stateside he collects more for me. We also brought a small supply of my middle son's medications (for asthma and his EpiPen) so we wouldn't have to scramble to find them immediately. Replacement medications are available without a prescription, but I felt better having everything on hand, at least during the time we took to settle in and learn the process.

NAOMI · LIVED IN INDIA AND SINGAPORE FOR FOUR YEARS

We sold our home in Cleveland when we moved to India. Because it was meant and intended to be a long-term move, we shipped over the contents of our entire house, including a baby grand piano! We did a lot of research and decided that because our two youngest children were so young (3- and 6-years-old), having the comforts of home would help their settling-in period. Looking back on that, I now know they simply needed each other, their mama and daddy, and a few lovies.

I was, however, really glad that my friend Ellen advised me to bring tampons. At that time, those were not to be found in India—anywhere! About one year after we arrived, some European grocery stores made their way to Delhi, which helped with the tracking down of our favorite items, but tampons were always elusive. Baby powder was a MUST but was almost impossible to find. It was a must because of the intense heat and... well, it helps create a barrier for sticky thighs and sweaty nether regions. It was also great advice to bring shoes for my husband and eldest son, as it was nearly impossible to locate shoes in their size. Photo books from home were much treasured. We wore those OUT!

Even though we missed a lot of creature comforts, part of the adventure is seeking out new items to try, instead of bemoaning the fact that the only Oreo cookies you can find are soggy, stale, and musty.

PART THREE

LIVING

14

CULTURE SHOCK

When you land at your destination—whether it is the first in a list as long as your arm, or whether it's where you plan to live for a year or more—you will absolutely experience some amount of adjustment. It's easy to assume that culture shock solely applies to your home culture ramming up against that of your host country. But for an expat, even a transitional one, it goes much deeper.

I expected that aspects of our new life would be a change. I counted on it, thrilled to it even. Pre-launch, when I desperately needed a way to shove suffocating thoughts about timelines and checklists out of my brain, I'd imagine chatting with local farmers as I shopped for fresh produce to fill what would surely be a tiny refrigerator. So tiny! Ah, that tiny fridge would be a challenge. I imagined sipping *espresso*, which I knew I'd need to learn to drink straight, not cut with milk. I imagined swapping out driving to piano lessons and soccer practice with leisurely strolls through olive groves as the sun slanted across the valley. That was what I expected of culture shock. A series of slight and charming hiccups that made me smile winsomely in the retelling.

What I neglected to envision was not having any idea what was going on half the time. Okay, that's not entirely accurate. More like 90% of the time. I remember a September meeting at the middle school to organize music lessons (offered free by the school system, and luckily right at the school, so my rosy afternoons were indeed not carved up by getting kids to lessons). The teacher talked and explained the structure of the lessons, and I concentrated on making an expression that belied the novel feeling of soporific panic that became a hallmark of our first six months in Italy. I reminded myself of a cat I used to have, who, whenever she was in danger, would flee up a tree and fall promptly asleep. The content stream of unknown words lulled my brain into a state of extreme boredom, all the while I knew that I may very well be tested at the end of the hour. As a matter of fact, there *was* a quiz, of sorts. The teacher stopped her speech and, in front of all the other parents, turned to us to ask if we understood. Only that was one more question I didn't understand.

I didn't understand how the school worked, I didn't even understand how *snack* at school worked. The kids informed me that students lined up to collect pizza (more like our focaccia) at snack time, but when I gave them my new resting expression of soporific panic, Nicolas and Siena assured me that it looked pretty bad, not nearly as tasty as what I bought them from the bakery, so they'd continue to bring their own snack, don't worry, Mom! Gabe must have been playing Legos when this interchange happened because not long afterwards, he burst out of school yammering about his free pizza. Now, I did know enough to know that the pizza couldn't possibly be free. Gabe must have blithely walked off with a piece. Keith and I attempted to have a coded conversation about what to do about this situation, but we weren't nearly as coded as we thought because Gabe cottoned onto what we were saying and collapsed into ready tears about how he was going to be sent to Italian jail.

Sigh. Parenting can be a tough gig, here or there or everywhere.

I ended up asking his teacher, who told me that the pizza man had indeed been handing out free pizza (whew!) because he'd brought too much that day. She also told us which bakery sold tickets that our kids could use to buy pizza, €8,00 for 10 tickets. Or they could just go in with a euro. Turns out, I had made that whole process unnecessarily complicated in my head. Also turns out, Nicolas and Siena were totally lying about that school pizza. It was awesome.

Not understanding or being able to contribute made me feel separate, different. People were very patient, but planning out what I wanted to say to confirm I'd be able to say it before opening my mouth exhausted me. And also made me a beat behind. I'm usually quick on the uptake. In Italy, not so much. My kids each had experiences like this. In fact, Nicolas was ecstatic when he started barely passing the tests his classmates received, rather than being handed dumbed down versions of those tests. He felt the progress of becoming the least bright kid in the class, rather than the kid who required interventions. This child, who once prided himself for his top marks, was now thrilling to just being "slow."

Even when language wasn't the crux of the issue, trying to parse out figure from background, exception from rule, took up more mental energy than I had allotted. At home, when a guest arrives for dinner laboring under a giant tray of appetizers I never suggested they bring, I know that's just them. But when Nicolas's friend arrived to our house with an over-flowing basket of goodies from quince jam to pastries, I had to wonder— is this how it is done? When we are invited to someone's house, are we expected to come bearing a basket of homemade treats? Or is this the child of a farmer, and this said more about the farming community? Or was this simply a gesture of welcome typical of this one family?

That friend of Nicolas's also brought his sister. None of us knew the sister. Siena gamely tried to engage her, but the girl was, if possible, more awkward and shy than my own daughter (thank goodness we had *Shrek* in Italian). Were we expected to drop our other kids off on playdates? At birthday parties, it certainly seemed like parents were surprised that we didn't bring our whole brood. Was this an Italian thing? A Spello thing? Were we unwittingly offending our hosts by not trusting them with our entire gaggle of little Americans?

I spent a lot of time trying to figure this out, partly because of my eagerness to understand our new home, but also because I am a rule follower to a fault. If there is an expectation, I feel the need to not just nail it, but nail it, polish it, and receive ample praise for a nailing job well done. Realizing that I was never, but *never*, going to understand the nuances of the rules was a process. And that process was a large piece of the culture shock. It wasn't so much adjusting to a country made of people fundamentally unwilling to form a line at the tollbooth—that's just a bit of humorous conversation over lunch—but rather adjusting to a new version of myself that my new location demanded.

For instance, after a few months of living in Spello, once locals realized we weren't just stopping though (enrolling the kids in public school pretty much broadcasted that fact), people wanted to chat. Now, I don't live in a big city where chatting on the sidewalk is unusual. In fact, I've always regarded Charlottesville as a laid-back, friendly community. And yet, I was surprised at my level of surprise at being hailed for a bit of conversation. Turns out, I was very used to greetings, but not at all used to connection. Now that I'm back, I realized those yard conversations in Virginia are primarily recitations of how busy people are. Before racing off again.

At first, this pull to stay and talk made me feel fidgety. Shouldn't I be getting home? Why was I having yet another conversation about my cats or the weather or the upcoming festival? Were people just being polite? I could restlessly hang in there for a few minutes, and then I'd make an excuse to get home.

By the end of the year, I was hanging out with old people, sitting on plastic chairs, watching the world go by and giving commentary, as Gabe played cards with the men and Siena braided my hair. Now street-side conversation is what I look forward to about going back. That and hanging out the window, watching neighbors amble down the street so I can hail them for a spot of talk. I no longer avert my eyes at the eye contact and bristle at the attempt to cleave together a conversation. I love it. But it took some getting used to.

Your own culture shock will depend on how ready you are to embrace change, how different your new community is, and how much your lifestyle changes as a result of your move. Transitioning from a classic suburban American home to living out of a backpack or a tiny apartment in Tokyo or a camper in Central Asia or a farm in Ireland will include some adjustments beyond acclimating to a different culture. You'll need to get used to not solely the omnipresence of full-fat dairy products and new social niceties, but also the small pinches in your daily existence that seem frustrating and inane, plus the demands on you that are different in a different place. Those demands could be entirely self-imposed or come from your family leaning into you in a novel way as your children and partner cope with their own adjustments. So many adjustments to make!

"Culture shock" is an umbrella term that covers a lot of ground. It references the head butting of one culture pitted against another, but also the feeling of being a fish out of water, of creating a new version of you or a new version of your family rhythm. And sometimes the shock isn't so much about the fact that your coffee now comes with a cookie or that your fellow citizens seem completely uninterested in line formation at the post office, and more to do with the fact that your old life is, well, old. In the past. Like a watercolor with too much water.

You can't entirely prepare for it. All you can really do is notice the differences between your new life and your old, with as little judgment as you can manage. When you are judging your new community for eating dinner at a time when good children should be tucked safe in bed, or judging your old community for failing to wholly embrace eating local, you are creating a dichotomy that is sometimes false and often energy intensive. Note the changes, without getting attached to things being one way or another. Without getting attached to YOU being one way or another. Transitions are hard. Be easy on yourself.

The Seven Lies of Living Cross-Culturally

JERRY'S STORY

W hen we first choose to live as foreigners, we are prime for the suckering. We are wide eyed and overflowing with enthusiasm. We soak up everything that Lonely Planet, Rosetta Stone, and Wikipedia have to offer about our soon-to-be new home. In our zeal, we are prone to misgauging our own proficiency.

We are pumped...and ready...and oh so naive.

Set for swindling.

There are seven great deceptions and most of us fall for at least five. I have personally tested them all. You know...for research. I lay them out now NOT for the sake of those who are packing up their lives and getting ready to go. That would be like telling newlyweds that marriage is hard. They just tilt their head and grin at you as if *you're* the cute one..."Yeah, we know it's hard for everyone else but we're sooooo in love...and it will never, ever be hard for us."

You're sweet and I would never steal this time from you. Proceed.

But for those of you coming down from the honeymoon (and possibly even some of you veterans), here are seven deceptions which you may or may not have noticed just yet.

1. THE "DUAL CULTURE" LIE

It's perfectly natural, when we relocate from one country to another country to focus entirely on those two cultures. Give me a spreadsheet with TWO columns and tell me how our cultures are different.

WE like personal space—THEY don't.

WE are direct—THEY are indirect.

WE use a fork—THEY use their fingers.

BOOM! I got this.

There are tests and inventories and boatloads of brilliant research that can help you size up YOURS and THEIRS. Culture to culture, side by side.

I love that stuff. I could get lost in it, but the big reality shocker comes when you realize that living cross-culturally is not simply TWO cultures but it requires MULTIPLE layers of cultural adjustment. Here's the kicker—oftentimes the OTHER cultures are more consuming than the one of your host country.

Expat culture—so different—You need another column on your spreadsheet.

Professional culture—different again—Another column.

International School—layers in itself—Multiple columns.

Faith culture—another column.

Generational gaps—more.

Subcultures—more.

This list goes on.

It's never just two.

2. THE "LANGUAGE BY OSMOSIS" LIE

Learning a new language is hard. Sure it's easier for some people than for others, and no doubt there are gifted learners who seem to have a flare for picking it up quickly. The rest of us are...what's the English word?

NORMAL.

Regardless, one of the most painful realizations is that new language doesn't just grow organically in your brain because you are surrounded by it. Expats are survivalists first and foremost. We pick up the absolutely essential phrases, we seek out picture menus, we print taxi cards, we download apps, and we are shameless masters of hand gestures and charades. Never has there been a group of people who have worked harder to communicate without learning how to.

In many places you can be (and you will not be alone) an expat for years upon years and never learn the language. Intentionally choosing the harder option is key.

It doesn't just happen.

3. THE "CULTURE SHOCK IMMUNITY" LIE

"Culture shock" is a deceptive phrase. The word "shock" insinuates some kind of unforeseen, instant jolt. As if you stuck your fork into an outlet and BAZZZAAAPPP!

"WHOA! Should have used chopsticks! Didn't see that coming."

Consequently, when we don't have the quick sizzle, hair-raising, eye-bulging zap followed by the easily distinguishable and obviously dysfunctional meltdown we assume (incorrectly) that we have beat the system. No culture shock for me.

"I am Transition Man! Your culture bolts are no match for my defenses!"

But transition from one system to another system is not a switch that we flip, it is a process that we go through. That process includes the stress of adjusting from the way you have always done it to the way it is now done.

It includes wrestling with *knowing*, without a doubt that your way is better...and then *thinking* that it probably is...and then *wondering* if it might be...and then *acknowledging* there may be two good ways...and then (sometimes) *recognizing* the new way is better.

For some people the process is harder, deeper, darker, more dysfunctional. Some people thrive on the instability.

It's not the same (by any means) for everyone but no one gets immunity.

4. THE "COOKIE CUTTER CULTURE SHOCK" LIE

Maybe you've seen something like this:

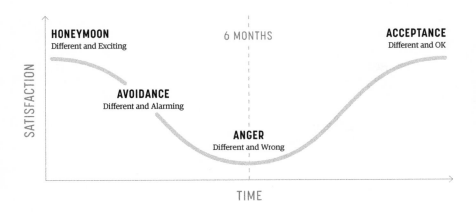

Tools like this are especially helpful when cultural transition feels like puberty. "Why am I feeling like this?! Why am I acting like this?! GET OUT OF MY ROOM!!"

In the complicated, confusing moments of adjustment, charts like this serve as a sweet reminder of a simple yet solid truth.

"I'm normal?? Waaahh, that's fabulous. But seriously, get out of my room."

The problem with the standard culture shock continuum is NOT that it is inaccurate. It is that we think it was designed to be more accurate than it is.

"I feel like my transition had more dips than that."

"I think my dip wasn't so deep but it lasted longer than six months."

"I don't think I ever got a honeymoon phase."

Yes. Yes. Yes. You are spot on. *Your* transition is *yours*. It is dramatically different from the next guy's and his is different from everyone else's. If you are expecting to fit exactly into the right schedule for adjustment, you're likely to slip back into feeling weird or abnormal or dysfunctional or superhuman.

There are too many variables for everyone to have the same transition. This was mine.

5. THE "SINGLE ANSWER" LIE

In human years expats move from 5-years-old to sixteen in about two months. Let me explain.

Expats are über-inquisitive on the front end. "What is that? How do you say this? What's that smell? Why do they do that? What's the history behind this? Who? What? When? Where? How? Why? Why? Why?"

Like a 5-year-old. We embrace ignorance in a quest for answers.

BUT (and this is where it ALL falls apart): We think when we get an answer we understand it (you should read that sentence again). Soon we "know" (finger quotes) *everything*.

Like a 16-year-old.

When we have answers we stop asking questions.

This can be a fatal flaw for expats. There is ALWAYS more to it.

"Ignorance is not your problem unless you think that you're not ignorant."
-Albert Einstein—*should have said this*
Embrace ignorance and stay five for a while.

For contrast, imagine describing the climate of North America as frigid because you spent Christmas day in Northern Canada. Check out Guatemala in July before you share your expertise.

There is *always* more to it.

6. THE "EXPAT BUBBLE" LIE

This one is doubly deceptive. It sneaks up on you and you never see it coming. There are no instant, clear-cut signs but one day...months from now...maybe even years, you realize you've been duped.

No one is more excited than the honeymooning newbies to engage local culture. "We're going to make lots of local friends and study language, learn their customs, and teach them ours. We'll share cooking lessons and laugh about idioms. It'll be great!"

Then...over time...and one interaction at a time you take the least challenging option. It's frustrating to speak a language you don't know. You don't connect with these people on sports or politics or food or fun, and it feels more like work than friendship. Being with fellow expats is just easier.

That's how the bubble is built.

For clarity let me just say...I love the bubble. Some of my best friends are in that bubble and I like hanging out there.

BUT I don't want to be STUCK inside of it. To live cross-culturally and never genuinely experience (deeply) your host culture is a BIG miss. To be surrounded by people who are SO different and could teach you SO much and never find a friend, is a sad thing.

The lie we believe is that it won't happen to us. However without tremendous and ongoing intentionality, it almost always does.

7. THE "THEY LOVE ME BECAUSE I'M A FOREIGNER" LIE

This varies dramatically depending on who you are and where you are living. It is painfully easy to mistake cultural hospitality for respect and admiration. "These people treat me like a rock star."

It's easy to let that misguided reaction go to your head (much like a rock star would). The result is typically tragic. This is where cultures get abused and foreigners leave a trail of mess behind them. In their arrogance they assume that they have all of the pieces —"They smile when they see me, they laugh at my jokes, they want to spend time with me...they must love me."

There is always more to it.

It could be culturally mandated kindness

It could be the art of war

They could be buttering you up to steal your wallet

Or maybe they love you.

Point is, you can't know until you stick around and build a real relationship. That's where the good stuff is. The real stuff.

Lies are easy to come by when you live cross-culturally. If you've been duped, welcome to the club. Actually, you've been here for a while but none of us wanted to say anything. Welcome back from your honeymoon.

This is where it gets good.

Adjusting to a New Normal

CONTRIBUTORS' STORIES

SARA · LIVED IN MOROCCO FOR SEVEN YEARS

Ahhh, the cultural differences could leave you crying, but we tried to have them keep us laughing. One aspect of Moroccan life that was challenging was the use of *inshallah,* which means God willing. The pure form of its use is beautiful. If God wills it, then the plumber will be there at 9 AM. But instead, this word has become a noncommittal way to be polite to everyone. So, the plumber may or may not show up at 9 AM tomorrow... or next Friday. Those test results, *inshallah,* will be available on Tuesday... or sometime soon after that. And it goes, on and on. An entire culture of people not committing.

Then there is the concept of time. In Morocco, it's soft and fluid. We were once invited to a wedding that began at 8 PM, so we arrived at 9PM thinking we were playing the whole Moroccan-time thing well. It turned out we were the first guests there and no one else showed up until 10:30 PM. It was just us, the caterers, and musicians. Talk about awkward!

Another cultural difference is that Moroccans will spend ten minutes asking about your family and their health before they get to any business. At first this was annoying when I wanted to ask a quick question. The worst of this was when a police officer reprimanded me for not asking him how he was before I asked him for directions. It was impossible to do more than one or two errands in a day because of the extra conversation or a hiccup of sorts that slows down the schedule. Eventually, we stopped fighting it and enjoyed the simplicity. Now that we're back in the States, I find myself trying to exchange all sorts of pleasantries with workers in the stores, all to be looked at with annoyance and a kind of "get to the point" look on their face. I hope this is one habit that I'll always keep from Morocco.

Besides the parts of our entry that were defined by our cultural differences, we also had to grow used to being conspicuous. Everyone in town knew about *the Americans*. That being said, there is a cool little thing that happens when you move abroad. Your host country doesn't expect you to follow their cultural and societal expectations, but there is *no one checking in that you're following America's expectations either*. So, you're given this free space to be whoever you want to be. It's this I love. I was probably seen as the crazy American, and that suited me fine.

HEATHER · LIVED IN ITALY FOR TWO YEARS

Getting used to driving in Italy was a challenge. Chris swears that drivers in Italy are safer than in the US, but it was a nail biter for me those first few months in Milan.

Chris struggled with how the Italians he worked with talked in circles. We both had a hard time with the lack of urgency. It could take nine months and ten appointments to address something as simple as getting our shower repaired.

Another thing I noticed is that Italians have a different internal thermostat. They bundle up in puffy coats and scarves even in April when it's close to eighty degrees. When the grocery store heater blew down harshly I wanted to strip off my light sweater but knew the reaction I'd get.

Then there were the aspects of Italian life that were easy to adopt. I loved the long dinners and not feeling rushed. Restaurants made me feel like a cherished guest. I love how Italians celebrate everything so brilliantly, with history and deep roots and specific foods, lovingly prepared.

CANADA-TO-FRANCE · LIVES IN FRANCE

We had to get used to the slower pace of Europe. When you are used to the North American momentum, it can be quite an adjustment. The

French take their time. They dine slowly, customer service in a store is slow, even bagging groceries can take time. I had to learn to slow down, which I'm now happy about. I mean, wasn't that the point after all?

CHERYL · RV-ING THROUGH EUROPE

Our biggest shock is lack of living space. Our motorhome is less than twenty-two feet in length. And with three children and two dogs, we are a *lot* of family. Lack of space can be both good and bad. Always being together has brought us closer; however, there's nowhere to go when your hubby is getting on your nerves and there's no time-out zone when the kids are bickering.

On the plus side, being a complete unknown in a foreign country is quite liberating. No one knows you, so no one has any expectations of you, and there's no pressure to be a certain way. Because of that, I now wear shorts. Every day. I've even worn a bikini, and I've not worn a bikini since before I had kids. At home I'd be too self-conscious to wear either shorts or bikinis. I know it's not a big deal to most people but for me it's huge progress in my confidence, and it's all down to being completely unknown.

NICA · SAILED THE CARIBBEAN

We didn't experience culture shock as much as acclimating to living in a small space. Two hundred eighty square feet is what I like to tell people (but that's an exaggeration—it was smaller than that).

I was shocked at how *social* cruising is. Any night, we could have people over or go to another boat for sundowners (when you bring your own booze/drinks) or dinner. There were beach potlucks. Shared dinghy rides to good fishing spots. There is endless time.

The thing that strikes me is the "we're all in this together" nature of cruising. Spare parts are shared, advice is freely given, and there is no expectation of payment or payback. If you can help someone, the next time you need help there will be someone there to help you. Everyone has different talents and they're all useful.

KRISTIN · LIVED IN COSTA RICA, THE NETHERLANDS, AND ARGENTINA FOR ONE YEAR

I did not expect that bikes in the Netherlands were absolutely necessities. We had to totally change the way we traveled in the biggest city we'd ever lived in with children. At the time of the move, we were primarily walkers, with my 6- and 4-year-old in a double stroller while I used a carrier for my 1-year-old. But in our non-touristed Dutch town, pedestrians with strollers were non-existent, and the bikers on the road had no idea how to navigate around us. So we were forced to bike. Before we lived in the Netherlands, I was a timid biker at best and suddenly I had to become a utilitarian highway biker on the fly with bikes zooming around me. Worse, I couldn't get accustomed to a biker life on a regular bike, but had to learn on a *bakfeit*, or cargo bike (I recommend Googling this contraption), filled with children. It was really hard and scary. There was no room for error, and although Dutch people are famously tolerant in lots of areas, they were incredibly impatient (rightfully so) with any biker errors.

AMANDA · LIVES IN MOROCCO

I walked into a different situation because I was the American wife of my Moroccan husband, so I had some expectations to live up to (or defy). Morocco is very relationship based so it was difficult to start over because we didn't have the connections to get things done. I really missed going out and seeing familiar faces and having small conversations.

It was hard to get used to the volume in Morocco, as conversations happen at a thunderous sound level. That took some getting used to.

Also, life happens later at night than I expected. It's very normal to eat dinner at 11 PM or later, and even children often don't go to bed until 1 AM. Another cultural difference is that in Morocco, what's yours is mine. Most everything is community property, and violating this can take a lot of maneuvering. We also had to adjust to the fact that in Morocco, kids come home from school for lunch every day. From 12:30–2:30 they're at home for the big meal. This is really hard for working parents, though in Morocco, moms or grandmas are always at home.

NAOMI · LIVED IN INDIA AND SINGAPORE FOR FOUR YEARS

I adored the Indian head bobble. Yes, no, maybe so! Even after our return to the US, we still find ourselves responding to questions with a bobble of our heads. In Singapore, I was struck by the concept of *kiasu*, or always staying ahead of your neighbor. I once recorded a video of a car creeping past ours, inch by inch, as my husband scooted forward at a traffic light.

More seriously, being in India, surrounded by people who were the same skin tone as me, was extremely interesting. I had grown up in a world where being biracial (my father is black and my mother is white) as a child of the 70s was not very common—maybe more specifically in the Midwest. Not until I lived overseas did I realize the power of belonging—visibly and physically—in a people group. Simultaneous to this, my white mother moved to Kenya as a missionary, and she is often greeted with *mzungu*, which means "white" and the contrast of our experiences is fascinating. She tires easily of standing out, being the source of attention and often speaks of the ease of blending in.

Now that we've moved back to the United States, our children are VERY conscious about diversity (or the lack thereof) especially as it relates to their education and the peers they are surrounded by. They will point out in restaurants when they see blended/mixed families, and are aware of advertising and media that does not represent diversity. I often wonder if that would be the case if we had not moved them from Ohio.

JOHN · RV-ED THROUGH EUROPE FOR ONE YEAR

It was absolutely delicious to not only be a complete unknown but to travel without obligations, expectations, or being defined by what you do for a living.

LISA · BACKPACKING AROUND THE WORLD

We have visited so many countries during our backpacking year, it's been fascinating to note the differences between them. It was hard to acclimate to the Hindu aspects of rural India, especially when my family was incorporated into the devotion. Many people in Buldhana have never seen a white person before, so they stared and touched us, asking to put our hands on their babies. Some believed we were gods sent to bring luck.

Then there are the cows roaming everywhere in Buldhana. Indian people feed them as an offering to their Hindu god—flat bread chapattis or other vegetable matter. Plus, there are goats with overflowing udders wandering the streets being pesky and stealing food from Sunday market stalls. There's also the feral pigs that live off scraps and the street dogs who chase the pigs and tear their ears for sport. It's gruesome, but it's part of the experience. For me, rural India can be summed up as the very best and the very worst of humanity. I would go back in a heartbeat.

Something I hadn't expected though was that though people loved hearing our global travel story, sometimes talking about it made me feel overrated and privileged. It was uncomfortable to talk about our trip with very poor people who had no chance of getting outside their village, let alone their country.

In Spain, we had to deal not just with the regular adjustment, but also with the adjustment of arriving from India. In India, we were constantly stared at, but in Spain, we were ignored. Even when we looked lost, no one in Spain came to help us; it was like we were invisible. Whereas in India if we looked the slightest bit lost, people assisted us immediately.

Spain also raised issues for us as a family because of our non-Spanish approach to bullfighting. We tried to get into the spirit, which was easier than expected thanks to the trumpets calling us into the ancient and ornate bullring, filled with thousands of cheering fans. But by the third bull slaughter we couldn't take it anymore and had to leave.

Morocco was a male-dominated society, and that was hard to get used to. The men sit at cafés beside side tables cluttered with their ashtray, newspaper, and their strong mint tea in a silver teapot. I loved watching silver teapots rise and fall as steaming amber liquid poured into decorative glasses. The men face the road, watching the world go by. Not once did we see a Moroccan woman sitting at a café on her own.

At first, we found the Vietnamese off-putting with their tendency to grab our arms and squeeze or pinch. It took us a bit of time to realize that people in Vietnam are not physically warm and cuddly, so this was how they express affection. It's a sign of burgeoning friendship, even while it feels like a reprimand. Once you've lived in Vietnam long enough—no one tells you how long that actually is—you'll become a regular Vietnamese family, and the people at the shops and the markets will give you a discount. It takes a awhile, but then you'll think, "I finally belong."

LEWIS FAMILY · LIVED IN MALAYSIA FOR TWO YEARS

The experience of being in a culture where you are the odd person out, where you do not understand the language or the culture, challenges your values and understanding. Too often people fail to question or reflect upon the values they have about life, the society they live in, and how this can be very different for other people and cultures.

One of the initial surprising aspects of the culture in Kuala Lumpur was that British women were viewed as "ladies of leisure." It was assumed that I would have a gardener and house help. In shops, if I had more than one carrier bag, assistants rushed to offer to carry my bags to the car. When they discovered I had walked to the shopping center, they were in disbelief. Also, retailers thought it a mark of respect to follow one step behind me. This was so different from UK culture that it was initially very off-putting.

I learned that "saving face" is important in Malaysian culture. People warned me, but it was still a struggle to deal with. This meant no trades-person says "No." Which sounds nice in theory, but in practice it meant that despite getting out diaries and seriously jotting in an appointment, my handyman or the telephone repair service often had no intention of keeping that appointment. It was left to me to figure out whether yes was yes-yes, yes-maybe, or yes-no.

Then there was the traffic and driving. Almost all the Malay people I met were pleasant and friendly—until they were behind the wheel of a car (or a bike). During peak traffic hours, two-lane roads would frequently become queues six cars wide, with cars and bikes weaving in and out of the traffic. Traffic lights were mere suggestions, and bikes would often mount the pavement and drive straight at you if they spied a parking spot. I was shocked to see mopeds with two adults and children aboard, and not a helmet in sight!

But those aspects of acclimating to a new culture were easy compared to adjusting to social inequality and local assumptions about people of various cultures. Or the Malay attitudes towards women. I was frequently referred to as Mrs. Henry as if I "belonged" to my husband. Sometimes this was amusing, but other times it felt dire, like when the bank refused to allow me to deal with our joint account because Henry was THE account holder.

One marvelous aspect of the culture was the celebration and acceptance of religious festivals whether they were Muslim, Hindu, Buddhist, or Christian. At each holiday, shopping centers and streets were decorated with elaborate displays that were colorful and joyful. Moving to a mainly Muslim country, I was surprised at Malaysia's acceptance of other religions.

STEPHANIE · LIVES IN ITALY

Moving to Italy is such a romantic idea, but the real-life experience has definitely been more work and stress than I anticipated. We don't yet speak Italian and even basic things like opening a bank account and establishing residency involve a lot of confusing bureaucracy. Finding an apartment was a real struggle that almost led us to give up on the whole shebang. We keep persisting though, and try to keep our eye on the big picture: We live in one of the most beautiful countries in the world, and eventually we may even feel at home here.

15

LEARNING THE LANGUAGE

I fell victim to the conventional wisdom that says that youngsters take to language as effortlessly as a thirsty plant soaks up water. I assumed that Gabe would be trilling Italian while he still had American soil clinging to his Keens. Turns out, that was 100% wrong. What determined our family language progress was a combination of experience in learning language and simple brazenness.

Nicolas, who learned French in middle school and was perfectly comfortable making mistakes, learned Italian far faster than the rest of us. At fourteen, he was dreaming in Italian while I was still conjugating in my head before speaking. Which gets at that brazenness. He made it his goal to *try*, not to be successful.

Nicolas's Italian lasted longer than the rest of ours. Possibly because he studied for the Italian Advanced Placement Exam (American high school exams that count for college credit, usually following a year of instruction) on our return to Virginia. This may have cemented and codified the Italian whirlwind in his brain. Even four years after our sojourn in Spello, I'll struggle to understand a friend on a return visit, whereas Nicolas, only paying partial attention, leans in to effortlessly translate. Speaking is harder, but after a week in Spello he can pontificate about American exceptionalism.

Nicolas must have inherited his brazenness from Keith. Since the language Keith learned in high school was German, one would presume he would have lagged behind my Spanish-infused brain. On the contrary, his ability to leap into the fray oiled his language-learning gears. Where I was translating every word someone said to me, somewhat panicked about understanding, Keith just let the words wash over him and had no problem with comprehension.

Keith developed a love of reading mysteries in Italian, supported by his Italian-English dictionary lodged permanently at his side. Because of this, his Italian vocabulary is rich with words related to murder weapons and rigor mortis. He also made a hobby of reading the newspaper, which not only aided his politics-related vocabulary, it made it easier for him to leap into conversations at the bar. Thus reinforcing not only his Italian, but also his connection with locals and consequently even more opportunities for language practice. I did eventually try using the newspaper to plump my language learning, and it was easier than I expected. I forgot that newspapers are usually aimed at a fairly low grade-level of reading comprehension.

In addition to his reading, Keith also managed (with significant assistance from Google Translate) all the bureaucracy. As with politics, this gave him a nuanced vocabulary in that specific topic area, as well as lending him conversational experience, since he was the point person for all things regulation and rule-bound in our family.

Keith would tell you that the two of us reached the same level of language proficiency. The people of Spello, though, would beg to differ. They consistently turned to him when conversations got tricky, even complimenting him on his language acquisition. I took lessons and got no such praise.

It must be said though, that in low-stakes situations where mistakes are expected (conversation classes or now when we run into friends on the street after long absences so they expect little), my language is more fluid and the Spanish accent aids my accent. It is when I'm anxious that my brain freezes. Things that help are wine, deep breathing, and preparing my brain by consciously thinking my thoughts in Italian.

Siena had learned a little French in school, but she was so scared about making mistakes that her language learning was only slightly faster than Gabe's. Both of them had this interesting phase of their language acquisition when Italian words jumbled in the bingo hopper of their brains, and would come out where required, but without the accompanying articles or specifiers. As time went on, those little words filled in until they were speaking complete sentences.

It's funny though, by the end of the year abroad, we'd go to a new restaurant and we'd chat with the waiter and then Gabe would order. As soon as the words were out of his month, the waiter would turn to us and say, "How does this child know how to speak Italian?" And we'd look at each other and wonder, isn't that what we're all speaking?

You see, though Gabe learned Italian more slowly than the rest of us, what he got more thoroughly was the local accent. Our friend Graziano mused that the rest of us probably used the written word as a broker between the words we heard and our understanding. Gabe arrived before he was reading, so he learned by ear, not by picturing marching letters.

We did a poor job maintaining the kids' Italian. I know another family that hired a tutor for their child on return and his fluidity benefited, but that didn't work for us financially. For a year after we returned home, we tried to compromise by hiring one tutor for all of them, but with three of them at different conversational levels and with different abilities to conjugate and parse apart language, it didn't work. The kids grew resistant and I got tired of fighting them. Their lessons stopped, and I decided that if they wanted to get their Italian back, that was on them.

Nicolas doesn't have an interest in pursuing language at this time, which saddens me. But given how easily it comes back, I think it's waiting for him when he decides he wants it. Siena and Gabe say that they understand most of what's said. I'm not entirely sure that's true because Nicolas can easily translate for us, and I find myself translating for the two younger kids, but I do believe they can get it back. What's more important is that now they seem motivated to try.

This summer we're returning to Italy for a month. For two of those weeks Siena will be living with an Italian family, taking language classes, and studying fresco making and art history (in Italian). She doesn't expect to get her Italian back in two weeks, but she wants some of it and wants to connect with Italian culture. Time was, living with strangers would bring on oodles of anxiety (oh the fear of the awkward situation!), but now she's confident enough that she's willing to hoist herself through uncomfortable situations for the sake of learning the language. Is that due to her natural development, or is it a by-product of her year in Italy when she had countless uncomfortable situations to navigate without dire consequences? Who can say? But the fact that my 15-year-old is asking to live with strangers and hang out with retired people learning Italian and spend afternoons with a native speaker, making art together—well, I can't imagine that would be anywhere on her radar if not for her year in Italian public school.

As for Gabe, he can't go off and live with strangers, but he does want to attend a summer camp when we're in Italy. Part of that is just wanting companionship, but he also wants to stretch his Italian brain. On our last trip to Italy, we stayed in an apartment that shared a wall with the public school. Gabe would literally stay up on that wall all morning, waiting to talk to the boys who would rotate coming out for recess. To his credit, he was able to communicate with them, so perhaps he retained some. Most of the interaction, though, was the boys tossing a ball over the fence to him, him leaping to get it, and then scrambling back to the wall to toss it back. Borders are inconsequential to children who want to play. Adults could learn something. But I digress.

The point is, language learning is a process. A process where a willingness to make mistakes matters far more than one's natural facility for languages. You can't teach kids to not fear making mistakes (dear God, how

I tried, and that backfired. Every. Single. Time), so don't push your child. Instead, model it. Make it explicit that you are a little scared, but you're going to try ordering a container of marinated eggplant. Applaud yourself for throwing in a question about the weather. Don't berate yourself when you accidentally order legs at the fish market. Let your children see you push past your innate timidity, and celebrate the power of even bumbling connection. Show, don't tell. And practice patience, for yourself, for your child. Words are our armor; it's hard to suddenly be without them.

You'll get there, one step at a time.

Language Connections

RACHEL'S STORY

Thirty years ago, I was a fluent French speaker. Those skills waned over the years, and by the time we moved to Barcelona, my French was rusty. When we arrived, I took Spanish conversation classes at a language school, but then I found a tutor through a women's group and started taking private lessons an hour or two a week. My prior French knowledge served me in terms of comprehension, but got in my way when I tried to speak. The French got jumbled in my head, and the Spanish word I was looking for came out French.

I made a point of going to my local vegetable shop and chatting with the shop owner everyday, even when it was hard. Also, I went to the same coffee shop daily. The shopkeepers were patient with my broken Spanish and never tried to speak to me in English.

Public schools in Barcelona teach in Catalan, but it was important to us that our kids learn Spanish, so we sent our kids to a trilingual school—Spanish, Catalan, and English. We were initially concerned that our younger son only hung out with the American boys. We didn't discourage him from playing with those boys, but we didn't work to make playdates happen since we hoped eventually he'd start to mingle with the Spanish kids.

Because we wanted our kids to interact with Spanish kids, we signed up for every extra school trip or activity. We hosted some Spanish students (from other parts of Spain) as part of school exchanges. We listened to Spanish music. We attended animated movies in Spanish. The animation was helpful because the singing and visuals make it easier to understand the plot. When those became easy to understand, we moved on to harder movies. Sometimes we understood more, sometimes less, but we were okay with that because our goal was to improve our Spanish. After all, when you meet foreign kids who speak English, many have learned the language from American TV and movies.

Our kids are nordic-skiers, and we joined, almost by accident, a cross country ski team based about two hours outside of Barcelona in the Pyrenees. This was transformational. The families there became our community. Every weekend, they patiently spoke to us in Spanish. They became the first local people we really knew. They included us in big team meals, and after-ski lunches and drinks, and chatted with us as we watched races. They had a range of accents as several of the families were from more heavily Catalan towns, which was useful for our language learning. Those few hours a week of listening and decoding the variations in Spanish, as well as speaking and thinking exclusively in the language, exhausted me. It was like a workout.

It all paid off. The kids' language skills took off around March, and by the end of our stay they were thinking and chattering in Spanish. They learned substantially more than the other American students and made good Spanish friends. They even picked up a fair amount of Catalan without even trying. One day, our youngest shouted, "Mom, I speak

Catalan! It's like I went from nothing to 80% all of a sudden. I feel like I was working so hard and then a door burst open, and I went running through it!"

Language

CONTRIBUTORS' STORIES

NELL · LIVED IN FRANCE FOR ONE YEAR

In France at least, if you want to be part of the community, you need to speak the language. I'm not saying you need to speak it well. I was pretty disappointed in my progress, actually. My husband and I took language classes, and we tried to speak French at home and talk to French people in French but by the time we returned to Virginia, I was not close to fluent. I was fairly functional, running errands and managing chit-chat, but I could not, for example, go to a cocktail party and understand the jokes. Talking to me was like talking to a fourth grader, and that only takes you so far in friendship formation.

So my advice would be to emphasize language learning as much as you possibly can before going. For me, reading books in French helped my French far better than doing loads of grammar exercises (particularly books I'd read and reread in English). I would definitely join one of those online groups where you can chat in your target language.

Anything you can do to get over the fear of making mistakes, do it. And one key is simply surrounding yourself with the language as much as possible—don't depend on a few classes a week, but watch movies and have the radio playing in the background in your new language.

HEATHER · LIVED IN ITALY FOR TWO YEARS

We all took Italian lessons. The kids took Italian both years at their International School, but all their other classes were in English. I had the hardest time of all of us. At first, I was dedicated and loved the language-learning process, but when we hit tough spots with our son, helping him took all of my time and energy. My studying went by the wayside. I am bummed that I couldn't really take advantage of our time to delve deeper into learning Italian, but I have to give myself grace. I know I focused on what I needed to at that time.

Also, in retrospect, I wish I hadn't worried so much about "fitting in." I actually think by not worrying I would have more easily found my place and fit in, if that makes sense. I was so concerned about looking or sounding dumb that I held myself back.

SUSAN · REMEMBERING SETTLING IN SINGAPORE AS A CHILD

Then, as now, English is widely spoken in Singapore and there was no need to learn a second language. Our Amah (nanny) did teach us some words and we were always scolded in Chinese.

AMANDA · LIVES IN MOROCCO

My husband, as a native speaker, obviously had no issues. My kids were speaking the language within a few months. I took a lot longer, mostly because I worked all day in English and didn't have the same exposure. I wish that I would have really focused on and spent more time learning. Moroccan Arabic is really hard because it's mostly spoken and not many schools teach it. I was in survival mode and wish I could have been more in learning mode.

Language was the biggest issue my kids overcame, and their process varied. One is really outgoing and wanted to make friends and play with the kids in the neighborhood. Even though he was older he picked up on Arabic faster than our younger son, who was more reclusive. Because we had planned to stay only one year, a lot of times they would insist, "Oh I don't want to make friends because we're only going to leave." The more comfortable they got with the language, the more they were able to adapt to life.

ELIZABETH · LIVING IN ITALY

We squeezed in a few lessons before moving, trying to learn verb conjugations while I fed my newborn and built a train set with my toddler. Once we were here, we used online language-learning sites and then as I integrated more with the mums from nursery, one kindly offered to tutor me an hour a week. My sleepless mummy brain doesn't always retain it but I can now, eight months in, understand most things.

LEWIS FAMILY · LIVED IN MALAYSIA FOR TWO YEARS

We tried to learn the local language, but English is the language now taught in Malay schools. We lived in the city, where almost the whole population spoke English. Every time I tried to speak to people in my novice Bahasa they would reply in English so beyond please, thank you, you're welcome, and good day, I failed at the language. If I had been living somewhere with less English in use, I may have made more effort.

ANDREA · LIVES IN ITALY

Tony's parents are from Italy, so he had no trouble with the language when we arrived from the UK. As for me? I knew nothing. Plus, I am shy and lack confidence, so integrating has been harder. Having young children and limited money meant I couldn't have lessons, so my learning process was slow. My education consisted of watching a children's program with the kids (see *Resources*) and using my English/Italian dictionary. Every day, I would practice by going to the bar and chatting with a friend. It took me a good six months before I could say a few words. Years in, I still struggle, but I can argue when necessary and read basic books or the newspaper. My aim was never to become bilingual. I just want to be a parent who is available at all times for our daughters.

ESTELLE · CROSS-GENERATIONAL LIVING IN ITALY

Learning language is the master key to getting the very most out of your stay. In my experience, learning a Latin language takes about eighteen months of living in the country, with lessons and daily interactions, to speak semi-comfortably in the present, past, and future tenses. It helps to read magazines (like national popular and women's magazines, which have simpler vocabulary), or watch dubbed American TV show or movies where you already know the plot. However, you will only be listening to a dubbed version and not watching the lips form the words, which is a drawback.

I always felt that not being able to speak the language in a country made others think I must be ignorant. This made me feel like a prisoner. I tried so hard to learn by watching the local news, understanding the regional events and politics, and buying weekly recipe magazines to know what to make seasonally.

If you can't ask the butcher for hundred grams of something new— because you are too embarrassed, afraid, or reluctant to learn—then you are condemned to eating the not-so-good stuff out of the plastic packaging, and your assumptions about the food in your new location will be false. That is a metaphor for any experience in your chosen location.

SARA · LIVED IN MOROCCO FOR SEVEN YEARS

An unexpected challenge of travel is how solitary it can feel to not be able to express oneself. I encourage would-be travelers to make an effort to learn the language as soon as possible. Even if it's only a few basic words, those and a smile go a long way. Language teachers can often be found on expat Facebook groups or language associations (e.g., French, Spanish or German Institutes). We also found Rosetta Stone to be helpful in the beginning.

Our kids learned French and Arabic much faster than we did, and to this day they are far more fluent than we are, and their accent is better. My son would mutter French in his sleep. My husband and I took classes, but we were so caught up in creating our new life there that we eventually stopped. Anything we learned was from immersion. I remember being so exhausted for the first six months after we moved because I spent all day trying to figure out what was going on in every moment. My husband and I used to joke that we usually only understood about 70% of a conversation, and we'd make up that rest with context and educated guesses. I sometimes wished I could express myself better in French. I know I'm a funny person, but I think most of the people I encountered only knew me as someone who demanded things "I want, I need," because I wasn't great with conditionals. And I definitely couldn't crack a joke in French or Arabic that fit the Moroccan sense of humor. It can feel frustrating not being able to share your whole self, day after day.

I remember a Danish friend expressed a similar frustration. She spent her days speaking French, and English with friends that she had met through her kids' American school. When she finally got to speak Danish, it was with 2-, 4-, and 7-year-olds. Not exactly stimulating. I remember when I was in China years ago, I found myself conversing with the BBC Asia TV channel just to hear myself speak in complete sentences. I came back to the States speaking broken English, because I had been speaking such simple English just to be understood.

16

HOW TO INTEGRATE

PART ONE · MEETING PEOPLE

Perhaps there are some travelers who would be perfectly happy landing in a destination and smacking their lips at a previously unknown sauce or appreciating the dramatic landscapes, while never interacting with a single local. Somehow, I doubt that's you. Parents who seek out an adventure across the globe are usually desirous of experiencing life in a novel destination. And life? It includes people.

Integrating can be a challenge, particularly if you are shy. Or if you are a pleaser who shivers in fear that your attempts at connection may be met with expressions of confusion, or worse, hostility. Or if you have lived your entire adult life within the confines of a familiar community, where you've rarely had to stretch out of your comfort zone to interact with people who look, act, or speak differently than you. I fit in more than one of those categories, so even the *thought* that I was going to have to speak to strangers and form connections was enough to make me want to hide in a closet in my house where our renters would never find me. Keith and the kids could send pictures, right? We could Photoshop me in later.

Besides personal factors, there are location-specific factors that complicate forming connections in your new home. Living on a farm in the middle of nowhere will throw a huge hurdle into the task of meeting people and integrating. Even if you have neighbors, some communities are suspicious of newcomers. I met a gentleman from Rome who had tried to move to Spello twenty years before and said that he couldn't make social inroads. But once Spello was on the tourist trail, locals became used to strangers and saw newcomers as less of a threat and more of an asset. Non-touristed communities do have upsides though. Locals may hold you separate for longer, but once you prove yourself as an open family willing to adapt yourselves to the community, locals can start to see you as "theirs." The bonds become tighter for not being diluted with lots of tourist incorporation.

There is a school of thought that it's harder to meet people in cities, but I'm not sure that's true as a general rule. Yes, there are cities where everyone is so busy and caught up with the split-second timing of their existence that their eyes will slide past a newcomer gripping a map. But there are many more cities made up of a collection of friendly neighborhoods that function like small towns and that offer an array of activities and opportunities helpful for expats looking to mingle.

A short foray into a community is also a barrier to integration, because real connections take time. Many families with a traveling (rather than landing) lifestyle report that they formed viable relationships with their landlords. This makes sense since that's a person you'll be forced to communicate with and is there to welcome you. If you are there long enough, landlords can also be conduits into a community. Ours had a pool, which was an added bonus.

There are plenty of anecdotal reports of colder locations correlating with less-open and gregarious communities. But even in a warm place like Spello, not all expats are welcomed as we were. Having children definitely was part of the calculus that tapped us into the town. Enrolling our children in the public school telegraphed the fact that we were there to integrate. Plus, our family had five points of contact (not all of them as shy as I am), not to mention all the socializing opportunities that come with school communities.

It is so odd, I spent years thinking the ship had sailed on living abroad, that the best I could hope for was a sunset cruise. I had no idea that if I really wanted to meld into a community, having children was my best resource.

So bringing your children means you have one piece of the integration puzzle in place. But there are other aspects of your new life to consider. Where you shop, your adapting to local rhythms and customs, how you engage—all these impact how others will view you and ultimately how well you'll integrate. For instance, in Spello there are some expats who shop at the German grocery story in Foligno rather than the little shop on the *piazza*. They never dine in the restaurants, they don't attend community functions. Locals mention them with a quizzical cock of the head, "Who are they again?"

Now, it should be said that integrating doesn't mean being mistaken for a local. I know that sounds obvious, but if you really sit back and think about your dream for your time abroad, it probably includes gathering with an assortment of locals, sharing the fruits of your collective table, with a sense of ease and belonging. The odds of that are slim to none. You will be outsiders for a long, long time. That's okay. At bottom, I'm not sure perfect belonging is what you really want anyway. What I suspect you actually want is to find your tribe. A group of people you gel with, that feel like a family of sorts. Your communality likely *won't* be that you live in the same small Romanian town. Rather, your communality may be that you are, for one reason or another, on the fringes of that small Romanian town. Or that you like dog shows. Or that you are involved with the International School.

Whatever your social network looks like, if you want to integrate, integration will have to be your goal. Not comfort, appearing competent, avoiding awkwardness, or looking like you belong for your social media posts. Integration, the moving from being unknown to known, is the intention. Look for opportunities and push yourself to reach across the divide. As much as you can, and a little more each day.

As ways to begin meeting people and integrating into a new community, consider the following:

Practice small talk. Will it rain today? How is everything? How is your family? Weather, health, and food are conversational entry points. A bit deeper, but not taboo as they are in the United States, are religion and politics.

Ask for help. Take a recipe from the back of the box to the café and ask what that strange ingredient is and where to find it. Ask how to prepare something. Ask where to find green olives. Ask where everyone is foraging. Ask what animal makes that cheese. Ask the word for bells when you hear them intoning above your head as you stop and chat with a neighbor about the weather. This lets people know you are invested in your new home, not merely sliding above it, and also gives you valuable connection as people love to share their knowledge.

Observe the social niceties. This means pay close attention so you can figure out what those are. In Italy, we learned that smiling at strangers is weird. But saying hello isn't. We stopped smiling like idiots at nothing and instead started greeting neighbors with words. We also watched and learned that at big grocery stores you bag your own produce and label it (always with the gloves provided!), but at small grocery stores, you point out what you want. Until you know the owner well enough; then he waves at you to just do it yourself. But not before that.

Rather than bristling at corrections in your pronunciations, thank your benefactor. That person appreciates you and their language enough to want the two of you to get along. Repeat the word a few times aloud until you get the thumbs up. This will help your language skills, always important in your quest for integration, and also ingratiate you with locals who will begin to see you as someone who wants to be part of the community.

Don't cringe at local delicacies. Pig skin soup may make your stomach lurch, but don't laugh at someone else's treasure. It's hurtful. Teach your children to ooh and aah in the market, rather than gasp and point.

Go to the same shops over and over. The more people see you, the more they will reward you with a hello and eventually with conversation. This is true for the vendors, but also the other people who frequent that shop. Becoming a regular at the bar where you get your morning coffee means you begin the day a part of the action.

Consider volunteering or asking if you can help with any project you see happening. The happiest expats I know are the ones who take the time to dig into a community through kindness (more on this in the next section). Sometimes that work will connect you with locals, and sometimes with others who share your values. In other words, your tribe.

Think about your activities and hobbies at home, and look for ways to continue them abroad. It will mean learning a new vocabulary perhaps, but it is easier to engage with people around a shared activity (again, more on this soon).

Recognize that no one owes you anything. I can only speak to the experience of living in the States, but here there is a pervasive assumption that we are owed. That we need to work to "get mine." Being a stranger in a strange land erases that core belief, leaving space for gratitude at any mark of kindness. Embrace that! Once you abandon the assumption that you are owed, the balance of the universe shifts. You will feel humbled and vulnerable, and while it's important to balance that (you and your family may be visiting, but that doesn't mean you don't have the right to protest when something feels wrong), this is one way that travel changes us and connects us to people everywhere. By taking every gesture as a gift, you will make yourself more receptive to the outreach of locals, and the kindness of strangers.

Take language lessons, preferably from a retired school teacher living in the community. This was our unintended godsend. Our tutor helped us understand the intricacies of the school system, cued us to area events, paved the way towards relationships in the community, all the while teaching us dialect and conjugation.

PART TWO · VALUES AND VOLUNTEERING

I n my work with couples, I've realized how important it is to be clear on what you value. I don't mean to talk about your values or to listen to ministers expound about values or consider your values once every four years while you tick off candidates at the ballot box. I mean *live* what you value, what you think of as important in your life. Once parents are out of the childbearing phase (which I define as lasting until your youngest is five) and have entered the child*rearing* phase, there's space to get intentional. To begin acting rather than reacting. You're getting sleep now, your children can wipe their own bottoms, you have a little space to breathe and look up at your partner and think, "So what about *us?*"

Years ago, I treated a mom for postpartum depression. When we were wrapping up our journey together I asked her what aspects of our work had been particularly helpful. She immediately said it was me telling her that she didn't have to listen to children's music in the car. Seems simple, but it was emblematic. I had told her that the greatest gift she could give her children was *her*. Not some sanitized, June Cleaver version of what she thought she should be for them, but rather who she *is*, what she loves, what moves her, what excites her. So that she is an actual person for them, not just an extension of themselves. That way, she'll be someone they find interesting, with opinions and ideas worth considering. When it's time to leave home, they won't feel a queasy mix of guilt and desperation, because they know that even though it's sad, Mom has a life and she will be okay.

So she ditched her awful "Wheels on the Bus" for the Reggae music she'd always loved.

Since then, I've made it a point to talk about values whenever I see parents for therapy. I ask them to think about what they love, what they want to share with their children, what they want to be their family ethos. And then to consider how to live that, not just talk about it.

Some families can mull over what they value when their children are still in arms, but that's complicated and depends on many factors such as how easy one's children are, how much childcare one has, and how much energy one has, and one's passions pre-children. Since you are reading this book, I know that no matter how old your children are, you are ready to dive into considering your values and how to create a family life around that. To which I say—Hooray! Good for you! You have decided that ditching complacency in favor of adventure or connecting with humanity across the globe is part of who you are or want to be as a family. What a gift you are giving your children, just by being clear on this.

Travel is one aspect of who you want your family to be, but I suspect it's not the only one. Families have all sort of passions, and it makes sense to consider what's important to you, your partner, your children, so that as you step off into your great adventure, you do that in a way that underscores more fully who you are.

Some of what you value may mesh easily with travel. For instance, our family places great importance on language. We love talking about how language defines reality, differences in how language is used across cultures, and historical roots of language.

Art and history and religion and food are other easy blends with travel. Some other interests may require a bit of consideration and creativity to incorporate with travel. But taking that time is critical. Not only will it make your life and your goals clearer for you, but it may well give your family a nexus to spin on, a sort of stitch that ties your travels together.

Confused? Let me give you some examples.

I know several families that have music as a shared interest. They seek out native music wherever they travel; they bring portable instruments to share music as a universal language; they think and talk about how musical legacies are shared across communities.

I know a family that loves soccer. They brought mini-soccer balls to Tanzania, handing them out to students at a school they visited. Their safari is obviously a treasured memory, but right up there with it are the images of playing soccer in the street with Tanzanian children.

I know several families that hold the natural world and environmental stewardship as a critical aspect of their family's value system. They prefer staying in remote places or national parks to learn about the flora and fauna, or designing trips around birding, or working to clear paths. They take nature journals when they travel, they think deeply about changes they see in landscape as they move up and down the globe.

I know a family that has biking as a shared passion. In their year around the globe, they did bike tours of just about every country they visited and made sure to catch part of the Tour de France.

But what I hear about most commonly (perhaps because it requires no specific talent, just a state of heart) is families wanting to give back. These families want to contribute to a community, not just glide through it. They want to connect, to help, especially in developing nations. Volunteering as a family, at home and abroad, gives their family lives a sense of purpose and mission that they relish.

If you value volunteering, there are ways to incorporate it into your travels. Some families jump from one volunteer experience to another, even using volunteering as their financial engine, since the sites I list in *Resources* offer food and accommodations in exchange for work. Some families intersperse volunteer experiences between traditional travel to spice up their global experience. And some families book travel first and then look for volunteer opportunities where they'll be.

There are websites that cater to matching people with volunteer opportunities as diverse as working on an organic farm to teaching literacy or English (again, see *Resources*). Make sure you ask fellow travelers and Facebook groups about potential agencies, to be sure it's what you are picturing and also that you are properly equipped (the occasional host may require you to provide your own tent, for instance). Particularly if you are not going with a website I include, research how legit an offer is, or if it is just a facade for bringing in tourist dollars. For instance, some travelers find the idea of helping at an orphanage appealing, but there are all sorts of human trafficking issues at play here, as well as child development considerations.

Volunteering, like other ways of expressing who you are as a family, is something to think about as you begin to sharpen your focus on what you want your family adventure to look like. I know of families that have traveled for years doing a combination of volunteering and house-sitting, which can be a rich lifestyle. If volunteering is something you want to pursue, I suggest seeking out volunteer opportunities with hosts who have children. They will be more understanding of your limitations and willing to work around your childcare needs. Also, they may have information about schools your child can attend while you work, and perhaps most importantly, there's a built-in opportunity for your children to have playmates.

Forming Global Connections

LISA'S STORY

In our year of traveling, we experimented with various ways to meet people. One solid route was volunteering. For a yearly fee, our family joined Workaway, which gave us access to myriad volunteer opportunities around the world. In return for volunteering, Workaway provides volunteers with housing. We stayed at the British Language Academy thirty-six kilometers outside of Casablanca in an industrial town called Berrechid. A Moroccan man called Mr. Harim runs and operates three English-language schools in the area to boost Moroccan students' English language learning as well as to break down cultural barriers between peoples. At these schools, both adults and high school children attend classes with a Moroccan teacher, and the foreign English- (or French-) speaking volunteers are scheduled into daily conversational classes for about half an hour in small groups. The advantage of this situation was not only that we had the satisfaction of volunteering, but we lived with fifteen other like-minded people. We became friends with our fellow volunteers, traveling to various Moroccan cities together. We also learned to appreciate and understand Moroccan culture by spending time with students and conversing about cultural, social, and political aspects of their country.

Besides volunteering, we discovered that a successful way to make friends with locals was to shop local, eat local, and be curious about other people. In Spain, we met a baker named José who sold his bread at the local market around the corner from our apartment. Each morning we bought a loaf of fresh bread from José and a bag of oranges from the stern lady opposite his stall.

Over the six weeks we stayed in Malaga, we grew close to José and his family. We ventured out for dinner with them to taste authentic

Spanish cuisine. We even attended his children's Easter concert. He helped us understand the hardships of running a business in Malaga, the high employment rate, and the inability for young people to carve out a successful future. Nothing was a given in José's life; he worked extremely hard for everything he had. Even so, José was friendly and upbeat, always including the girls and offering his assistance.

In Vietnam, we became especially close to our landlord family— Chuong, Dao, and their little boy, plus their extended families. We enjoyed dinners together on the weekends, taking special tours on the river, or just having a beer in the afternoon with the Google translator app working overtime. In my mind, this is one of the perks of traveling and living in one place longer than the standard brief tourist visit: You certainly get to see the sites and taste the food, but more importantly, you get to connect authentically with the people.

In some locations, integrating into the expat community is a great way to form connections. We found expat groups on Facebook, as well as by researching meet-ups in cities for language exchange nights, language lessons, or social nights at restaurants. Some expat groups have a long list of activities and suggestions for get-togethers where we could meet people.

A resonant message from our year abroad is that it doesn't take effort so much as intention to connect with people. We meet people by making it important to let others into our lives.

Integrating into New Communities

CONTRIBUTORS' STORIES

LEWIS FAMILY · SETTLED IN MALAYSIA

When we arrived in Kuala Lumpur, I was exhausted from organizing children, family, house, and work. All I wanted was to put my feet up for awhile. However, after three weeks, I started to think, "That was a nice holiday, but what am I going to do now?" Henry was at work, Richard at school, and I had help in the house, help in the garden, and even a pool man. I had gone from living life at full speed to a life of leisure. It was uncomfortable.

Fortunately, Henry's company offered a support group for spouses. Through this group, I was introduced to the Association of British Women in Malaysia (ABWM). Thanks to contacts I made, I started volunteering at a local children's home with a group of other women. I not only was able to connect with children and workers at the home, but also became close friends with some members of ABWM. The organization also offered courses and outings to increase our understanding of Malaysia, which was an excellent way to learn about the culture.

Some of the parents from Richard's school invited me to regular lunches and through them I learned of a group that did volunteer work at a local hospital. I helped the group with weekly visits to ill children, as well as fundraised to provide toys, books, puzzles, and other items for the patients. Through the work, I not only got insight into the local health-care system but made great friends as well.

Part of the fundraising work I did involved holding several Beer and Curry events in our garden. The friends we had made were generous in their support, and we enjoyed those evenings.

Many of the staff Henry worked with were Malaysian, so at work events I met locals, who I found consistently to be friendly and welcoming. Nonetheless, most of our social life was with other expats. We were also involved with the American Marines at the Embassy and that was great fun, especially when our two daughters were home, as we became quite popular with the young marines.

JOHN · RV-ED THROUGH EUROPE FOR A YEAR

The traveling community in camping grounds is sort of like a gypsy affiliate program. Most people are welcoming, sharing of their experiences, and free for "wine-o'clock" every evening. Often we would catch up again and again with the same people; each time creating a new opportunity for celebration.

HEATHER · LIVED IN ITALY FOR TWO YEARS

Our community was difficult to integrate into. I think it would have been easier if we had tried to interact with locals right out of the gate. But at the beginning, I kind of enjoyed the novel feeling of being an unknown. It was freeing, like I could reinvent myself. Eventually that wore off, and it felt strange to be among people, but not connected with them.

At that point, I worked harder to integrate. But by then, our neighbors were already a bit cold. Maybe they would have been anyway, as they didn't seem keen on yet another expat moving into their neighborhood. There were some people who were friendlier but their English was about as good as our Italian, so it was difficult to form a real connection.

I wound up getting my connection needs met at shops and restaurants. My foodie Italian is my strongest, so I enjoyed practicing and connecting through talking about food. We made friends at literally every restaurant in our neighborhood. Those friends started recognizing me on the street, and that made me feel like a local (even though I knew I'd never really be one). It was satisfying to feel part of the community in that way.

It's funny, before the move, my goal was to have an "authentic" experience. I crazily assumed I would make friends with locals and wouldn't need other expats. Boy, was I wrong. It was the expat community where I found my forever friends. I suppose it's different for everyone, depending on your circumstances, location, chapter of life. But I couldn't have done it without my expat peeps and my friendships and adventures with them are some of the best memories. Even the mishaps we had were fun, it's so much easier to laugh through the craziness with someone else.

CANADA-TO-FRANCE · LIVES IN FRANCE

Aix-les-Bains has about 25,000 people, and since we live in the center, we are very much part of the community. My husband goes to the same coffee shop every day and meets people that way. I volunteer at my daughter's school teaching English, so I have made friends with other parents and also my daughter's teacher. Most cities have a newcomers group within the mayor's office, and that's a resource.

People warned me that the French are very rude and pretentious and that I would not be welcomed, even though I speak French. That is so far from the truth. As soon as I start to speak, locals know I am Canadian, but they love our country and the people. Everyone is intrigued about our move, so there's ready conversation.

ELIZABETH · LIVES IN ITALY

I can't believe how friendly people are here. Once we started to go to the nursery gates and functions, we quickly made friends with families of our eldest child's friends. We are the only English-speaking family in the area and that made us quite a novelty. Things eventually settled, and everyone is used to us. Now we have a steady little group of friends.

SARAH · LIVES IN THE NETHERLANDS AFTER YEARS OF WORLDSCHOOLING

For most of our time moving around, we were active members of our church, and found a local congregation in each new home. It helped to have an instant group of friends, both for ourselves and for our children. We've also made friends at our children's school, sports teams, volunteering, work, and neighbors. Meetup is a great place to find friends in different places. My husband likes to check out the board-gaming and basketball groups in a new city.

NAOMI · LIVED IN INDIA AND SINGAPORE FOR FOUR YEARS

If I need something that does not yet exist, I create it. For instance, I started a buddy system and school tour program in Delhi and a crossing-guard campaign in Singapore. That allowed me to integrate with the school more swiftly. I also met people by volunteering at the embassy and at a local NGO (Non-Governmental Agency). School, though, was my richest source of connections. I wonder what it would be like to move to a foreign country without the automatic introduction children provide.

ESTELLE · CROSS-GENERATIONAL LIVING IN ITALY

At one point I realized I was calling people "friends" just because they also spoke English. This was not a good feeling. Patience is key because sometimes friendships happen quickly and sometimes they don't. The difference is mostly luck or coincidence. Hobbies like quilting, walking, biking, and hiking open the doors a little wider. Also, bear in mind that you have a commodity people value highly—you are a native English speaker. Language exchanges benefit both parties and increase connections.

In larger cities, there are federated International Women's Clubs that host activities. Many women in these clubs are married to citizens of your host country. Knowing people who straddle cultures can give you a window into your new home. For instance, it was the bi-cultural mothers who assured us that our 6-year-old's slang learned on the Spanish soccer field was not as inappropriate as it sounded to us. They helped us realize that those words gave our expat child a sense of belonging. Another example: When we lived in Madrid with our teenage children, we were shocked at kids' freedom. However, we learned from bi-cultural friends that bars served only nonalcoholic drinks to those sixteen and under. Then at 10:30, older teens arrived and the younger ones cleared out to ride the train together, where parents would carpool them home.

Smaller towns may lack an International Women's Club or many opportunities to meet bi-cultural families, but they invite more curiosity and care. In our case, Leonardo, the realtor who found us a place to live, took a continued interest. He made us lists of where the best "butchers, bakers, and candlestick makers" were in our neighborhood. Being closer in age to our kids, he invited them to events he thought they would like, showed them restaurants, and was a general goodwill ambassador for our family. You'll most likely find your Leonardo too, with a bit of luck.

CHERYL · RV-ING THROUGH EUROPE

We recently got into a situation with our motorhome. We set out for a supermarket in the hills of Portugal, and ended up wedged between the buildings, as the road was too narrow to allow us to go further down, and too steep to allow us to reverse our way back up. A local family came to our rescue. Despite a lack of common language, a mother and her children entertained us in their home for nearly two hours while our husbands set about getting us out of the mess. Thankfully her husband had a small tractor to haul us back up the road.

As travelers, we aren't ever part of a community, but in times of need we have always found kindness and people who are happy to help, despite any cultural differences.

SARA · LIVED IN MOROCCO FOR SEVEN YEARS

There is a vibrant community of French expats in Morocco, but the American community is limited mostly to Embassy Diplomats. Some embassy families welcome connections with those outside their "bubble," but far more are not interested. This made meeting people who wanted to befriend us challenging.

Joining a new community, no matter where in the world, is a bit like going on first date after first date. There is a temptation to become friends with anyone and everyone who speaks English. But after a while, I began realizing that those connections felt forced, rather than authentic and meaningful. It was at this point that I made the decision to re-prioritize friends and a social circle. I'd rather have a few great friends—or even just one—than lots of people in my world who I do not jibe with.

Throughout our time in Morocco we tried to create friendships with locals, but most of those hit a wall. I think it would have been easier to make friends in a westernized country, but being in an Arab/Muslim country changed the dynamics. We discovered friendships only developed so far. There are ingrained cultural differences that we are unaware of, and we found those differences challenging, particularly in approaches to parenting, notions of personal boundaries, and the concept of a friend's place in the world as compared to family. For example, our children would go to playdates and the nanny didn't watch the kids, leading to needless accidents. Or, our daughter went to a sleepover and wanted to call me late at night to come home and the mother ignored her requests. So, for this reason, except for our Moroccan friends who had lived in North America for a time and were more "western minded," we did not build deep friendships with Moroccans. Not because we didn't try. We did try to adapt our ways and be open minded to differences, but ultimately we recognized we weren't willing to compromise who we are and our core values. This still saddens me, but I know we weren't alone is this experience and I have just had to accept this was the reality of the situation.

17

SCHOOL DAYS

A t the time we moved to Spello, Nicolas and Siena had only ever attended a small, private school and Gabe had attended a tiny home-based preschool called The Bunny Gardens (which should paint a picture). Italian public school was a towering adjustment. In fact, when I have tried to reread my own memoir, I actually have to stop at the point when we are preparing for school, because I'm blinded by the deranged idiocy of sending these tender humans into what seemed the lion's den. They got through it, obviously, and have only grown stronger. In fact, Gabe was a pretty anxious tot, and going to school in Italy seemed to scrub that right out of him (I suspect watching himself get through it made him surer of his abilities, and therefore trust himself too much to be anxious). Yet, the start of school remains a painful memory.

Everything seemed hard. Shopping for school supplies, which isn't usually listed among common panic triggers, sent me into a tailspin. I had to will myself to not crumble on the linoleum floor of the SuperConti grocery store. Ostensibly, I held a list of what we needed, at least for Gabe, but there were notebooks with subject names, did we need those, too? I didn't even know how many days a week my kids would be in school, how was I supposed to know what size grid they needed in their graph note-books? That was the moment I realized only Nicolas knew how to ask to use the bathroom.

So, yes, that felt impossible. It got easier when I realized that it wouldn't kill them. I was so busy defending my heart against the image of the school swallowing my children whole I hadn't stopped to tell myself, "It will be hard, but it's not actually dangerous." After that, it became far easier. I stopped alternating between aggressively cheerleading and stiffening my upper lip, neither of which was helpful. Instead I reached a weird level of calm that if you have met me you'll know is rabidly unlike me. Maybe Keith was slipping Xanax into my morning *cappuccino*. Some things are better left unasked, and in any case, my settling the hell down had a positive impact on all of us. I communicated to the kids that it felt scary because it *was* scary. That was expected, but the feeling wouldn't hurt them. When I stopped trying to make it okay, they started making it okay for themselves. They realized that even though they wouldn't see each other, they would know they were all experiencing the same thing and that was a comfort. They were scared, but resolved.

Even with my realization of limited danger, and even with my children's bravery, that first drop-off was a nauseating challenge. Nicolas, bless his heart, had stated that it would be best if Keith and I accompanied his siblings into school, and he'd make his way to the middle school on his own. Watching his back recede down the hill, through the crowd, and having no idea what happened afterward made me want to crawl back in bed—a feeling that only exacerbated when Gabe's eyes swam with tears as I was shuttled out of the classroom by his teacher. Keith's goodbye with Siena was much the same. Miserably, I waited five long hours for them to be done. But at the end of the day, they each burst out of school with happiness radiating from their fingertips.

The first day, despite the agonizing apprehension, was none of their hardest. Those days would come later with spanking, and being yelled at, and feeling small and alone. But by the end of the year, they had all found their feet.

Along with learning Italian, their learning they can teeter without toppling was the greatest gift of educating my children within Italian public schools. If our move had been longer than a year, however, I might have been less pleased with the option. A year is easy to "lose" in the academic life of a child. Any holes can be made up on returning. If it had been longer, I would have been far more interested in their acquisition of critical thinking and writing skills and creativity. This isn't to say that Italian public schools *don't* provide that. They might. But what Nicolas told me at the end of the year has stuck with me. While talking about what it would be like to stay longer in Italy, he said he was looking forward to getting back to the American school system because from his perspective, Italian public school was great for teaching students how to put pegs in a pegboard, but not great for teaching kids to figure out how to *create* the pegboard. If we had extended our sojourn in Italy, I would either have had to decide that what they were getting was worth more than my previous educational values, or I would have had to start supplementing their education.

I feel for these traveling kids, I do. They don't have a say in this decision, and all of a sudden they are trying to navigate the icy waters of a new and totally different school experience. That can happen with any school choice. Contributors told me about their homeschoolers feeling the ache of missing other children and growing progressively more withdrawn until the parents figured out how to meet kids while traveling. Or their extremely shy child who nonetheless craved social connection floundering for a bit at an International School. One of the contributors shared with me that her son recently reported to a therapist that he found the first few days at his school abroad some of the scariest of his life. I know we all have an ache in our heart for this mother. Watching our children suffer is the most debilitating aspect of being a parent. The mom went on that in retrospect, she wished they had talked more to her young boy about the transition. She added, "He was young when we left and hadn't been through many big life transitions. Transitions are easy for me and my husband. We should have thought more carefully about the difficulties he'd have with understanding what we were doing. He had no way of knowing why we thought a temporary move to a foreign country was going to be valuable for our family and for him in the long run. We were going through our own transitions and by the time we realized he needed so much extra support, it had become scarier for him."

I should hasten to add though, that even on home soil, school is rarely a daily treat bag of glittery lollipops. Can you name one child in your acquaintance who has never struggled socially, academically, or emotionally with school? Of course not!

The problem with being abroad is that it's the *devil you don't know,* and that unfamiliar can make it a scary kind of hell at times. That doesn't mean you need to fling yourself home and huddle with your children behind a locked door. Rather, communicate with your children with compassion and interest, but also with a matter-of-fact manner that tells them that they can do this. Until they can.

Schooling in a French Village

NELL'S STORY

One of my goals for the year was for my children to become fluent in French, so we chose to settle in a small village (811 people) and toss them into French school. I wanted them to make friends and feel partly French by the time we had to leave. Enrolling them was easy, all we had to do was contact the local school to tell them we were coming.

When we arrived in France, we weren't yet able to move into our rental, so we were staying in a *gîte* (a small vacation house in the country) about an hour away from our village. Even so, I decided to go over to the school to say hello. I was very nervous, as my French was practically nonexistent, and I desperately wanted to make a good impression on the principal. I bucked up my courage and walked up to the school. It was then that I realized that I had gotten the dates wrong. School was already in session.

My face burned with shame as I walked into the principal's office. I felt like the worst mom ever. But he could not have been friendlier and more welcoming, not the least bit concerned about a few missed days. "Just come when you get here!" he said with a big grin. I felt like I had met a kindred spirit who wasn't so big on rules either, and that assessment proved true over the course of the year. He was a problem-solver and an inspiration, not one to blame or get hung up on how things had always been done. I had been worried about not being welcomed and being seen as interlopers, but the rural villages of France are losing population, so the more students they get, the better their funding. They were happy to have us. There were at least four British children, as well as Dutch and Spanish kids.

I held my breath that whole first day. I was sure I had made a terrible mistake. Both of my children had taken French in school in the States, but not enough to matter. Worse, I had just discovered that my daughter would have to take a bus every day to a different school in a different village; we had expected that at least they'd have each other on the playground. How would we make it through the year if they really, really hated school and were miserable? But they came home chattering and looking for ice cream, as though spending a long day at a new school in a new country was nothing. "Did you understand anything?" I asked. "Nope!" they answered cheerfully. They didn't care. It was all fine.

I had no expectation of academic leaps during the year—I mean, I didn't care how much math or history they learned. I figured fluency in a new language and fitting into a new culture were plenty. But I did appreciate that my daughter had to memorize and recite poetry every week, and that both of them emerged at the end of the year with the most beautiful handwriting ever (now lost, sadly).

Since my daughter was only seven, she picked up French quickly and was speaking in sentences within a few months. It was harder for my son, who was in the French equivalent of fourth grade. I thought his teacher handled it in a masterful way. He allowed my son to sit at his desk and read during class. Books in English! Which sounds crazy, right? But it had two big effects: My son thought this school where he was allowed to read all day was the best school on earth, and even though he was reading in English, French was coming into his ears. He was learning French without realizing it.

Bit by bit, as the teacher saw his comprehension improve, he asked my son to put his book away for a minute or two here and there. Until he was thoroughly part of the class. The process was so gentle and slow that he had no chance to protest; instead he was pretty pleased with himself. As he should have been.

I credit enrolling our children in the local school with our becoming part of the community. And my children did make huge gains in language. My son refused to speak French in front of me so I can't really gauge how fluent he became. But my daughter was chattering away with her French friends so that my foreigner's ear couldn't tell them apart.

The School Experience

CONTRIBUTORS' STORIES

LISA · BACKPACKING AROUND THE WORLD

Australia's Distance Education option was flexible regarding when and where school work got done. All the girls had to do was follow the curriculum laid out for them. The constant drawback was that we required excellent Wi-Fi. We ended up having to abandon our month in Morocco because Internet was such a problem. Also, even though we had a lot of flexibility, we did have to carve out time to follow the weekly structure, which limited spontaneous traveling. Another challenge was that my husband and I were forced to be both parents and Distance Education supervisors, which is hard when the students (our own children) didn't want to work or were unhappy with us for reasons that only teenagers understand. By the time we arrived in Vietnam, our teacher-student relationships were unraveling. We sought help from various expat teachers who took over the roles of motivating the girls to complete their schoolwork, and in fact, get ahead. This left us to just be parents again.

CANADA-TO-FRANCE · LIVES IN FRANCE

Our daughter is very timid and shy, and we worried that she would have issues fitting in or finding friends. In fact, it was the opposite. When she started school in France, her classmates already knew she was coming from Canada and welcomed her with open arms. She soon found her group of close friends and has since blossomed, proud of her experience and grateful to be here. We often ask her if she misses home, and she answers that while she does miss her old friends, she has made such a life for herself here she can't imagine going back.

ELIZABETH · LIVES IN ITALY

Currently my 3-year-old is in *scuola materna* in a private nursery. He is fully immersed in Italian, with one teacher in another class who speaks English to him if needed. At first he struggled, and it was heart breaking to send him, but I felt I needed to just push on, as there were few other options for him interacting with other children his age. He now happily goes and has lots of friends. He still speaks to them in English, expecting them to understand, but he is slowly picking up words and trying them out. His teachers say he definitely understands now but is shy when asked to speak Italian.

AMANDA · LIVES IN MOROCCO

It took a good two to three years before our sons really felt like they fit in, which I attribute to being in a community where they were the only foreign kids. We tried to connect with other expats to give them a bit of an outlet. They also have cousins nearby to play with.

School was the hardest for our oldest son. He had to go back two grades because he lacked the foundation in Arabic. Thankfully he accepted this, at least at first. Once he was older and demonstrated he had the skills, we were able to have him skip a grade.

NAOMI · LIVED IN INDIA AND SINGAPORE FOR FOUR YEARS

We were not able to tour the school prior to the first day (something that I helped to rectify later by creating a school tour program), which caused all sorts of anxieties. We showed our children as many photos as we could of their new school so that it would feel familiar, and we also did a dry run of the school route and morning routine so that it would be comfortable.

What we didn't expect was the welcome we received thanks to the fact that Delhi is a hardship posting, which means that because of its climate and poverty there aren't many expats. We were accepted easily, and we fit in immediately. The school's on-site coffee shop added to our feeling that the school was amazing.

As we went throughout our school experience in both Delhi and

Singapore, I was astonished at the opportunities my children experienced overseas. Our oldest son played American football, and his championship game was in South Korea. Our middle child was given exposure (in elementary school!) to the study of world religion and global civics, subjects that continue to inspire him. Our daughter—in the midst of challenging hearing loss—thrived because of the support and confidence the medical professionals instilled in her. Thanks to their experience integrating with new peers and teachers, my kids grew in confidence, empathy, social justice concerns, and listening before speaking.

JULIE · WORLDSCHOOLING IN MEXICO AND BEYOND

My kids were all in public school before we left, so homeschooling has been an adjustment. My younger two children use workbooks and online resources like Khan Academy and Duolingo for their schooling. The older two use Time4Learning, which we don't love (it's very cheesy) but gives the kids the credits they will need when they return to public school. We've also discovered a music app called Yousician which has taught all of them—even the 6-year-old!—to play the ukulele. My oldest child also does two classes with Texas Tech University Independent School District, which is a good program but costs more. Transitioning to online school has been hardest for her. It would be easier if she was self-motivated, but it's sometimes a challenge to get her learning without a teacher.

NICA · SAILED THE CARIBBEAN

Boatschooling was easy. Our kids' elementary school allowed us to borrow textbooks, so our simple plan was to have each child work through each book completely. We set it up so that the kids had a certain amount of work to do each week, and once they were done, they were free for the rest of the week. Get it all done on Monday? Great. The rest of the week is yours to play and explore and goof off. Also, our focus was NOT on school. Our philosophy is that travel teaches far more than you can ever hope to learn in a classroom, so lessons in local history and culture, snorkeling and fish identification, reading, and journaling were far more part of daily life than the book stuff.

That said? If we were to go again, and the kids were the same ages as they were? I'd want to travel in company with another family, and they can homeschool our kids and I'll deal with theirs. The multiple roles you play when you're teacher and parent can become hard to distinguish.

KATE · WORLDSCHOOLING

The first year of trying to motivate my son to do his work was like pulling teeth. The second year, we were feeling our way with curriculum, connecting what school required to what Oscar was interested in, and constantly making sure we were doing enough. Now, in the third year, my husband, Eric, and I share the homeschooling. I do two days a week, and Eric does two days a week, and we send Oscar to the Living Earth Camp outdoor school one day a week when we're home. At this point, we feel comfortable with our curriculum.

Most importantly, Oscar now gets that it's a privilege. It's no longer "mom and dad are forcing me to do schoolwork." He's excited about school, and he's taking more ownership of the process. He's thriving in the two-and-a-half hours a day that he gets to sit with his parents and talk and learn.

Part of what's made the homeschooling work this year is that we're no longer shunning YouTube and other media. We realized that if we give Oscar access to the Internet, he wants to learn more. When he's on YouTube, he's learning about fishing and lures and drone photography. I'm not totally hands off; I do secret spot checks to see what sites he's on. The other day, I started wondering, "God, what videos have you been watching all day??" I snagged his computer and discovered he was researching kids' exercise and how to get a nine-pack ab. So now? I'm less fearful, and more trusting. He still watches stupid vines and learns stupid words, but that would happen in school.

The homeschooling really works for him. In fact, I debated sending him back to school this year. Oscar told me, "I will go back to school if you make me. But I want you to be clear that that's about you. And not about me." That hit me. It's true, he's thriving. My wanting to change our schooling was about wanting nine to five to myself.

Eventually, though, I think he'll go back. There are certain aspects of education that he can't do from home, like giving a presentation in front of the class, physics labs, and standardized tests. I'd like him to have those skills before he goes to college.

For now though, we've developed a rhythm. We homeschool for two to three hours a day, and he pursues his other interests afterward. Or we go to the gym together, and he can work out. Gotta get that nine pack ab. Now that he's twelve, he'll sometimes stay home alone to complete a book assignment that we'll discuss when I get home. Or he'll meet up with friends downtown. Most often, he'll come to work with us at our shop, hosting or working the coffee cart. He feels a part of the business, gaining skills like how to make change, how to be polite, and how to see what needs to be done instead of asking what to do.

GABRIELLA · LIVES IN MEXICO

The first day of school we only sent my eldest child. We figured if she liked it, then we could send the younger ones. At the end of the day she didn't want to leave! The next morning we walked all three to the building. My daughter ran inside with her new friends, the smallest one found a "pretty teacher" and held onto her as she led him inside. The middle one, the daddy's boy, cried and cried but eventually relented and went inside when tempted with a small toy. When we returned, they were having such a good time, *none* of them wanted to leave. There was a period of about two weeks where we had to coax them out of bed and drag them on the one-and-a-half mile walk to school in the morning, but by the afternoon, they had settled in so much they wanted to stay. It was a surprisingly positive experience, and now in their second school since moving, they're old pros.

SARA · LIVED IN MOROCCO FOR SEVEN YEARS

Before our move, we were clear that we wanted our kids in school, rather than worldschooling or homeschooling. We enrolled the kids in a private, trilingual, Moroccan school until the beginning of my daughter's second grade and my son's kindergarten year. That was when I discovered the gaps in their education. They were so busy learning languages, that history, math, and science were being pushed to the wayside. Also, the kids were constantly given mixed messages on *how* to learn.

Even though the school espoused an appealing philosophy, we discovered that what actually influenced a teacher's style was where they themselves studied. The English-trained teachers took the western approach of encouraging kids to ask questions, the French-trained teachers expected perfect repetition and memorization while discouraging questions and creativity, and the Arabic-trained teachers lectured and yelled at the kids. Our kids had no clue which mode to expect.

We made the decision to pull the kids out of school on a Friday and homeschooling started that Monday. We didn't know how we'd manage, but we knew anything would be better than what our kids were experiencing. I spent the next few months teaching them in the day, then spending the evening reading about educational styles and how children learn.

Our first year of homeschooling looked more like school at home, because that was what I was comfortable with. But over the years we've broken form more and more to create a space that works for us. I primarily teach the classical method. Our language arts and history meld into one another as the kids read literature from or about the time period they are studying. Unschooling does not suit my children. I think some kids are very self-driven and seek out new topics of study, and others have to be guided towards various topics so that they can narrow down to what interests them. My kids are the latter.

18

MEDICAL CARE

ile this chapter under the heading, "Things Someone Should Have Told Me." Only, I'm sure someone *did* tell me, and I was too busy dreaming of gnocchi napped in cheese sauce to pay strict attention. Plus, I figured everything would be fine.

This reminds me, I must pause here and share a dirty little secret you need to know, right now. It's about you. And it's about me. And it's about the people you will be surrounded by on your journey. See, there's one quality that we expats have in common that makes us both invigorating to have in company and also insufferable to love. *We trend towards relentless optimism.* Show us a problem on paper and we *pshaw* and tick off ways to get through it with grace and aplomb.

Living it is another matter.

Living it, we flounder like the next person. Only we labor under a layering of shame that we *should have known better.*

So, I'll just say it—we should have known better.

We should have hooked up with a doctor in the first week that we landed. Yes, it's true we are a healthy lot, so haven't had broken bones or stitches or even cavities to ingrain in us a deep-seated tickle of our vulnerability. But we had plenty of warning signs. Gabe struggled with wheezing the very day we arrived. A week in, Nicolas wiped out at the playground and saw stars, stumbling as he fought fainting. Months later, he developed an upper respiratory infection that left him breathless and so exhausted that the prospect of stairs left him ill. Every time one of these pokes from the universe were over, I wiped my brow and congratulated myself on a dire emergency avoided, and a return to non-medical-intervention lifestyle.

We didn't seek out medical care until Gabe's double ear infection wound us up in the emergency room.

But even *that* didn't prompt us to say, "Maybe we should find ourselves a doctor so if something *else* happens we can avoid the ER?"

A month later, I had bronchitis and Keith had pneumonia.

This is all to say—have a medical plan.

Routes towards medical care vary by community. For example, it was only when Gabe had hives all over his body (did I mention that one?) that we discovered a medical clinic right off the main *piazza* in Spello. We had ducked into the *farmacia* looking for cortisone cream, and learned that cortisone requires a prescription (while the inhaler that requires a prescription in the US is sold over-the-counter in Italy), so we were directed to the unmarked clinic. It has spotty hours, but when it's open, you can pop in, talk to a doctor, and get a referral or a prescription for the pharmacy. No insurance cards, no credit card machine, no receptionist. We tried to give our contact information for billing, but the doctor just cocked his head at us like we were offering him an expired yogurt. He waved us out.

It wasn't until Keith was hospitalized that we realized that the hospital system itself varies by country. In Italy, you are expected to bring your own water, towels, forks, and (super odd considering it's *Italy*) coffee. More than that, there isn't an assumption that patients need to know the diagnosis, prognosis, or plan. It took actual work to find out what medications were in the IV and the expected discharge date. Meanwhile, everyone in Spello knew all this before we did. There is no HIPAA in Italy, so your *barista* may well know the results of your CT scan before you do. I say roll with it. Sink into the belonging and community that come with lowered boundaries, which, to my mind, is worth the sacrifice in privacy.

My suggestion? Spare some time while you are researching local paleolithic cave drawings to also read blogs or other expat accounts of interactions with the medical system in your host country. When you are coordinating housing, ask your landlord about the medical system, particularly the location of the hospital and the name of a doctor you can contact. And if you will be in a country for any length of time, set up an introductory meeting with a doctor that you'll be able to call if you run into trouble. Forewarned is forearmed. This is not something you want to be figuring out on the fly. Spontaneity has its place, and that's not while you are clutching your screaming baby and trying to figure out how to patch your world back together.

One last pro-tip; bring ibuprofen. Advil and Motrin are super-expensive in other countries, and sometimes you can't find (my favorite) gel caps. Do yourself a favor, get a large bottle, and lug it around if you have to. You'll be glad you did. Ditto for other medications you take with any regularity like Dramamine or allergy medications.

The Worst Moments

THE LEWIS FAMILY'S STORY

Most of the difficult moments of our time in Asia centered around illness. Thank goodness we had an excellent hospital near our house as my husband, Henry, needed two major operations during the time we were in Kuala Lumpur. One was a surprise operation that happened just a day before we had been slated to leave for Laos. It was frightening to realize that if this had happened just 24 hours later, I would have been in a country with limited support and a very ill husband. As it was, our surgeon was excellent and the procedure successful.

The other medical fright happened in China. I was so glad that we didn't save visiting the Great Wall for later in our trip because I succumbed to severe food poisoning on our second day. I assumed I got the food poisoning in China, but my doctors actually suspected I got it in Malaysia. But that didn't make the experience any more comfortable. I had to see a doctor at a Chinese hospital where there was very little English spoken. Eventually, we gave up on our holiday and returned to Kuala Lumpur for treatment.

Then in November 2008, I caught chikunguna. The frequent rain in Kuala Lumpur had led to a rise in the mosquito population, and a consequent outbreak of this mosquito-borne illness. Chikunguna is similar to dengue fever but affects joints for a longer period. It was so bad, I had to be hospitalized. I felt absolutely awful, but grateful for the exceptional medical care in Kuala Lumpur.

After that, I was absolutely neurotic about mosquito bites, regularly dousing myself with insect repellent. My family joked about my "*Eau de Off*" scent, but I was determined to not get reinfected. After my experience with chikunguna, the UK felt like a much safer place to be!

My advice to anyone traveling is to get excellent medical insurance and also to research the nearby medical facilities. It's best to find one that you would be happy to use, especially if you have children, and especially before you need it.

Seeking Out Medical Care

CONTRIBUTORS' STORIES

HEATHER · LIVED IN ITALY FOR TWO YEARS

We only saw a doctor for minor things our first year in Milan. With the help of local friends, we discovered where the doctor's office was, and then discovered that he made house calls. The Italian belief that a sick person shouldn't be moved was handy on several occasions when our son had strep throat.

Being a huge city, Milan has several "English Clinics" that I visited on two occasions, but it took about forty-five minutes to reach the closest one (with a drive/metro excursion and then a walk—not great when you are sick).

My son got braces before we moved to Italy, so we had the adventure of finding an orthodontist. Our orthodontist was billed as "English Speaking," but his English was as good as our Italian. So we had lots of misinterpretation, which I was not in the mood for at 8 or 9 PM (our appointments were often at this late hour). My son also had to get a wisdom tooth removed. I'll just say, we should have waited until we moved home.

JOHN · RV-ED THROUGH EUROPE FOR ONE YEAR

We carried a full medical kit with us in the camper. Twice, though, we had to seek out medical care, and it was easy. Campground managers all had recommendations. One doctor even did a "home visit" to our van in southern Morocco when the kids had the stomach flu.

SARAH · LIVES IN THE NETHERLANDS AFTER YEARS OF WORLDSCHOOLING

We have loved our experience with the medical system in the Netherlands. It is mandatory to have health insurance from the moment you set foot in the country, and the premiums are set by law (we found the plans much cheaper, and with far lower deductibles, than in the US, see *Resources*). Visits to our family doctor are 100% free, and he has walk-in hours almost every day. We've been in for a variety of small complaints during our two years here. He always takes time to listen and examine carefully. The most serious medical issue we've had was when my husband came down with shingles. Our family doctor diagnosed him and scheduled an appointment with an ophthalmologist who called the prescriptions to the pharmacy near our house. This sounds terrific, but it took a couple of tries for the message to actually make it through. Dutch doctors are not big on medication, and my husband would have preferred stronger painkillers. But other than that, it was a good experience. The doctor's assistant called several times to check up on him, and he had a follow-up appointment with the ophthalmologist to confirm that there was no damage to his vision. Most of the prescriptions were covered by our insurance (no copay even), and everything is so centralized that the pharmacies and doctors just look you up in the national system and submit the insurance claims automatically, so it was all very easy.

NICA · SAILED THE CARIBBEAN

We didn't require medical care on our trip with the kids, but when Jeremy and I did our sailing trip in the mid-90s, I had a bad boil/staph infection under my armpit that had to be lanced and treated in the Bahamas. The doctor was UK-trained, but was only on the island once a week. I saw a nurse at the clinic (also UK-trained) every day for ten days to have the abscess drained and repacked with antibiotics. Total bill (handed over with an apology for how high it was) was $50 USD.

We carry a well-stocked medical kit, complete with prescriptions and even a suture kit and EpiPen (though none of us is allergic to anything that we know of). Chances of being nearby a medical clinic when you need it is slim for sailors cruising the Bahamas. "Close by" might mean two sailing days.

NELL · LIVED IN FRANCE FOR ONE YEAR

Both children got sick with the flu while we were in France. It was so bad my daughter vomited on the street on the way to the doctor's office. The office was a room in the doctor's house, full of interesting art and furniture. There was no discussion of money and how we would pay; the attention was on treating the sick person. The cost was so low I did a double take.

KRISTIN · LIVED IN COSTA RICA, THE NETHERLANDS, AND ARGENTINA FOR ONE YEAR

We didn't need a doctor in the Netherlands, although it would have been easy to find someone. Their medical system is great and simple to access.

We did need input from a doctor in Costa Rica, but we were in a rural area so had to send pictures of what we were worried was a flesh-eating rash from a black fly (it was common ringworm). It wasn't as stressful as it seems now, but when we arrived at our house in Costa Rica, I remember thinking that we should have been closer to the hospital (it was four hours away).

In Argentina, my then 2-year-old fell off a play structure within two hours of arriving at the new house. He landed on his arm and head. The next day he was still crying so my husband took him to the Argentine hospital. That enabled us to form a relationship with some doctors there.

Later we took all of our kids there for their school entrance forms (it was tremendously difficult to fax and get that information from the US). It was different from an administrative perspective but not that different from a practical, medical-advice perspective, and I felt better knowing we had a relationship with a doctor. I had tried to develop relationships before we were on the ground but found it very confusing and difficult. We needed to wait until we were there.

CHERYL · RV-ING THROUGH EUROPE

During our recent stay in Portugal, our 2-year-old split open the back of his head. It was only an inch-long gash but it was extremely distressing. Luckily, the apartment we were staying in while our motorhome was at a garage for repairs was right across the street from a pharmacy. We rushed him in, where a pharmacist cleaned his wound and stopped the bleeding. We were in a small town where almost no one spoke English. The pharmacist called us a taxi and told the driver the situation. The driver drove us straight to the local hospital. He also escorted us to where we should be and helped us explain to the emergency department receptionist what had happened. We have travel insurance that we purchased specifically for our journey; however, as we are a part of the EU (being from the UK), we were entitled to free healthcare using our European Health Insurance Card (EHIC). Overall, the treatment we received was fantastic, and we feel much less anxious about using medical care in future.

NAOMI · LIVED IN INDIA AND SINGAPORE FOR FOUR YEARS

How I wish I had been told before we moved abroad that I would become a family health advocate—without any qualifications except the title of Mama. I quickly discovered that you need to bring hard copies of your medical records to each appointment. Also, given some health professionals' faith in the curative powers of "wear a hat and drink only warm liquids," I often needed to push for further reflection and more specific treatment. Nonetheless, we adored our doctor in Delhi. He did house calls, and there was nothing more reassuring than to know that he was literally one phone call away.

One of the most meaningful experiences with medical care while abroad was with our youngest, Mia. She had hearing issues and chronic ear infections. As a result, she had difficulty with her speech, so we had to seek out an ENT (ear, nose, and throat doctor), an audiologist, and a speech therapist. After many dead-end introductions and mediocre recommendations, we found ourselves in a cramped basement audiologist office. They checked us in, and soon we were being asked questions about Mia's history. I began answering, and the doctor looked at me, tilted his head to one side and said, "Can Baby Mia answer please?" She was 4-years-old, but was always called "Baby." To this day, she remembers that moment, and it is the catalyst for her desire to want to study ENT medicine when she grows up.

LISA · BACKPACKING AROUND THE WORLD

During a dentist visit in Vietnam, my husband swallowed a piece of the drill and was rushed to the hospital to have an x-ray. They didn't find anything. The next day they took Steve to Da Nang to have a gastroscopy to locate the drill bit. After a lot of dry retching as a 90 cm garden hose was fed down his throat, they found nothing. Again. Finally, a CT scan located the missing part—it was already in his lower intestines and on its way out.

Worse was when our eldest daughter developed a really high fever for a couple of nights while we were in Cyprus. Doctors were few and far between (as it was August and holiday season), so we were directed to the local hospital. X-rays and blood tests revealed that Charlie had a 12% consolidation on her lungs, which required a drip, strong antibiotics, and a week of bed rest.

The worst moment of our backpacking year was when Steve's mum broke her femur in Laos. For two days, she was forced to stay in a Lao hospital without adequate pain relief or medical attention while we tried to get her out. The travel insurance agency organized a medical evacuation to Bangkok, where she had a major operation to mend her broken bone. Then there was the rehabilitation to get her able to sit upright so she could get on a plane back to Australia. That took ten days.

What I learned is that even with the very best travel insurance, the wheels move slowly in third world countries. Paperwork moved slowly, getting doctors' reports for insurance purposes moved slowly, getting approval for a Thai medical plane moved slowly. Lesson for anyone traveling overseas—take out proper travel insurance. You just don't know what can happen.

19

COPING WITH HOMESICKNESS

I n our family of five, four of us experienced zero homesickness. Sure, I missed Chinese food delivered to my door, and in the winter when it took days for socks to dry I longed for my dryer, and I would have loved to instantly "port" an old friend to my dinner table, but compared to my daughter's homesickness? Walk in the park.

Siena struggled, and that's putting it mildly. Part of that is who she is, or was, more accurately (whether because of the year abroad or predictable development, she doesn't sweat change anymore). Change was impossible to manage. So *that* much change really did her in. Add to that her shyness, which made her cringe at the outpouring of Italian love that my boys soaked up like sunshine, her awful teacher who shamed her relentlessly, and her perfectionist streak which delayed learning Italian...well, she floundered. The kind of floundering that is virtually indistinguishable from drowning.

She missed her friends and she missed her knowable life, but like most expat children, those were smokescreens for what she really missed. Which was *her*. She missed having an instinctive sense of who she was. Banging up against her limitations made her have to examine herself and her needs and her vulnerabilities more than she, or anyone, would choose. She's all heart, our Siena, and she was essentially a walking wound for some time. How long? Well, it's hard to say, because there would be a month or more when things seemed fine, and then BAM! A teacher would yell at her, and suddenly she refused to go back to school and cried about missing home. Early spring was when I noticed her blossoming, and then it seemed like she laid down the last of the homesickness and skipped away.

But I'll be honest, there were moments when I literally thought my child was cracking up. I'm a child psychologist, and that's the diagnosis that ran through my head. I'll be honest again, I dealt with it poorly. I pushed her to exert herself when the right thing was to just hold the space for her. This is why I wrote about working to hear your children, rather than convince them of the irrationality of their reality (*see* "Involving Your Children"). Do as I wish I had done. Because when I finally realized that I needed to back up and let her find her own way, that was when life turned around for her. It helped that her language had come along by then, and that we started giving her freedom that increased her sense of competence (she became my bakery runner, and also would collect pretty flowers for our table from the fields around the town). Everything suddenly seemed to click. She created real friendships, she ran into school with a grin, and to the audible dropping of my jaw, she answered a friend's question of, "How do you feel about leaving Spello?" with "I don't want to go." I was in such disbelief I translated for her, even though by that time her Italian was better than mine. She nodded and said, "I know what she asked."

And how bitterly my daughter wept when it was time to return home. She had nightmares about it weeks in advance.

I'm going to share with you what I learned through trial-and-error application of tools in my therapy basket. These are not child therapy tools; it would be wrong to ask a parent to assume the mantle of therapist. Rather, these are the tools I teach *parents* for dealing with a struggling child. While these strategies lack the systemic power to change that is inherent in the solution-oriented, cognitive-behavioral work I do with children in my practice, those techniques backfire when doing them as a parent (as I discovered). So therapists out there? Take off your therapist hat when dealing with your expat child. Just be a parent. If you feel like your child is so stuck that therapy would be beneficial, consider trying to get a therapist from your hometown to do a spot of Skype therapy (I know a family that did this during their year abroad, and I've also done this for families). But if you are just stumped on how to support your child during this painful period, here are strategies that I find the most useful, based on what I've learned about children by doing this work for twenty years. They are what ultimately helped in parenting my own child through her homesickness and anxiety.

Reflect what your child is feeling. Mirror what you hear, "Sounds like you are lonely." Rather than trying to fix the problem by asking, "Why don't you talk to that nice kid who always smiles at you?" You have to admit, that's not a rocket-science sort of solution, your kid can generate that on his own. What he needs is space to feel his feelings, to be heard, so he can come up with his own solutions. There is little doubt his solution will be better than yours. No offense, his ideas will be better than mine and I do this for a living. I know it's difficult to not offer solutions. So if you simply must, then do, but put a pause on it. Try hearing your child first for a bit. Practice just listening and saying what you hear.

When you reflect, don't ask questions, and give "why" questions a particularly wide berth. The last thing a child needs to do when she's wrestling with heavy feelings is to have to defend those feelings. Here's an example. Let me ask you this—what did you have for breakfast? I know, I know, it's silly, but tell me anyway. Okay, now *why* did you have that? See? All of a sudden, when you have to explain it, the assumption is whatever you chose for breakfast was the *wrong* choice. So don't ask questions, stick with reflective statements like "I can hear how hard it is" and "It sounds like you feel confused about if they really want to play with you or not" and "You must really miss how easy it was to be with your friends back home." Being heard is a balm. Try it with your partner some time, too.

If your child is building a narrative that feels harmful, like he is "too shy to talk to anyone" or she is "never going to make a friend" you can gently challenge the assumption by asking for exceptions. Best if again you stay away from questions and instead wonder. "I wonder if it feels that way some days more than others" and "I wonder if it's easier to talk to some people, like another student, rather than a teacher."

Bad days are seldom unrelenting. Build on the positive days that are sure to pop up now and then. Not with too many questions, as you've learned, but with wondering. "Today seemed easier. I wonder why." See if you can divine the reason for the shift, and if there was something structural or in your power, see if you can repeat it. For instance, the days Siena went to our friend Paola's shop to make macramé were always great days because she had that to look forward to. So she did it once a week (God bless Paola). Also, when Siena was given a task that stretched but didn't snap her, it built her confidence and made her feel strong. So we sent her to the store even when we didn't need anything. Basically, look for places your child can feel connected and competent (lack of these two are the stinging shards of being an expat child). Build on those.

Be careful of asking the impossible, like clear speech and eye contact, even if you are trying to make a good impression, say, on a potential landlord. Asking for high-level social behavior sends a message to kids that they aren't "enough." Struggling kids already feel "less-than." Just let them muddle through. They are aware enough of their limitations, don't send the message that their every move is being observed, micromanaged, judged. That's hardly the way to reduce anxiety.

We ended up taking danger words off the conversational table, especially labels. For us, the word was "shy." We even stopped noting when Siena *wasn't* shy. At first we had a misbegotten notion that the praise would be helpful but a) see the advice above, avoid the microscope, and b) when your child shifts her behavior, she knows it, and can feel that as her own reward. It's not about you, so don't make it about you. We also stopped asking if she felt shy stepping into situations. After all, if she agreed, then she had to *be* shy. Plus, we were highlighting the feeling she least wanted to feel before a social interaction.

Stay calm. Anxious children are sensitive children, and sensitive children will pick up on your worry. I'm not saying to project something you don't feel. Rather I want you to trust that your child can weather this expat storm and communicate that trust.

Normalize, normalize, normalize! Of *course* this is hard. A child that believes his anxiety or homesickness is weird or different will only feel the shackles of those painful feelings more. Be matter-of-fact. It's a tough spot, and you know he'll move through it. Ask if there is anything you can do to be helpful. If your child offers a suggestion for you, listen, reflect, and consider it.

As for more specifics about homesickness and coping with the adjustment to life abroad, I asked all the expats I know and got these ideas.

* Sketch out in advance that the adjustment will be difficult, but worth it (and why).

* Ask a child what experiences he or she really wants during the adventure (like climbing the Eiffel Tower or going on a gondola ride or ziplining) and put one of those in the itinerary. Even if it's a ways away, it's something to look forward to, which tilts the balance of homesickness. Plus just the act of looking forward creates a surge of dopamine, one of those neurotransmitters that is fundamental for happiness.

* Go to the market and get lots of little things to send back to friends.

* Skype or FaceTime can be fantastic, though not particularly for an introvert to communicate with a class he left behind. That can be overwhelming.

* Sometimes Skype or FaceTime are *not* fantastic, because they make a child aware of what they are missing back home. Try using these and

not using these to see which is more helpful for your child, bearing in mind that what works in month four may not work in month eight. The contrary is also true, so feel free to bring out coping strategies that didn't work earlier. Development is a wonder, they may work now.

* Buying postcards and sending those can be a fun way to connect. Get postcards for your child as well to festoon around her room, as a reminder of her travels, and implicitly, how much she's seen and done and can feel proud of.

* Try to connect with other English-speaking families, especially ones you know. Encourage people to visit or have their vacations collide with your own. Bantering in English can remind your child of who she is and what is likable about her.

For us, homesickness (for lack of a better word, though again, it's not about wanting home, even though that's often how kids will describe it, it's more that they miss how they felt when they were home—safe, easy, comfortable, connected) was akin to a dark patch in the forest. There is no way out but through. Trying to rush the process only serves to confuse and ensnare. Trust your child, trust yourself, and the soft light will dapple through the boughs again. In other words, your best healer may well be time.

When Homesickness Spirals

HEATHER'S STORY

The hardest part of living in Italy was my son's homesickness. Ben was ten when we moved to Milan and so excited about the adventure of it all. Before school started, we met a few expat families, so he started the year with familiar faces, which I assumed would be helpful. It was, but things changed rapidly once school got underway.

Ben was starting sixth grade that year and had a locker and different teachers for each class for the first time. That was new and overwhelming on its own. But add in feeling out of place and homesick? That was a bad mix for him. It didn't help that he was going through puberty and outgrowing his clothes in the blink of an eye. I erroneously chalked his moodiness up to a passing phase.

His homesickness initially presented as illness. He got sick and couldn't get better. I thought he might have mono or strep, but the tests came back negative. The Italian doctor was kind, coming to our house several times. But all he could tell us was that Ben was ill from not wearing a scarf. A very Italian response, they are obsessed with air drafts.

We realized Ben was homesick when he started talking about how much he missed the familiarity of home—his room, his friends, his school. That homesickness soon spiraled into depression and anxiety. He began resisting leaving the house and had panic attacks at the prospect of any kind of appointment or trip.

Our first step was talking to the counselor at Ben's International School. She normalized Ben's feelings, by telling him how common homesickness is and how scary it can be to be far from the familiar. She also worked with his teachers to make a specific plan to help Ben manage his way back from missing so much school. She also set Ben up with a mentor, his band teacher. The teacher was the neatest guy and helped Ben not only with studying and catching up, but with self-esteem and anxiety issues. That time with his mentor was one activity Ben looked forward to.

The school counselor also provided ongoing support to me and Chris. I never felt judged or ridiculous as I fell apart in her office, time after time. We tried connecting Ben with a child psychologist, but it wasn't a great fit. Ben felt stressed and uncomfortable with the whole experience, so we ended up canceling our return visit.

Emotionally, it was a roller coaster of a year, and we were exhausted when we visited Idaho that summer. We took Ben to his doctor, who diagnosed the throat issue as a virus that would flare with stress and cover his throat with sores. We also had him tested for allergies, because of his ongoing stomach pain. The doctor ended up determining it wasn't allergies, but anxiety.

We returned to Italy for year two, with a better understanding of what Ben was dealing with, and medication on board to help him with depression and anxiety. It was definitely a better year. The medications helped, as did Ben's burgeoning ability to verbalize how he felt. He learned the language for talking about self-esteem and anxiety, describing how hard it was for him to feel out of place. As a historically outgoing kid, it rocked him to be an outsider. Most of the kids at this International School had been expats for years, or were European and knew four languages. He struggled learning just Italian. He felt inadequate, like everyone else had it all together and he struggled just to make it through the day.

I learned that Ben needed time to process. We began talking about events coming up in the week ahead, and took it week by week. Chris and I worked to make our conversations with Ben feel safe and encouraging. With all of us clearer and calmer about Ben's anxiety, he began opening up more. Talking and working through difficult feelings prevented the anxiety from spiraling out of control. Chris and I also began choosing our battles. We thought hard about what we'd push him to do because we thought it would ultimately feel good for him, versus what we would let slide.

Most days we still felt like we were walking on eggshells, and every time he said he was too sick to go to school I went into panic mode. Maybe it sounds minor, but it was a huge stressor that affected the whole family the entire time we lived in Italy. I dreamed of the day that he could look back on the experiences he had had living abroad and see them with new eyes and hopefully have some good memories.

As our time in Italy came to a close, I watched Ben come back to life. I don't know if it was the promise of our looming move back to the USA, or that he finally was getting his feet under him, or the medications doing their job, but regardless, it was great to see him enjoying his life and friends. As we walked to dinner the night before we flew back to Idaho, he casually said to me, "Mom, I really love Italy." I laughed and told him I was so glad he could feel that way before we left. I may have cried a little, too. It's all a blur.

Looking back, I think Ben was dealing with anxiety way before the move, we just didn't realize it. It seems now that the move and the changes in how Ben saw himself made the anxiety spiral out of control. I think Ben assumed that once we returned to Idaho, everything would magically be better. He was surprised that things weren't so rosy. We've been home a few years now, and he is in a great space with school and has a wonderful group of friends, and a supportive counselor and effective medications. Only occasionally does his anxiety flare up, and we know better how to help him.

When Ben remembers his struggle in Italy, he sees it as anxiety rather than homesickness, although he acknowledges that homesickness was a big part of it, perhaps the trigger. My daughter and I also experienced some homesickness, but nothing like Ben. Everyone is so different. One thing I know is that I could not have coped with the pain of Ben's suffering if not for the expat friends I made in Italy. They heard me and supported me when I shared the real, raw stuff.

Last year, Chris and the kids joined me at the end of a tour I led in Italy. It was the first time back for all of them since we moved home. Prior to that trip, Ben talked a lot about how he hoped being back in Italy would allow him to release the bad memories so he could really enjoy being there. I was nervous before they arrived, wanting so much for him to be happy. They deplaned, and before my eyes, Ben fell in love with Italy. Like he was seeing it afresh. Made this mamma's heart happy.

Homesickness and Loneliness

CONTRIBUTORS' STORIES

NELL · LIVED IN FRANCE FOR ONE YEAR

We all had brief patches of homesickness, though short lived and not very intense. For the adults, it was more an occasional wishing things were easy and familiar. Like, if the heat goes off, you know whom to call and can effortlessly make yourself understood.

The kids missed their friends at first, especially when it hit home that they couldn't actually communicate with their new classmates. But that also gave them motivation to learn French—so much so that my second grader would come into my room at 6:30 in the morning, begging me to quiz her on verb conjugations. After a couple of months they had friends, and felt no homesickness after that. Being on the young side, seven and nine, definitely helped. And it was wonderful to see how tight the kids got with each other in those months when it felt like they were all they had.

HEATHER · LIVED IN ITALY FOR TWO YEARS

We joke about how much we love "Vacation Italy." When we were actually traveling, none of us were homesick. It was fun and delicious and full of adventure. We couldn't get enough! It was the days of "Everyday Italy"—the chores, the homework, the language, the culture differences, dealing with our crazy Italian landlord, figuring out how to take care of a sick kid or sick animal—that could sink our mood. If I was already feeling off, any one of these could push me over the edge.

ELIZABETH · LIVES IN ITALY

I struggle with loneliness so much more than I thought I would. Maybe it would be different if my children were older or if my husband wasn't working. But with a baby and a toddler, I often regret the lack of family and a support network. I keep in touch and phone as much as possible, but it is not the same.

KRISTIN · LIVED IN COSTA RICA, THE NETHERLANDS, AND ARGENTINA FOR ONE YEAR

Of the three places we lived, I got the most homesick in Argentina. Part of that was that the community was less welcoming, but I also think not having external connections exacerbated my missing home. My husband had his job and my kids had school. In retrospect, I wish I had taken Spanish lessons, even though I already speak Spanish. It would have connected me more, given me something to focus on, and maybe helped with the homesickness.

CHERYL · RV-ING THROUGH EUROPE

We haven't once been homesick. The kids never mention our house, their rooms, friends and family, nursery, or any other significant aspect of home that we, as parents, were anxious about leaving. It's strange, before we left I was incredibly sad about selling the house, where we felt safe and secure and where we made memories together. I felt our home, bricks and mortar, was what connected us. But very quickly, living like this, you realize that it's not the material things that make a family feel "at home." It's all of us, being together.

NICA · SAILED THE CARIBBEAN

Our daughter struggled with the adjustment. Since she was eight, we thought it would be fairly easy, but she is very social and being away from friends was tough. When our family visited us in Hope Town, Bahamas, for Christmas, she slept in their rental house every single night while our son slept on board. It was hard on her when they left.

Contacting friends back home wasn't all that helpful because of the experience barrier—there is just no reference point for another 8-year-old when someone is going on and on about how they had to snorkel fast back to the dinghy to get away from a barracuda, or how cool it was to find beach trash to make a monument at this one anchorage. The vocabulary is out of context; conversations were not very satisfying.

Meeting up with another family was a turning point for us, as their daughter was just a year older than ours. She too was having a tough time with the loneliness of being aboard, and the girls hit it off and are still close. We altered our sailing plans to meet up with them (skipped a few islands to get to an anchorage we could share), which was a great decision.

RACHEL · LIVED IN SPAIN FOR ONE YEAR

At the beginning of the year, my 9-year-old would always say he wanted to go home to Seattle. No matter what was bothering him, if he was tired, mad at his siblings, whatever, he would say, "I want to go home." About a month before we were slated to leave Barcelona, he got teary at bedtime thinking about leaving. He admitted he was excited to go home, but that he was going to miss people. He added, "It's like you leave a little part of your heart in all the places you've been, and it's never whole again." I tried to reassure him that it's like your heart is bigger, but he wasn't buying it.

20

SAVING MONEY WHILE ABROAD

The penny-pinching doesn't stop once you heave yourself across the big, blue ocean. Most of us have to continually be mindful of preserving our financial reservoirs. Particularly since the money in other countries doesn't register as "money." It seems more like Monopoly cash, to be tossed about without compunction or consequence. (Dear Lord, I hope that's not just me.)

In all seriousness, it can feel like this is the trip of a lifetime, so budget be damned! But I know too many families who returned home without any sort of financial cushion to soften the landing. We are a prime example. If not for the generosity of our friends Emily and John, we wouldn't even have had wheels, as they sold us their car in three easy monthly installments.

If nothing else, you'll want to save money so that you can travel while you are abroad. In fact, many expats report that their biggest outflow of cash is given to traveling within their travels. I know this may strike you as silly while you are still in your planning stages, particularly if your itinerary is comprised of landing in one idyllic destination. Your eyes are on your new home. Thoughts of vacations within vacations seem like an irritating distraction. But no matter how exotic and spectacular your destination, you are still a wanderer, and you will feel a pull to explore your new corner of the globe. Particularly once you realize how cheap regional flights are in many parts of the world. I remember when we were in Italy and realized we could fly to Brussels for €11,00 each. I wondered how far I could get from Charlottesville for that price. Answer, I could take a Greyhound bus one hour to Lynchburg. It's a charming town but the language, history, and food-ways are all virtually indistinguishable from where I currently live. The mind fairly boggles at the travel opportunities available in many other parts of the world for a virtual song.

Once we discovered how cheap regional airfare was, we decided to go somewhere for everyone's birthday. We took two trips by car (Venice at Christmastime, and skiing in the Dolomiti) and the rest by plane (Paris and Normandy, Brussels, Seville, plus a non-birthday bonus trip to Sicily). That meant a trip every other month. To afford that much travel, we developed ways to save money while living in Spello, and strategies for cheap travel.

Saving money in Spello was easier than expected because the cost of living is lower than home. Yes, we ate out more, but phenomenal Italian food can be easily found for €12,00 a plate, and anyway, we ate pizza more than anything else. Our groceries were less than half of what we currently spend. So even with our daily hit of coffee at the bars, and our summer-time splurges on almost daily gelato, we were consistently surprised at the affordability of our luscious lifestyle. It helps, of course, that what we really enjoyed was the *life* in our lifestyle. Rather than looking for enter-tainment or expensive meals or fancy toys to brighten up a hectic and scattershot existence, we glided through our days, happy to pop into the church for a free concert or walk to the park together in the afternoon.

The other thing we did was limit gift-giving. We told our friends and families "no gifts," as we didn't want the hassle of trying to mail gifts to the States or mess with trying to meet up with a postman for parcels (our apartment door only allowed slender mail). Even our gifts to each other were sparse, since the birthday trip was the major gift. It was liberating to be free of the expectations and obligations that come with gift-giving.

When it came to traveling, our budget was quite modest. We have a no souvenir policy, which saves us needless accumulation of stuff as well as annoying stretches of time in gift shops. We did purchase a postcard from each place we visited to festoon Gabe and Siena's room and also to bind into a memory book once home. But postcards are cheap. When we went to Rome or Florence, we weighed the financial advantages of taking the train versus driving and paying money for gas and parking. We took new friends up on their offer to stay with them in Le Marche for a weekend. We researched inexpensive restaurants to find quintessentially local meals.

For longer haul trips, we chose destinations based on what was cheap to fly to in our chosen month. We researched departure airports, and were willing to have our outgoing airport be two hours away in Rome, rather than the more convenient Perugia airport, if it meant saving money. We always stayed in vacation rentals, which are reliably less expensive than hotels, and also gave us the cost-cutting option to eat in. We tried to go places where we wouldn't need to rent a car. We limited costly tourist attractions (even cheap ones add up in a family). We went so far as to convince the kids that the copy of Michelangelo's David standing in the Piazza della Signoria was the actual statue to save on a museum entry. They can see the actual one in the Accademia on their own dime when they are older.

Rather than focus on sights with their ticket fees, our low-cost travel consisted of wandering through historic areas to arrive at a lunch destination, heading back to the apartment for *pausa* (even when not in Italy, we kept to the Italian midday rest to keep us fresh and energetic for the afternoon), then a leisurely wander to dinner. Followed by a starlit stroll back for sleep.

Our travels during our year in Italy remain some of our clearest memories of the trip. Here's how I can explain it. In Betty Smith's *A Tree Grows in Brooklyn*, Francie describes how once in awhile, she buys a pickle with her meager funds. After that pickle, her standard fare of re-purposed bread tastes good again.

Traveling is my pickle. Traveling is where our family jokes are born, it's when we make the biggest realizations about ourselves and our world, and coming home clicks the lens of gratitude back in place. I remember on the flight from Brussels back to Italy, we overheard the families behind us chattering with emphatic phrasing. We leaned back, smiling as those tones washed over us. When we arrived back in Spello, the hills looked greener, and did the old ladies plant even more flowers in the alleys?

As an added bonus, vacationing when you are already abroad is far more spontaneous, leading to less planning time. I'm convinced that the greatness of a trip is inversely proportional to how much I plan and therefore to my number of expectations. Our best trips were the ones that were so spontaneous we had no time to research. No expectations means everything is a surprise and everything is a gift. You just don't get that when you are poring over websites for the six months leading up to a vacation. Think about it, if you drive over a hill and discover a stunning beach with mysterious drawings all over the cliffs, it is far more powerful than if you drove there to see it and have an imprint of that beach and the backstory of those drawings already in your mind.

So if you can take advantage of travels within your travels, I highly recommend it.

Even if you don't, it's a good idea to be mindful of your spending, and keep some of your practiced money-saving strategies. It will allow you to return home with a bigger safety cushion, especially important if you don't have jobs lined up, or will be hit with a series of bills for things like a vehicle or school tuition, right when you are shaking the travel dust off your suitcases.

Traveling within Travels

SARA'S STORY

One Christmas in Morocco, my children received the DVD of *The Sound of Music*. After the presents were opened, they popped it in, and there were these gorgeous Austrian Alps and images of Bavaria in the opening credits. My husband and I have wholly embodied the belief that a clear intention is all that's needed to make an idea possible. We turned to one another and both of us said that *this* was where we were going that summer. I instantly began to search for places to stay in Bavaria, without much luck. I was convinced that I could find the fairy tale image in my mind, so I started thinking outside the box. I jumped on Google Translate and began translating the key words "farmhouse" and "vacation home" into German. Once I began searching for the German key words, loads of sites popped up for what were obviously aimed at Germans looking for Bavarian getaways.

I eventually found the most idyllic farmhouse, complete with cows, chickens, rabbits, geese, rolling hills to run over, and a play structure for the kids. I began corresponding with the owners, again with the help of Google Translate, and we booked a summer at their farm. We took the ferry across the Straight of Gibraltar and camped our way through Spain, France, Italy, and Switzerland, to Bavaria (something I suggest to every person who loves camping—European campsites are incredible AND cheap).

Once there, we played lots of charades with the owners and exchanged laughter and smiles, eventually figuring out the necessities for our stay. The kids went over to the farmer's home each morning to collect fresh milk and eggs, and we bought a jar of their heavenly farm-made honey. Each Tuesday and Thursday, the bread truck arrived at precisely 8:30 AM with fresh bread and rolls. The kids spent much of their days running around the farm, free as can be for the first time in their lives. In Morocco, homes are surrounded by walls, and although many of the yards are quite large, the kids were ultimately limited in how far they could explore, since letting them play out on the street was not an option. This farm was pure heaven—free and open, with limitless opportunities.

On some days we ventured out, visiting little villages and Lake Chiemsee, riding our bikes and hiking. There was a German family staying at the farm with whom we grew friendly, and though our kids didn't speak the same language, they were happy as can be jumping together on the trampoline or pushing one another on the swing. The parents spoke English and laughingly told us that the farmers were totally stumped at how we found their farmhouse considering we don't speak German. It turns out, they had never hosted Americans.

Taking the road less traveled (and the language not spoken) proved to be the best decision in this trip and all our others.

How to Save Money

CONTRIBUTORS' STORIES

ESTELLE · CROSS-GENERATIONAL LIVING IN ITALY

If finances are an issue, my advice is to live like average people in your location. Aim for an apartment rather than a house, with smaller rooms and fewer bathrooms than you are used to. Don't buy a lot of clothes and use a smaller car or public transportation. Splurge on good food, and use the wealth of historic sites, nature walks, forests, mountains, and local events to entertain yourselves.

CANADA-TO-FRANCE · LIVES IN FRANCE

With a sluggish Canadian dollar and the euro quite high, we do what we can to save money. Since we both get paid in Canadian dollars I am constantly converting prices in my head as I shop. Food costs are quite low in France, so we still seem to come out on top and our rent is reasonable for what we have. Some luxuries can be expensive and we have to be creative. I learned to make a lot of things instead of buying prepackaged items in the grocery store. I also never waste food; we eat everything in the fridge/freezer. Since we love to travel, we are not stuck on particular destinations and simply go where the sale fares send us. We don't have a car here, which saves us a ton of money in car payments, insurance, and those high European gas prices. We chose an apartment that is central, so we walk everywhere.

ELIZABETH · LIVES IN ITALY

Southern Italian food is phenomenal. Simple. Affordable. Delicious. I eat well, cook with fresh ingredients daily, and spend a lot less than I did in Scotland. I admit there are days where I miss using online shopping and delivery by a big grocery store, but it's so much more satisfying going to all the local stores and sellers to buy my cheese, vegetables, and meat.

JOHN · RV-ED THROUGH EUROPE

Living in a motorhome was a cheap way to travel, mainly because accommodation averaged €20 per night and we could cook most meals. We also free camped at times, and embraced the lunch menu specials across countries like France, Spain, and Portugal. As a family, we rarely ate out at night, as it was more expensive.

KRISTIN · LIVED IN COSTA RICA, THE NETHERLANDS, AND ARGENTINA FOR ONE YEAR

We had a hard time developing a budget since prices varied across our locations. We generally decided to prioritize experiences and admission fees to things like UNESCO heritage sites and to skimp on meals out which was not a sacrifice, given how young our children were. We saved for four years but didn't go through most of our savings. Actually, we learned that living overseas is cheaper in many ways; for instance, no extracurriculars, birthday parties, or nights out with friends. We didn't buy new clothes because we were in backpack mode. And we didn't pay for babysitters because we didn't have any. If we wanted a night out, we just ordered drinks and appetizers, then ate dinner at home.

NELL · LIVED IN FRANCE FOR ONE YEAR

One of the very best, and unexpected, outcomes of the year in France was that it showed all of us, kids included, how much our lives in the States had involved *buying stuff*. We arrived in France with huge duffel bags (I let my daughter bring an unconscionable number of stuffed animals, worrying about her getting homesick—mistake! She would have been just fine with one or two), and we did not have much room for adding anything new. So we traveled around and lived our lives in the village without acquiring much of anything that would need to be transported.

We weren't impossibly strict. The kids bought little glass animals in Murano, plenty of Pokemon cards, and some toy knights. But (aside from books, in those pre-Kindle days) everything we bought that year fit into a knapsack. It was eye opening. It wasn't only that we didn't miss having more stuff—we liked the freedom and emphasis on experiences, food, and being in the moment.

A side benefit was that the house was easy to keep neat, because there was no stuff clogging the place up. We felt lighter. We spent our money on food and taking trips, both of which we still talk about ten years later.

CHERYL · RV-ING THROUGH EUROPE

Traveling as we do, we need to pinch pennies. It's easy to get carried away, especially in those first few weeks when you are still in "holiday mode." We free camp as much as possible, whether that's free parking spaces or wild camping. There's plenty out there so it's just a case of planning ahead. After France and the lure of all the attractions there, we try now to stay away from the really touristy places. Small towns and villages are often just as special and pretty, you get a better sense of the culture, and they are a lot less expensive. We also try to travel toll-free options when driving any distance. This can sometimes save money, although often it makes the drive time a little longer, so we weigh which is more cost effective.

We try to be self-sufficient. We have solar panels to run all our electrical appliances and gas for the cooker, heating, and fridge. We make all our meals in the motorhome, avoiding eating out as much as we can, especially in more touristy (and therefore expensive) locations. If we are going out for the day, we try to take a packed lunch. I guess it's all about being sensible. We set a monthly limit, we transfer that amount onto our cards, and we make it last.

LISA · BACKPACKING AROUND THE WORLD

We make sure we travel during shoulder and off seasons, for cheaper flights and cost of living. We research flights about three months in advance and set alerts for watched flights. Skyscanner and Cheap Flights are awesome. We stay in Airbnb's longer than twenty-eight days to get an extended stay discount. For shorter trips we seek out six-person or family dorm accommodations. Those often include a complimentary breakfast.

Rather than spending money on dining out, we invest in cooking lessons to learn how to use the local produce. Cooking lessons are an excellent souvenir of our trip, without creating the stuff that clutters and chokes our lives.

I've also come to realize that even though we won't necessarily admit it to anyone, especially ourselves, we all try to maintain the image that we are successful and accomplished through what we own or how we appear. It takes a strong character to withstand the societal pressure to buckle into "keeping up with the Joneses" mentality. We are very happy with our decision to forego funding that new car and home renovation in favor of a trip around the world. We are grateful for experiencing what living a minimalistic lifestyle can provide—joy and freedom.

AMANDA · LIVES IN MOROCCO

Honestly, we live better here than we did in the US because of stronger purchasing power with our money. Food is MUCH less expensive. We walk a lot more so we don't have the gas expenses. Living with family means no mortgage or rent. The first year we didn't have extra money, so we got by with a basic stovetop for cooking and fans for cooling rather than buying a big oven and air conditioner unit. I think that one big mistake people make is assuming they need to replicate their life when they go abroad. This will cost you a fortune. If you can afford small luxuries, go for it. But otherwise, decide what expenditures are really important to you, and make do with the rest.

21

STAYING CONNECTED
TO YOUR OLD LIFE

Some expats throw off the mantle of their previous existence like an itchy sweater long outgrown. But most of us want to maintain some connection to our old lives. This is easier than it used to be, thanks to technology, but the jury is out on if this effortless way of clicking into old dynamics actually serves us. I wish I'd disconnected more, but it was a challenge considering I was blogging, which necessitates a certain amount of connecting into the ether. I sometimes grew annoyed with myself for watching American movies or TV shows. After all, wasn't I supposed to be soaking this Italian thing all in? But sometimes at the end of a day, when everything was hard, it felt amazing to tune out and not really be anywhere. I told myself it wasn't like I was missing out on anything so late in the evening, but I still felt weird about it.

Ultimately, you'll need to choose what's right for you. What I hope is that you read the experiences of our fellow adventurers and act with intention, rather than just reacting to stimuli. Come up with how you want to envision connecting versus disconnecting. That vision can shift over time, but ask yourself if you actually *want* to change that plan, or if you're just too tired to fight your instincts.

Pay particular attention to what Heather says about social media. I've heard this from so many travelers, and I've watched the same dynamic unfold on friends' Facebook pages. People will have this image that you are some big-shot person living a perfect life in a perfect way, and if you complain about anything, you may well get shot down.

I remember asking for support on Facebook when Siena was struggling and was told by a friend, "You chose this, so now you'll just have to live with it." Not the encouragement and comfort I was looking for. A mutual friend private messaged me and told me how her kid was having a hard time at school, suggesting that maybe it was just the age, and of course it was hard, but it would all be okay. Much better.

This is all to say people's responses to your social media postings may get testy if you either wax too rhapsodic about how lucky you are and/ or complain when you are frustrated, like when it rains the entire week you'd arranged a cabana on a Thai beach. You see what a fine line that is to walk. You have to be happy, but not too happy. Ridiculous! I want you to be authentic and honest and let the chips fall where they may. But if that's hard for you, at least know that when you get flak, we've all been there.

Beyond sharing your new life with your old friends, you need to consider staying connected to who *you* are. That's easy to lose sight of when you are on a grand adventure. Are you the sheepish tourist clinging to the door and apologizing for taking up space? Or are you the bright-eyed explorer later in the day using large gestures to request the meal special posted on the wall? Are you the one dreaming of your featherbed millions of miles away? Or the one bounding out in the morning, ready to greet a slew of new sights and sounds?

Those superficial and artificial distinctions mask a deeper divide—are you the old you or the new you? This is a question complicated by the fact that you may have a fairly good idea of the old you, but the new you is a work in progress.

You don't want to lose who you are. Yes, growth is important, but you need to connect to what matters to you in this world. You have your little twists of fate to kiss goodnight, so that's grounding and reminds you of who you are as a parent, but how about the rest of who you are? What aspects of the old you matter to you and deserve to be woven into this new tapestry of your adventurous life? How do you identify what matters, how do you dig into it to keep it real for you?

Being clear about who you are and what moves you has the added side benefit of connecting you to a logical niche in your new community. That is, if you love organic gardening, you'll find your tribe by seeking out organic markets and scrolling through forums for gardening resources in your area. If you love cooking, ask locals about recipes, ask what's in dishes you enjoy, look for opportunities to take a cooking class. Often locals are so tickled by your appreciation for their cooking that they'll offer to teach you themselves. Don't demure, take them up on it. If you love skiing (remember Rachel's story?) join a group that treks out to ski, learn the vocabulary around skiing and snow. Create a micro-community within your community.

You'll find that being you in a foreign location is far more satisfying than trying to pretend you are a cookie-cutter local. You aren't. It's a difficult row for expats to hoe, and, at the same time, one that we are uniquely suited to—we thrive in liminal space. When we are in our home country, we live on the margins, refusing to blend in and be one with where we are. When we leap into a new wilderness, we can't sink completely, we will always stand out. Becoming comfortable with our role as margin dwellers, and connecting with others who do the same either because they've chosen a similar path or because they don't entirely fit their community of origin is part of the joy and the work of this life we choose. Join the skiers, the aspiring chefs, the organic gardeners in your community.

So while embracing growth and change is a profound part of this process, allow yourself to be *you*.

Keeping up the Fiction

HEATHER'S STORY

I t's good to be prepared to connect with your old life. Then you can disconnect if you want, but you'll have the tools and resources to connect when you have a rotten week and all you want to do is watch your favorite show. For instance, I didn't watch regular TV at all while we were in Milan, but we had access to our iTunes library of movies and shows. We tried various VPN services to be able to watch Netflix/Hulu (they weren't in Italy when we were there) and finally found one that worked well for us, halfway through our second year.

FaceTime was fantastic to keep in touch with our close family and friends and show them around our house and town via iPad. Our kids kept in touch with friends from home via iMessage and FaceTime. Even brief contact seemed grounding for them.

Facebook Groups were great for interacting with friends we met in Italy, to organize outings or have a built-in forum to ask everything from where to find sour cream or kid-friendly hotels.

Social media with people from home, though, was more complicated. On the one hand, it served to connect us to those people who wanted to see and hear every detail of what we did. But people assumed my life was the highlight reel that I chose to share on Instagram or Facebook. The *one* time I let myself be vulnerable and share a struggle I got feedback like, "Oh, it must be sooo hard to live in Italy and travel the world." That bothered me so much that I never let myself be vulnerable like that again, carefully choosing what or how often I shared. Usually I don't care that much what people do or say, but I think because I was struggling so much at the time it made me feel more like I was broken and OMG, why couldn't I just suck it up and enjoy my wonderful Italian life instead of complaining? But there has to be a way to live this crazy double life and be able to enjoy it and receive support in the struggle too.

Even now, when someone asks about the good and bad experiences, I find myself downplaying the hard spots because I don't want to look like a failure or a crazy mess, even to myself. This is why I strongly advise travelers to find friends. Ones you feel safe with and can lean on and thank God for, every single day.

Connecting and Letting Go

CONTRIBUTORS' STORIES

JOHN · RV-ED THROUGH EUROPE FOR ONE YEAR

I am a strong advocate for disconnecting and have presented a TEDx talk on this concept titled "The Power of Time Out." I believe that if you truly want to immerse in your travels, smell the roses, listen to that violist, or connect with your family, then repeated distractions and interactions from "the real world" can only divert your attention away from the pure joy of being in the now. "Email days" at an internet café were fun for a few quick messages from home, but inevitably contained bits of admin and bureaucracy that brought us down. Lose yourself and disconnect as much as possible.

That said, sanity breaks to connect with *you* are important. My wife and I enjoyed what we called "the big day out." We each treasured our alone time so occasionally, when staying in one place for a few days, we took turns exploring museums, sights, going to the cinema, or just aimlessly pottering about while our partner stayed with the kids.

LEWIS FAMILY · LIVED IN MALAYSIA FOR TWO YEARS

Keeping up with news was easy in Malaysia. The BBC world news was available on TV as were many programs from British and USA networks. The Malays are avid supporters of the UK football league—much to the delight of my husband—so that was frequently televised. Even the local people who could speak little English could always speak about football!

I volunteered a lot, which is something that matters to me. Because I was not content to sit at home or socialize all the time, it was also important to me to revive my skills in sewing and other crafts. These were activities I hadn't had time for when my children were young and I was working. We had a pool and local gym facilities that offered classes like yoga. The hard part was that our favorite exercise is walking, and that's challenging when it's 30°C and humid. Sunday afternoons we often ended up walking around one of the large modern air-conditioned shopping centers.

HEATHER · LIVED IN ITALY FOR TWO YEARS

Music and books are extremely important to our mental health and well-being and that was especially true while living abroad. I took way too many books, but I don't regret it. Familiar board games from home were great to have (apparently you can bond over Portland-opoly while living in Italy). Having familiar family activities was a comfort, especially in the rough days.

NICA · SAILED THE CARIBBEAN

We listened to the radio nets every morning for weather and other big news. When we had the Internet, we posted a blog and checked Facebook. Email worked. The important things had a way of sifting into our consciousness, even the news of the massive snowstorm in Charlottesville in January 2010. Honestly, I wish I could live this way now.

Mail is problematic when you're sailing because it can't really catch up with you. We had our parents acting as mail drop and they'd open anything that looked important and email us. We did have one major gear failure, and the manufacturer sent the replacement part to us via someone we "met" via the HAM radio in the Turks and Caicos.

KRISTIN · LIVED IN COSTA RICA, THE NETHERLANDS, AND ARGENTINA FOR ONE YEAR

We didn't really have Internet in Argentina and Costa Rica. Disengaging ironically made it easier to tolerate being separated from family and friends, as we were less aware of their day-to-day lives.

NAOMI · LIVED IN INDIA AND SINGAPORE FOR FOUR YEARS

We had a VPN and used it fastidiously so that I could keep up with some semblance of normalcy around television programming. I can still remember watching the entire series of *Friday Night Lights* and feeling connected to my home town. Our library back home offered audio and digital books—highly recommend that! Other than that, we immersed our children in local television and they soon grew to love Indian cartoons. My news source was Al Jazeera and the online version of NPR news.

SARA · LIVED IN MOROCCO FOR SEVEN YEARS

As our time went on, we became more disconnected with the news. We took the attitude that if it was important we'd hear about it from our friends and family, or in passing conversations. Sure enough, this worked.

22

PARENTING ABROAD

There is nothing like moving abroad to shine a light on how culturally constructed our parenting is. I would never have defined myself as a helicopter parent pre-Italy, but once there, I was uncomfortably aware of my hovering. More than that, I realized where it came from. When my children were young, I might have been able to hoodwink you as I pontificated on the value of letting children fall and scrape their knees so they can learn to dust themselves off and leap up again. But I didn't live that. Why? Because I was just too damned anxious. Their disappointment, discouragement, despair seemed the end of the world to me, a feeling to avoid at all costs.

Now? I'm a lot more relaxed.

Not because I don't care, but because I trust in their innate resilience. I don't long for them to struggle, but I also know a struggle won't kill them. On the contrary, only overcoming a struggle will teach them that they can overcome a struggle. I can tell them until I'm blue in the face that they are strong, but if I intone that while I'm yanking them off the bike before it teeters, well, what will they believe?

This was brought home to me on Nicolas's first day of school after we returned from Italy. Up until this point, his school experiences were limited to nine years of a small private school that caters to honoring the whole child, and then a year in an Italian school that was once a palace (the elementary school was a former seminary), being loved on by teachers and students alike. Now we were idling outside a giant public high school, housed in a former prison. Okay, I've since heard the prison thing is a myth, but it's a myth we were buying as Nicolas slowly shoved his individual pencils into individual slots in his giant binder. Finally, he confessed, "I'm scared I'll get lost."

A fair fear. We'd looped through those halls multiple times together and I still had no idea how to tell what floor I was on. Perhaps the school wasn't the former prison that those things that looked like barbed wire-topped towers would suggest. But it was indeed a warren, a maze.

Time was, his fear would have let loose a blade of ice through my gut. But after a year in Italy, I shrugged and said, "I hope you do." Nicolas gaped at me, sure he was being pranked. I smiled, "Of course you'll get lost. And you'll only stop fearing it once you do it and realize the world doesn't fall apart. Go. You'll be fine."

He went.

He got lost.

He was fine.

Did he learn anything by my shrugging off his fear of failure? Who knows? But I do know I felt a whole lot better about seeing his anxiety as a ring of fire one must leap through to get to the place where the fire evokes less fear. I have to think that at the very least, my lack of anxiety kept him from redoubling his.

I wonder if this wasn't even so much of a conscious "my children will benefit from hard times" realization and more my getting a lot of practice watching my children suffer. I couldn't go storming into the principal's office when Gabe got spanked because I didn't know where the principal's office was, or even if she had one, or really how to pick the principal out of a lineup. I couldn't set up a meeting with Siena's awful math teacher to tell her to lay off, that my daughter was doing the best she could, and that the teacher's sarcastic impatience was not to going help Siena accelerate her comprehension skills. I only knew a handful of those words.

I couldn't solve their problems. And Siena made sure I couldn't fix her internal ones. All my ideas for homesickness, loneliness, and shyness were met with a wail of resistance. She struggled and she chafed and she cried and there was nothing I could do.

And then it would be Tuesday and the sun would rise patiently over our town of pink stone, and Siena woke up with a smile, and it was like the night's storm had never been. I had to grow comfortable with her pain, with all their pain. Not take it on, not panic, not resist it. Just let that pain be, until it ebbed away.

I'm not perfect at that, even with the practice. But I'm better. And even when I do let my children's angst rock me, at least I have the ballast of, "You know this is probably one of those things to let be." I might not always heed that voice, but it's a comfort to have it.

Besides getting out of the way of my children's nascent competence, there were other parenting changes, ones that live on and make my current life more joyous.

One is that I learned that not everyone is special. And that we can live happier lives if specialness is not our goal. It became clear early on that Italians had no such striving to be special. I couldn't understand why Nicolas and Siena's new friends would rave about their art. I love my kids, but they aren't prodigies. Suddenly, I realized. These Italian children didn't feel the need to stand out, to be special. In America, one kid's art ability can make another kid frantic to find their "thing." In this country, we spend so much money and time seeking our kids' talents. This was not the case in Spello, where children are valued just for being children. So they praise each other and delight in each other. One person's success feeds the community.

Marvelous.

Since then, when Gabe complains he's the worst on his soccer team, I don't figure out how to pay for a coach or pull him out of soccer and try to find a sport for him to excel. Instead I tell him that someone has to be bottom of the heap, and who cares? It doesn't reflect how valuable he is. It's just a reflection of some amount of genetic loading, plus how much he's practiced, or maybe even how much he ate that day.

It's a more relaxed way to parent. I don't need my kids to shine. They shine in my heart and that's plenty. Being a good person is so much better than being special.

What an important lesson that was for our family.

I want to hasten to add that there may well be aspects of your parenting that you do not abandon to fit in with local culture. That's wise in my book. I'm not in favor of throwing out all your cultural norms so much as I want to encourage you to insert a pause to learn to parent in a way that is most authentic to you.

For instance, I knew about Italian breakfasts before we left. I fully intended to stretch and yawn in the morning, before reaching for the cookie bag and proffering it to each child as they marched out the door. When in Rome and all that. But I couldn't do it. I couldn't bear the idea of sending my children into the thicket of Italian public school with about eighty calories of simple carbs in their system. I come from a community that values protein, and I lived that. Eggs for my children. Which made my mornings not the relaxed time I anticipated, but I couldn't have done it any other way.

So definitely have some ideas about what matters to you before you go, but be ready to shake that conception up when you land. Somehow the world looks different when you are making breakfast in it.

How Our Parenting Changed

THE WAGONERS' STORY

O ur parenting has changed a great deal after traveling and moving abroad. Before, we lived the typical American suburban life, complete with the big house and a yard, two cars, and a dog. We both worked full-time jobs, plus some extra hours. The kids were very busy with school and activities, and we had very little time for a true family life. We were all busy going different directions and trying to "divide and conquer" our responsibilities. As parents, we constantly worried about the kids going beyond our comfort zone in our safe neighborhood or about strangers or spending too much time playing.

Our life now, in Spain, is all about quality family time and allowing the kids to be kids. We have been in Spain for five years, plus one year of nomadic travel in Southeast Asia. We have become far more relaxed as parents and less worried about the kids being perfect and belonging to everything, and we have also relaxed knowing we don't have to be perfect parents either. Our town in Spain has a population of about 30,000 people, and we don't worry at all about crime or safety. The atmosphere here is to allow kids to be part of the family and to just be kids. They go wherever you go and are accepted. They don't have to sit still at a restaurant and "behave" or be quiet. The kids just play out front or alongside a restaurant with other kids or hang out at the table with the adults.

As parents, we are now far more relaxed and accepting of change, and that trickles down. Our kids are very active. They know that we can trust them and that they are allowed to be human and make mistakes. They have many friends, but can also hold conversations with adults on just about any topic. They are well-rounded, understanding that life doesn't need to be perfect and there's room to accommodate the unexpected.

Parenting on Foreign Soil

CONTRIBUTORS' STORIES

SARAH · LIVES IN THE NETHERLANDS AFTER YEARS OF WORLDSCHOOLING

Moving abroad changed the way I parent. It quickly became obvious that everything—from what to feed a baby to how to handle a tantrum to expected behavior of children in restaurants—was open to cultural interpretation. I first moved abroad with my kids as a new mom, and noticing these differences made me realize that there is no one right way to parent. After all, kids all over the world turn out just fine, in spite of the many different parenting norms. So I let complete strangers give my children candy on the bus in Italy. I let my kids walk to the corner store alone in Tunisia. I closed my eyes and breathed and let them ride bicycles without helmets in the Netherlands. The kids survived. In fact, they thrived. And so did I.

NELL · LIVED IN FRANCE FOR ONE YEAR

At ages seven and nine, the children's main desires were access to ice cream and finding other kids to play with. And that play was wonderful—not based on electronics but outside, all day, no matter the weather. They made forts, constructed skateboard ramps to hurt themselves on, battled with seed-pod grenades, rode bikes, took off their clothes and painted themselves with mud.

That freedom and focus on the outdoors was something we all missed terribly after returning.

AMANDA · LIVES IN MOROCCO

We quickly realized families here don't adhere to schedules or routines.

But our kids had a bedtime hours earlier than other kids, we had expectations, and they needed to participate in family life. Eventually, we realized we had to loosen up and relinquish some of our American need to schedule so our kids could be like local kids and not alienated.

RACHEL · LIVED IN SPAIN FOR ONE YEAR

In Spain, our kids were learning without us, riding around the city on public transportation, in a culture where kids have more autonomy. They gained confidence in overcoming the language barrier and the challenges of living in a foreign country. At the end of our year, my 14-year-old daughter flew home to the US through London, alone and without the unaccompanied minor service, through customs and the border and with lots of bags. She did it all without batting an eye.

SARA · LIVED IN MOROCCO FOR SEVEN YEARS

One of the best things that came out of our time abroad was a re-envisioned view of parenting. I felt like parenting abroad placed a microscope on my parenting style. I was constantly witnessing other approaches to parenting, some of which I admired greatly, and others that made me cringe, but ultimately they brought into focus how I wanted to mother my children. Having moved from New York City, I think I was a bit of a "helicopter" mom. In New York, I had to be, or my daughter could easily run into an avenue in the blink of an eye. In Morocco I was encouraged to let my kids roam. One Swedish father told me that his goal for his children was for them to make every kind of mistake possible while they lived under his roof, so that he could support them through the natural consequence, rather than try to protect his kids from mistakes and accidents, only to have them struggle with how to overcome similar situations alone later in life. He suggested that many Americans do the latter. This idea hit home for me, and I've made this concept a part of my parenting.

On the other hand, there were numerous parenting approaches that I just as adamantly did not condone. During our time in Morocco, I regularly saw parents hit their children. This was hard to witness, and hard for my kids to witness as well. Thank goodness for our family phrase of "every family is different" because sometimes that's all I could say so that I was not conveying judgment. I continuously aimed to teach my kids about differences with an open mind, because ultimately I could not understand what had led parents to hit, either in their upbringing or culture.

There was also a prevalent parenting approach in Morocco of not respecting children's boundaries. Whether it was telling the kids how they felt—they were hot, cold or hungry—without giving the child an opportunity to speak for themselves, or forcing the kids to give kisses and hugs when that wasn't comfortable. I consciously worked to make sure my children felt their boundaries were protected. It was difficult. People criticized me for allowing the kids to politely say, "No, thank you," when a stranger would try to touch their head or kiss them on the cheeks. Of course, I explained norms to my kids, I encouraged them to loosen them in situations where it was advantageous for them to experience the cultural difference. But in general, I maintained that if they felt their personal boundaries were being crossed they could politely decline. I would be the one to apologize; they did not have to.

I feel that parenting abroad requires constant attention to one's family values, while never assuming that another family holds those same values.

23

THE DAILY ROUTINE

I ronically, your vivid adventure is a reminder of how much of life is made up of mundanities. No matter how extreme and glorious your road, much of that road will still involve feeding whiny children and cleaning grass stains out of clothes. Those things can be harder or easier depending on where you are, the language divide, and the culture of amenities where you've landed. It's something you don't think about when you are curled up in American suburbia, scanning through Airbnb listings—life, even on the most extraordinary adventure, is still made up of necessities and obligations. It's important to remember, here, now, because families often experience some amount of a letdown in their new lives at some point. Maybe the day getting dark so early sinks your mood. Or you're tired and don't want to explain to the butcher how you want your beef ground. Or maybe you're hauling yourself out of bed to make breakfast, and you catch yourself muttering, "Wait, wasn't I doing this back home?" In short, when you realize that this life you are living is just not what you imagined, it can feel like you are rubbed raw.

It's okay.

Every (honest) expat story includes low moments. Teenage tantrums, couples sniping at each other while lost and running out of gas, bullying landlords, exhaustion, blowing up at little things because the big ones are too scary to confront, confusion about why anyone thought this would be worth all the fuss and bother.

All of that is simply part of the process.

For me, it hit in late winter. I suspect that timing matches up with many expats, particularly those who do the summer-to-summer gap year in a place where December is cold. By the end of winter, I had been away from the things that defined me and my family and "home" for about six months. The short days definitely affected me, and it was hard to graze my fingers lovingly against the pink walls of Spello when they were weeping from the pervasive fog. My language had plateaued at a clunky phase that felt impossible to budge. I had cabin fever from being stuck indoors, safe from the rain-slicked cobblestones. I loathed the sight of the drying rack set up in front of the radiator so that socks would dry in two days rather than three (was a dryer really so much to ask?). I was irritable at most things, but mostly myself because what was wrong with me that I wasn't enjoying my dream? Even cooking felt flat and boring. Same old meals. Same old routine. Different zip code.

Luckily, spring arrives on the early side in central Italy. Before I knew quite what was happening, my daughter transformed from a homesick shell of a child to a young woman filled with joy and wonder at the poppies blossoming across the valley. The shutters around the gelato display case were thrown open. And best of all, people filled the streets again. My Italian melted into an easier place, and I threw myself into the opportunities that spring brought—asking virtual strangers if they would take me asparagus picking and questioning new products in the butcher case. Suddenly, I was caught breathless by the beauty of my life.

It helped that spring brought visiting groups of friends. It's tempting to assume that this filled my emotional well, but really, the friendships I formed in Spello were quite sustaining. Rather, our friends brought fresh perspective. They were in love with Spello, and that helped me see anew the place I fell in love with. I started taking photographs again, documenting the beauty and color I saw all around me, which allowed me to keep alive that sense of discovery I had when friends were pulling me by the elbow to gesture widely to another magnificent view.

This is why I advocate for taking a beat and considering where you are and how it fits with what you want, rather than self-flagellating for not feeling the way you expected to feel. Stepping back and thinking about how to get your bearings is far more constructive than berating yourself for having the doldrums.

It's important to recognize those stalled moments for what they are—temporary. As I mentioned in the "Staying Connected with Your Old Life" chapter, your friends back home may snipe at you if you post any sort of blues on Facebook. They'll insist that you should be happy all the time because you're living a fantasy! Why can't you just enjoy it God Dammit, instead of complaining?!?

They don't get it.

But we do. No matter what your adventure—sailing, RVing, plopping in Spain—your days will begin to take on a routine and yes, even some measure of monotony. Own it, address it, and start looking for joy again. Be clear about what you want for *you*, what would make this experience fit what you need *now*, not what you thought you needed while you were in line at the embassy.

How to Wait

NICOLAS'S STORY FROM LIVING IN SPELLO

How did it begin?

Well, my pre-piano-lesson tactic is normally to waste my time until about thirty seconds before I have to go, in which time I gather my music, find my shoes, fumble with my laces, and get out the door. So in this hectic getting out, it's really no wonder that I'd forget the keys that my parents told me to bring five times already.

So, I forget the keys. I walk out with that nagging "you forgot something," in the corner of my mind, but I steel myself and continue onward.

I arrive at my piano lesson and everything goes as usual until about ten minutes before the end. At that point, the nagging suspicion has turned into full-blown knowledge that something is missing. But what? Five minutes later, I realize. My keys! Of course! I must have smacked myself a little too obviously because my friend sitting next to me, asks in slow English "What is it?" I manage to get out in ragged Italian that I forgot the keys to my house. He looks surprised, and immediately starts to think about how we could remedy the situation. He asks if I know my parents' phone number. I think, "No, but their number is in my backpack, but that's at home, so..." I say, "No." He thinks a little bit longer, but there's really no way to fix the situation. He looks disappointed, so I reassure him with the fact that I'll buy some chocolate, and I'll be fine, because everything's okay with chocolate.

After the lesson, I make sure to fulfill my promise with two packs of peanut M&Ms (one pack if a family member is reading this). I amble up the hill; after all, I've got nothing but time.

I reach the steps of our house. No lights seem to be on, and I begin to feel dejected. I halfheartedly ring the buzzer. No answer. I try again. No answer. By this time, I only have one pack of M&Ms left. I make a mental note to go slower on this one. I sit on the stoop for a while before hesitantly ringing the buzzer of our downstairs neighbor. Silence. One more time; still nothing. By now the sky looks as if a bottle of ink spilled on it, staining the blue with swirling darkness.

After a little bit more sitting, I see one of the nice old ladies who live in the alley near us. She's coming up the hill, two black-and-white cats following at her heels. As she gets close to me, she calls, "*Buona sera!*" and we talk a bit, about school, about cats...wait. "What are you doing out here?"

she asks. I say the phrase that will become my mantra for the rest of the evening: "My parents are out and I don't have the keys to get back in." She nods gravely, then realizes I'm wearing a short-sleeved shirt. She says, as will so many others, "*Senti freddo?*" or "Aren't you cold?" I tell her, "No, it's not that bad, don't worry." She understands my novice Italian, and after emptying her trash into the trash container, begins to walk back down the hill. One of the cats, the one named Veronica, stays for another minute to keep me company. After about a minute, she trots back to her home, and I'm left alone. Just me and my chocolate wrappers.

After a few more minutes and more hopeless doorbell-ringing, a few of the elderly ladies see me. The one who already met me has explained my situation to them. They conference with each other for a few moments, before stepping up to me, one by one, and offering their ideas. I get asked in Italian whether I wanted to come stay in their houses multiple times, to which I reply, "No, they'll be back soon...thank you, though." They look disappointed that they can't help, and talk among themselves some more. After a minute or so, one comes out of her house carrying a jacket. She offers it to me (although it's not so much an offer as an instruction to take it), and I take it, thanking her profusely. She smiles and tells me to just come by her house when my parents return.

The next fifteen or so minutes will be cut out of this entry because they consist of me sitting on the stoop, huddled up against the cold.

After that oh-so-engrossing chunk of time, I walk up to the parking lot to check if anyone is there. My family isn't, but instead I see one of the aforementioned ladies and a new one, who gives me a quizzical look as if to say, "ONE jacket? Not enough! What is that child thinking?" The other one explains my situation, and the woman responds, in shock, "Well, come to my house!" I decline, saying that it was very kind but my parents would be back soon. As I walk down, I hear the lady from before telling the other, "He told that to us a half hour ago!" True.

After a few more minutes of waiting, I see my little sister running down from the parking lot. I hastily greet her and run down to return the jacket to the lady. After that, I am let into the house by my parents, who aren't too pleased with my key-forgetting.

But really, it was all their fault.

The Day Abroad

CONTRIBUTORS' STORIES

JOHN · RV-ED THROUGH EUROPE FOR A YEAR

Sleep-in, breakfast, empty the chemical toilet and refill the water tanks, drive somewhere having long breaks on the way, sightsee, find a café for lunch, camp up early before witching hour, wine o'clock with camping neighbors, dinner prep, eat under the stars, and early bed. The most grinding aspect of the daily routine was showers—most campsites have those annoying timers, coin-operated machines, or push buttons, all impossible to use by small kids. Consequently, Mandy and I took turns each night getting wet while pushing the screaming children under disappointing shower sprays. It was a great night when it wasn't my turn.

NICA · SAILED THE CARIBBEAN

Each morning began with checking the weather on the radio. Make coffee and drink it in the cockpit. If it's a moving day, get underway. Kids wake up when they want. Fishing, shopping, laundry, school, reading, projects, cooking, exploring, cleaning...maybe a blog post or check of the Internet. Always we were discussing the weather and what our options were in terms of anchorage or safety. Afternoon snorkeling or beach walks.

Shower by jumping in the water and soaping up and rinsing off, then a fresh water rinse and clean(ish) clothes. Sundowners in the cockpit every night, with friends or just by ourselves. Catching fish and sharing it with friends, after an hour of cleaning it on the side deck and washing fish blood and guts back to the ocean. Stargazing on the foredeck, a sky filled with endless pinpoints of light.

Of course, there were nasty weather days, when we were pretty much confined to the cabin, watching movies, reading, or making muffins. There were the occasional rough nights at anchor, up listening to the wind and checking the anchor holding, the panic of hearing a boat dragging. Hopping in the dinghy to help with that dragging boat, even at 11 PM.

NELL · LIVED IN FRANCE FOR A YEAR

A typical day for our family in a small village in the Dordogne? Up in the dark to make coffee and hot chocolate. The kids would eat toast and jam. My husband walked them to school. I would drive about fifteen minutes to the market and spend at least an hour going from stall to stall, trying my best to chat with the vendors as I figured out what to have for dinner depending on what looked good that day.

French class in the afternoon with a teacher who knew exactly which things to correct and which mistakes to let slide so as not to discourage us. And a class of expats from all over the world, a smart and funny group.

I walked to school to pick up the kids, noticing how after-school pickup was bedlam, with kids and dogs running into the street. Very unlike the ultra-regimented systems in the US. Every day I asked about the school lunch menu and the kids would tell me—some days rapturously—details about the three-course meal they had eaten, before the hour-long recess in the middle of the school day. Since the kids didn't have school on Wednesdays, a different typical day had us in the car, out for exploration, headed to see cave paintings or a castle or something odd like the Walnut Museum.

CHERYL · RV-ING THROUGH EUROPE

A typical day begins with us waking up when the dog decides it's time to go for a walk, usually 7:30. Because of the tight living space, when one of us is up, everyone is up. We fold the beds away so we have somewhere to sit and eat breakfast. Breakfast tends to be whatever bread or pastry is customary where we are parked. France has been our favorite so far. I could eat croissants every morning for the rest of my life, and the kids thought each day was Christmas with *pain au chocolat* for their daily breakfast.

After that, we either plan our exploring for the day or head off in our home-on-wheels to a new destination. We try not to drive longer than four hours between places for the sake of the kids and the dogs. We haven't got a set route or timescale; we are fluid and plan only one country ahead. When we get to that country, we spend a day or two researching where we want to go and what we want to see while we are here. Then we plan a basic order to follow. If our plans change or we discover something else on the way, then we just simply change route.

Other people probably prefer having a detailed and mapped out route, but we like to take each day as it comes. We spend roughly one month in each country, but if we want to stay longer (or a shorter) then we just adapt our plans and go with it.

TANIA · ROAD-TRIPPING THROUGH EUROPE

A typical day starts with breakfast together. Sometimes we send the kids to pick up rolls at a nearby bakery, or one of us wakes up early to make a big breakfast. Eating French toast and fruit salad our first morning in southern France, on the balcony overlooking the Pyrenees, was a morning I won't ever forget.

After having breakfast and planning our day, we usually spend our mornings working and learning. Then after lunch, we usually get out with the kids. For us, learning happens both inside and outside, and outside is where all of us are happiest. We'll walk around town, go for a hike or bike ride, walk the dog on the beach or whatever the area offers. We spend our days trying to live as the locals would and enjoying wherever we are.

GABRIELLA · LIVES IN MEXICO

Our children are enrolled in school, so our days are pretty routine. Kids are on the yellow bus by 7 AM and return at 2:30 PM. In the interim, Vernon and I work on our businesses from home or from an oceanfront café, work out, run errands, or perhaps have a leisurely brunch. Once our kids are back from school, there's homework and a little homeschool, and then they head out to ride bikes or play at the park. Two days a week the kids go to *futbol* practice. I cook a lot, though it tends to be my healthy standards from home. I have yet to learn how to cook the local cuisine. After a year of living here, you would think I would have, wouldn't you? My children are pretty basic eaters, and it's too hot to cook every day, so I don't cook a whole lot of fancy new foods. We eat out for that. I would like to learn how to make tamales. I don't particularly like them, but the process is fascinating.

After dinner, it's bedtime, around 8 PM.

On the weekends, our daughter takes ballet every Saturday from 9 AM to 12 PM. In the evenings, we go to a local Spanish-language story time. Sundays, we typically have family day, which includes watching church on the computer, going to the beach, movies, or park. While it's a magical life, it's also somewhat routine and mundane.

24

A SPOT OF ADVICE

I can't hear the word "advice" without thinking of Helen in E.M. Forster's *Howard's End*, "I require no more advice."

And you don't.

No matter how much advice you accept or ignore, there will still be moments that feel insurmountable. In those moments, you will marshal your reserves, and you will solve the problem. A blessing, since part of the adventure is figuring it out for yourself.

So my advice is stay loose, stay flexible. Push past what seems rigid and unyielding. If you can't get a visa to Spain, but you can get one to Costa Rica, consider it. If the local International School winds up being a snooty band of expats that keeps you from connecting with your neighbors, consider the public school. If the idea of sailing gets your heart pitter-pattering, but you've never sailed and live far from the sea, consider moving, taking lessons, saving for a boat. If the apartment you booked gets rented out from beneath you mere weeks before school starts, ask at the local bar where a real estate office is and march in with a willingness to give up your hope of a garden for something closer to the town center. In short, don't get rigid. Watch your tendency to get inflexible in the face of the unknown.

Take what's given and find novel ways to make it work for you.

Another habit I'd advocate for is abandoning over-thinking. It's tricky because planning a move abroad requires so much frontal cortex activity, it's easy to adopt a pattern of checking, double checking, and panicking about triple checking. Parenting can be the same, especially in those early years of stocking diaper bags and keeping track of feedings. The problem is, life isn't really suited to that kind of minute analyzing and hamster-wheel consideration. Over-thinking is as muting to the mind as a straight-jacket is to the body. I know whereof I speak when I say that if you plan and check what you want to say to your neighbor in the street, the conversation will run off without you. Ask a stupid question, pop into the café without rehearsing what you'll say, go into the bike store without knowing what the rental process is like in your new country. You may say it or do it wrong, and someone will give you feedback, but as you are a fully formed adult human, you can accept that course correction with a smile of thanks and move on.

Over-thinking can sometimes be a by-product of perfectionism. You might not consider yourself a perfectionist because perfectionism and Type A/high-strung personalities are often confused. So let me change the frame a bit. If you call up a swim center and sign Sally up for group swim lessons on the day that it's convenient for you to drive her, without soliciting reviews on swim instructors or weighing the advantages and disadvantages of group versus private lessons or recruiting a buddy to make the experience more palatable for Sally, you are likely not a perfectionist. If you are having friends over for dinner and you give your menu a scant few minutes thought and your centerpieces not one, you are likely not a perfectionist. If you are choosing a hotel in Paris and you pick one that is in your price range without comparing reviews of the included breakfast, the proximity to a revered cheese shop, and the orientation of the room to the street, you are likely not a perfectionist.

Which must be nice. I myself am a total perfectionist and a typical Wednesday might consist of all the over-thinking in the above paragraph. At least I know it, and work to temper my tendencies. I can recognize when the monster of perfectionism is stirring. I recognize that flutter of anxiety, and I know it means that I'll no doubt be "what if"-ing and "what about"-ing something awful if I don't steer this ship into friendlier waters. I have found it expedient at that moment to forcefully but lovingly say to my brain, "Get over yourself, it doesn't amount to a hill of beans" (my inner voice, as it turns out, is surprisingly folksy) and then fling myself into a situation before I can over-prepare.

For example, in the expat context, if I'm standing in the *alimentari* and I'm wondering what the difference is between the grappas, and I catch myself starting to practice how to get Corrado's attention and how I'll phrase the question and evaluating which label looks better, I remind myself that my stalling is buttering no parsnips. It's time to make hay while the sun is shining, already! And then I'll ask the next person I make eye contact with. There hasn't yet been a time I've regretted forcing myself to impulsively engage rather than slowly drown in the miasma of my insecurity.

The secret is valuing actions over perfection. When you make *trying* the goal, it's much easier. When you make trying to release perfectionism the goal, *everything* gets easier.

One more plug for letting go of over-thinking. Not to freak you out here, but I want to remind you that your children are always watching you. If you over-think, over-rehearse, over-plan, you are setting your children up to do the same, sure, but there is one more side effect. You may be reinforcing their own fear that they can't handle difficult situations. Think about it, if you run yourself ragged trying to create the ideal playdate for Johnny, then Johnny may well begin to believe that he is fragile and in need of coddled circumstances. Throw him into the deep end of the pool (metaphorically speaking, please), and Johnny will learn that you believe he has what it takes to cope with less than optimal circumstances. Even if the playdate is a dud because you failed to get construction paper, it's better than a seamless playdate that your child watches you over-plan.

So, let yourself go a little. Be clear on your goals for yourself in this process, and consider the value of increasing flexibility, decreasing over-thinking, and embracing imperfection. But if you are like me, and some-times find yourself fixating and fretting and ruminating, remember: Don't be too hard on yourself. Note it and move on. Berating yourself will get you nowhere. And anyway, making a mistake is better than a stick in the eye.

The Value of a Good Goodbye

NAOMI'S STORY

I n our community of internationally mobile families, there is often talk about the term "leaving well." What IS leaving well, you might ask? It's the practice of gracefully and artfully (and intentionally) navigating from one place to another. The act of moving often conjures up images of boxes and piles of paperwork, and let's not forget the sound of packing tape as it's ripped from the roll. The art of leaving well, however, offers opportunities to honor the time spent and memories created in a place you're leaving.

There is a reason that we don't all practice leaving well when we move to a new location. You see, our brains are wired to protect us from fear and sadness, and so it is preferable to focus on whatever is new or exciting. In settings with an upcoming relocation, fear and sadness often align with the place we are leaving, and new and exciting match more closely with the new home. My advice to families is this: Rather than ignoring the pain that is associated with leaving a beloved place, tackle that goodbye head-on.

One of the first things our family does on leave-taking is identify a list of the places we want to visit again to say goodbye. Typically, this includes our library, a favorite restaurant, a local coffee shop, and our favorite thrift shop or second hand store. It has also included nearby nature walk spots, and in one place we called home, a post office! Once we've identified the locations, we clear time in our schedule and we revisit those locations. Often, we take selfies of ourselves in front of the place, or with our favorite employees. If our children were younger, I can imagine we would hand THEM the camera to allow them to capture memories in their own way. We eat our favorite foods or collect keepsakes from the parks or purchase a memento from the shops. It may seem silly, but it allows us to intentionally stamp and imprint our hearts with those locations, and reduces any regret for not making time for those practices.

We also schedule and plan our own goodbye parties. Instead of asking someone else to take on that responsibility, or end up with party details that don't suit our family, we put our heads together and plan something that provides an opportunity for our favorite people to see us off, and say goodbye. We make sure we tell friends what they have meant to us, and if language precludes that, at least let them know through a touch and a warm expression. Often, we split these into several different events—perhaps a sleepover for one of our children, or meeting at a restaurant or movie for the teenagers. Nothing says "easy" like a happy hour (at home with adult friends), especially if the new location doesn't allow for the shipment of your alcohol collection.

Regardless of how you decide to say goodbye to a community, at its simplest form of a tradition, comes the practice and the intention. Make space in your life—amidst the busyness of packing and researching the new digs—to make leaving well a part of your relocation.

What We Wish We Knew Beforehand

CONTRIBUTORS' STORIES

TANIA · ROAD-TRIPPING THROUGH EUROPE

While we loosely stuck to our plan, we learned early on the importance of flexibility. We planned to have all our houses booked before we left, and I'm very happy that didn't happen. It was an asset to stay in some places longer and cut other stays short. Plus, a month into the trip, just as we were approaching Copenhagen, we got a cancellation notice from our Airbnb. There were no affordable houses left in town, so we turned around and headed to southern France, where we found an incredible last-minute deal on a villa with a pool. We ended up having a great two weeks in this tiny French town that we never would have found if our Copenhagen plans hadn't fallen through. After that, we knew we needed to stay flexible.

HEATHER · LIVED IN ITALY FOR TWO YEARS

The summer we arrived, Chris was working, and I was in this new town, new country, new house with the two kids and two dogs and lots of bugs and no A/C. I was trying to figure out things like which bottle was the laundry soap and which was the fabric softener, and how to run my tiny washing machine without blowing the fuse. Now, of course, I laugh, but at the time it drove me crazy.

We are from a high desert climate and Milan is humid, so the heat was unbearable and made us all super sticky and grumpy. Sometimes the kids and I would go drive (terrifying at that moment in the timeline) just so we could have A/C. By the time the summer was over, Abby was so sick of being "stuck with us," she practically ran into school.

We had imagined a summer spent exploring and getting settled, making friends with neighbors, and eschewing an expat community. What we didn't know was that the International School community leaves for the entire summer as soon as school gets out. That was an essential support system I didn't realize I would require.

After our experience that first crazy summer, I have advised several people to time their move to when school starts. Ahhh, hindsight.

NELL · LIVED IN FRANCE FOR ONE YEAR

I wish we had heeded the advice not to speak English to each other except in dire emergencies. It would have ramped up our language learning so much, which would have made everything even better.

ESTELLE · CROSS-GENERATIONAL LIVING IN ITALY

First order of business in any destination: Write down the emergency numbers for ambulance, police, fire, and hospital. Make a dry run to the nearest hospital. Travel means new habits, new stairs, new knives, new germs, etc., which means increased vulnerability. Be prepared.

CHERYL · RVING THROUGH EUROPE

I recommend UK travelers to Europe register for an EHIC card, which grants access to medical treatment in all EU countries without the need for travel insurance. Having your child hurt or sick in a foreign country where you don't speak the language is horrendously stressful. The EHIC card has made things easier.

NAOMI · LIVED IN INDIA AND SINGAPORE FOR FOUR YEARS

One practical tip I have is to make sure that you have all necessary and required immunizations BEFORE you leave your home country, as sourcing those in your host country may be difficult. This can be particularly important for school enrollment.

I wish we had taken less "stuff" with us. The only things we really needed could have fit in our suitcases. The hassle and stress of packing up your lives into shipping containers are more easily set aside if you are clearer on what matters.

From a practical standpoint, I am so glad I researched and connected with people in both locations before we landed. We walked off the airplane into the arms of a mini-community, ready to help us settle in.

LEWIS FAMILY · LIVED IN MALAYSIA FOR TWO YEARS

Henry's employer managed our visa process to live in Malaysia, but we needed to renew the visas, as well as apply for visas to visit other Southeast Asian countries. I would advise soon-to-be expats to keep track of their visa expiration date and allow plenty of time to coordinate with consulates.

I wish I had taken more time to research the country and the culture we were going to. I also wish I'd thought ahead about how I'd use my time in Kuala Lumpur. I could have been more proactive in about how to use my social work skills.

SARA · LIVED IN MOROCCO FOR SEVEN YEARS

My suggestion to those looking to enroll their kids in International Schools is to research the teaching approach at the school. It is easy to look at the curriculum and check that important subjects are taught, but it's another thing to understand how that information will be given to your child. I remember a friend telling me about her 5-year-old son coming home from his French school with a big X through his drawing because he had drawn the branches of his tree purple. My friend went to speak with the teacher who insisted that kids must learn exactly how things are in the world, with no personal interpretation. Needless to say, my creative and curious kids did not attend a French school.

KIRSTY · ROAD-TRIPPED THROUGH NORTHERN AFRICA AND CENTRAL ASIA FROM HER ADOPTED HOME IN ABU DHABI

I wish we had traveled slower, with more down time. But we had a family commitment further down the line that required complex logistics, so we had to sacrifice time, resources, and miles. Our best times were when we traveled slowly and soaked up places.

I'm glad we listened to ourselves about what countries to visit and used our own judgment. Otherwise, we would have missed so much.

AMANDA · LIVES IN MOROCCO

Have way more money set aside than you think you'll need and be as outgoing as possible.

NICA · SAILED THE CARIBBEAN

Pick a date to go and GO. There is always more to do on a boat than you have time for, and if you wait for everything to be perfect you will never ever go. No matter how prepared you are, casting off those docklines is always a leap of faith.

So, go. Go small. Go simple.

Go now.

PART FOUR

COMING HOME

25

ROSE, THORN, AND BUD

U nless you've decided to remain in your new location, you'll eventually be packing up to come home. As if waking up in somebody else's dream, the adventure will just be...over. I know, it will seem utterly impossible. How can these people, this place, be part of your history rather than part of your life?

It's so much to process, some find it easier not to process at all.

But I don't recommend that.

Like talking about your day around the dinner table, thinking about your experience helps you make sense of it. It allows the flurry of images to form themselves into understandable pages in the photo album of your mind. It helps you hang onto the memories, and formulate your takeaway messages.

Our local Montessori school helps children learn to process by thinking of experiences as having a rose, thorn, and bud. The rose is the highlight, the thorn is the hard patch, and the bud is something that is in transition, that you are still mulling, or that you are looking forward to.

It's a useful construct for processing an experience as small as a day at the beach and as large as a chapter in your family narrative.

My roses were many, but mostly bloomed with the spring poppies. The Infiorata festival where we spent the night laying flower petals on the street in intricate patterns alongside our neighbors, the air scented with fennel and coffee. The next day, standing with our team as the priest and his procession walked over the flower carpets, and realizing that the priest consecrated our work by (essentially) ruining it, which prompted me to consider the holiness of imperfection. Regular Aperol spritzes on the patio of Bar Tullia watching the swallows dip and swirl in the cobalt sky. Hearing Siena chatting with her friends in Italian, fluidly and freely. Watching Gabe play cards with the old men, who pretended disgust when he "won." Nicolas's piano competition with his duet partner; watching him manage the whole process and play intricate music as if he were just another Italian boy.

Our travels were also definite roses. My kids came up with silly songs and their "harmonizing" was our soundtrack as we meandered the green hills of Normandy. Then there were the scents and flavors of wild oregano in Sicily and crisply sweet waffles in Brussels. The thumping of flamenco guitar that filled my ribcage in Seville. At each trip there was the surge of gratitude to return to our pink village perched above the Umbrian valley, the church bells pealing out a merry welcome.

The biggest rose in a garden just full of blooms was growing into feeling that I *belonged* to a place I hadn't known existed a scarce few years before. A feeling that culminated when our friends and neighbors threw us a party, and presented us with the seal of Spello that commemorated our citizenship to this town that had stolen our hearts.

But there were thorns. Of course there were. All of those centered on moments of panic coupled with feeling marginalized by my lack of language skills. When Siena refused to go to school and in my state of overwhelmed demoralization, I threw her backpack to her feet, sending her into school with tears in her eyes—that I have yet to forgive myself for. When Gabe's raging ear infection sent us to the pediatric wing of the hospital where we had to contend with roving clowns and a doctor who grew rapidly disoriented at our lack of fluency and flew out of the room at the sound of an alarm, leaving Gabe hooked up to an incessantly beeping heartbeat monitor. When Keith was hospitalized, and we misunderstood the word "TAC," and thought the doctors were afraid his pneumonia would lead to a heart attack, when in actuality they wanted to schedule a CT scan.

While the roses and thorns have stayed the same through the five years since our return, the buds have shifted. At the time of our leave-taking, I would have said our bud was the anticipation of our return to Spello. For at least a year after our return, I hungered for it. Now, the pain of being gone is less profound, and that bud is only a bud when we have a trip in the works. Today, I'd say the bud of our year abroad is the seed that it planted for travel as a dedicated pursuit, not just a cavalier by-product of "what should we do this summer?" We are always looking for opportunities to stretch our vision through travel. Since our return we've traveled to Southeast Asia, Quebec (twice, as it turns out to be a relatively inexpensive way to be surrounded by French), the west coast of the United States, and we are gearing up for our third trip back to Spello. Our big bud, however, is one we hadn't even considered when we left Spello, but wouldn't have been on our radar if not for that experience, and that is our year around the world slated for 2020. Living in Spello and traveling so easily from there made us realize how vast and fascinating the world is. We don't want to limit our travels to swinging through a country, we want to dig into destinations. Hence our plan to live a month in each of twelve places. We don't pretend that we'll get a real understanding of any place in that time (which is a hard value to relinquish, I sometimes wonder if settling into one place again would be preferable), but we want a real taste.

There's a part of me that places importance on a global trip because we'll be empty-nesters in seven years, and Keith and I want eventually to spend at least half of the year outside this country. Italy seems like the best fit for us, but I relish the opportunity to sample the wares of other parts of the world, just to make sure. Much like I stroll into the *gelateria* sure I'll be ordering pistachio, but I like the agony of indecision when I'm offered tastes of chocolate or green apple.

I asked our fellow adventurers to process their journeys by thinking of the wonderful moments, the hard moments, and what they have on their horizon, so you not only get an idea of what a journey abroad looks like through the rear-view mirror, but also to create a framework for processing your own experience.

How to Backpack the World with Four Teenage Girls

LISA'S STORY

W e are an average Aussie family of six, currently nearing the end of our year-long backpacking trip around the world. Before this epic venture, we had backpacked to countries in Southeast Asia for shorter periods of time. In fact, it was our five week trip to Vietnam in 2012 that planted the seed for long-term travel. While in Hoi' An, we met an English family of five who had been traveling for eleven months. I had never heard of a family traveling with their kids long term. Could we do that too? For a year?

Meanwhile, I transitioned from being a stay-at-home mom to working full-time at a lucrative marketing job, which allowed us to finally pay off our debt. We decided to put off our travel dreams and instead use our growing surplus on a new car and house renovation. After all, that's what people do.

Yet, something continued gnawing inside my heart. One night, I whispered to Steve, "When we're old, like eighty, do you think we'll regret not choosing to travel for a year around the world with the kids?" And Steve responded, "*Yes!*" So the next day we tore up the renovation plans and turned our focus to planning and saving for a one-year family travel adventure.

We chose backpacking for the freedom, flexibility, and lower price tag. With our four girls schooling via Distance Education, we planned to stay two to three months in each country (Spain, Portugal, Cyprus, India, and Vietnam) so that we could school during the week and explore on breaks. This meant that each home base had to include exceptional Wi-Fi, which limited our range of budget options and became especially complicated in rural India and Morocco. Plus, we needed a suitcase full of books, modules, and study tools.

Given how much we move, it's astonishing how easily we've been able to integrate into new communities. Having four daughters is an easy ice-breaker, especially in Asian countries where people love kids and place a high value on family. Nonetheless, our four teenagers struggle to form friendships, since they are not in school and most other traveling families have younger children. At times, the lack of social resources causes heartache and loneliness, and they resent the amount of time they have to spend with their parents. Thank goodness they have each other. They form a small tribe—being very close in age (ranging from twelve to sixteen) means they have become the best of friends while on the road.

This journey has changed them more than I anticipated. Sure, we've had explosive moments of teen rage, which has at times left me wondering, is this really worth it? But then I realize, we would get angst at home. I'd much rather have a family meltdown in front of the Taj Mahal than in suburban Melbourne.

The most intense mood swings came early on, in rural India—the heat, the dust, the staring. Yet it was India where we witnessed our most profound shifts. After nine weeks of bathing with a sponge and bucket, we realized that *one* bathroom is a luxury. Let alone two. In rural India, there was no need for expensive makeup, tanning products, skin care products, or trendy clothes. My daughters learned to distinguish between a need and a want, and developed a deeper understanding of what's important.

We have had to push ourselves through uncomfortable situations more challenging than that bucket bathing. Every day, *anything* could happen. Embracing changes and obstacles and going with the flow is an empowering experience, one we never had snug inside our comfort zone.

Our volunteering in Buldhana for nine weeks is a great example. As a family, we worked with an untouchable doctor I'd met while volunteering with an immersion program the year before. Dr. Kharat offered to introduce us to Nikita, a 15-year-old Indian girl who lives with her grandparents in the local slum. Her home is a tin shed, the door a small opening. The temperature inside her home must have hit 50° C, and the sweat dripped down the arch of my back all the way down my legs as I stood inside her home chatting away. Nikita's home houses the many goats and one cow that her grandfather tends. During our visit, the animals were all lying down in the back room out of the hot, harsh sun. That was Nikita's bedroom, which she eagerly showed us, lightly leaping over the cow dung and goat poop while my girls followed grumbling about the searing heat and soiled floor.

Nikita had no material possessions, just her grandparents and a tin roof. But she is bright and yearns for a chance. When we discovered that she wanted to learn to sew garments, we raised money from family and friends and purchased a sewing machine as well as a new pink bicycle. She had been walking to school each day, carrying heavy books, and we wanted to make that journey a little easier.

Her humble happiness when we arrived with the bike and sewing machine made me grateful to be able to help someone that little bit. My girls looked at me with tears in their eyes, and I have yet to get Nikita's beautiful face out of my thoughts. At the end of the day, not one person gets to choose where he is born. It's the human lottery for all of us. My teenagers understand that now, in a way they never could before.

With Nikita and other people we've met all over the world, it's become clear that it's not what you do but who you're being that makes the most meaningful connections. What a powerful realization for our daughters, who now know the complex layers of humanity and life all over the world.

We have not only learned to adapt to other cultures, we've learned to adapt to each other. We can't escape to school or work when we're bothered; we have to find ways to accommodate our individual needs. For instance, each time we arrive in a new country, one of my daughters grieves and takes time to settle. Now that we understand her reaction to upheaval, we intentionally give everyone landing space. It takes a whole week to find our bearings, so we don't expect much from anyone. It helps that we set our own schedule, and everyone gets to sleep in. What teenager wouldn't love that?

Similarly, we've had to learn to be flexible about eating. There was a time when our third daughter was living on grapes and cashew nuts, such was her struggle to adapt to Indian flavors and her fear of getting sick. Once we found a couple of reliable places to eat and we started purchasing our own fresh food from the market to cook at home, she slowly came out of her shell and started trying different things. It took time.

Children are directly impacted by their parents' relationship, and I can definitely say that this trip has altered my marriage. Without the pressure of full-time work, I'm a lot more relaxed, actually present, and our marriage has shifted in terms of equality and opportunity. My role is no longer the family chef and cleaner and chauffeur. And Steve is not viewed as the lone breadwinner. Our marriage is stress and argument free, and we are more in sync with each other and our daughters. We find connections in the little things because we have the time.

Steve is due back to work on the 27 December, and I'm job hunting. The girls are excited about being reunited with their friends; they are in reverse countdown mode, counting down until we're home. I'd much rather be oblivious.

Looking back, there's not much I would do differently. For the Distance

Education, I wish we'd bought one laptop per child, rather than the iPad for the younger girls we were told would be sufficient. Submitting work, storing files, and backing work up are better on laptops. I'd spend money there rather than expensive footwear they agreed to but never actually wore. Grrrr! All they wore were Havaianas flip flops! We carried around expensive footwear for the entire trip, a waste of money and luggage space. Teenage girls are fussy—if they don't jump at it, don't buy it!

We still want to travel to the Americas, Mexico, Cuba, and parts of Canada, the Caribbean and Galapagos Islands. Also Iceland, Mongolia, and Romania. The travel thing, it's in my blood and bubbles up at the merest provocation. Our future travel dreams continue to inspire us. Returning home feels right now like drawing the short straw, but it gives us the opportunity to earn again and save money for another epic trip.

Processing the Experience

CONTRIBUTORS' STORIES

CHERYL · RV-ING THROUGH EUROPE

Our first week was the worst. We had zero experience and zero clue what we were doing. Everything that could go wrong did—an oil leak, lots of things didn't work in the motorhome, it felt like everything we touched broke, Jason got tonsillitis and had to go to hospital. Just everything! That was a hard week, and it was a huge learning curve for us. I think if it hadn't been for pride, and the fact we had sold our house and everything with it, we would have turned on our heels and headed home. But we didn't, we kept at it, and in time we have fixed the broken things, had the motorhome mended, and found our groove with motorhome living and traveling. I'm so glad that we didn't give up and go home when things got tough.

For us, it's the everyday moments that catch us off guard. We are living the life of our dreams. And for us that's all about being together, every day, showing our kids the world and getting to experience it all for the first time as a family. We've had loads of "firsts" together; climbing the Eiffel Tower in Paris, swimming in a fresh water lake in Spain, eating our very first authentic French macarons and Spanish tapas, having our first-ever ride on a *tuktuk* or riding a cable car and eating freshly roasted chestnuts in Portugal. The list is endless, but it's these small moments that we will cherish forever.

Our initial plan was to travel Europe for a year and then be done. However now that we are living this life, we can't imagine going back to "normal."

AMANDA · LIVES IN MOROCCO

The biggest challenge was integrating with my husband's family. Learning the social norms and protocols of a place is hard. Privacy and space was a major concern. We had to learn to navigate our expectations and theirs. About eight months in, I hit the depression part of culture shock.

One of the hardest aspects of living in Morocco was the reliance on physical punishment of children. It's technically illegal, but accepted by most parents and some teachers. When our children first started school and exhibited normal distractible behavior, the typical advice was, "Well, you need to hit them." Just hearing this offered as an obvious strategy was heartbreaking. We had to reaffirm constantly that we did not condone physical punishment and that our children must never be touched. Fighting this cultural norm continues to be stressful.

The best moment for me was when my kids were happy to go to school and could communicate easily with my in-laws. This was the reason we moved and to see it actually happen was satisfying.

After the 2016 US election, we decided to stay in Morocco for another four years. But there are other places we consider moving for a time, perhaps Norway, Sweden, or Finland. Scandinavia reminds us of where we used to live in the United States, but with the pace and feel of Europe. Also, I really respect their educational systems, and, hard as it is to believe, I love the climate.

KIRSTY · ROAD-TRIPPED THROUGH NORTHERN AFRICA AND CENTRAL ASIA FROM HER ADOPTED HOME IN ABU DHABI

On the day our Iranian visas were set to expire, our car broke down. We were far from the border, twenty kilometers from the nearest town, outside a church on the side of a mountain, in a closed border area, guarded by the military. It makes my stomach lurch to think of it now. But people stopped to help us, they called friends, they fed us, they drove us back to the town, they found us a mechanic who then drove us an hour to another town, and back, to get a car part, then fed us again, and then—six hours later—fixed our car in the dark on what was by then a freezing cold mountainside. We made it out of the Iranian border with fifteen minutes to spare before our visas expired, all because of strangers' generosity.

Also, we once had to reroute a thousand kilometers to avoid airstrikes. It took us two extra days, but worth it to avoid the rioting and murder in the border town we had planned to drive through. Realistically we knew the chances of us being caught up in it were slim, but we couldn't take the risk with children.

Those challenging moments were dramatic. The good ones were quieter. While staying in a very average one-bedroom apartment in Morocco—which was so cold we had to buy a heater—I woke up every morning feeling blessed. We had these long days together and could get up and decide what we wanted to do without any other pressures or constraints. Our life was so simple and easy, and I loved it. I think once we'd got into our groove with traveling there was just this feeling of contentment that there were no insurmountable challenges. Even if some days finding accommodation was hard or we couldn't find fresh veggies to cook, we could figure it out.

The kids loved camping—being in Cappadocia in Turkey was an absolute highlight for them, and they both discovered countries they want to go back to and live in.

NICA · SAILED THE CARIBBEAN

There were rough times. Our children struggled with the lack of kid companionship and with the awkward attempts to connect with people back home. There weren't any hurricanes, but there were a couple of weather systems that pinned us to the boat for days at a time, and one almost-disastrous dinghy ride through the surf to see Dean's Blue Hole.

The wonderful part of the trips was sunsets. Celebrating sunsets is a tradition on cruising boats, and there was maybe only one sunset the whole journey that we didn't celebrate with reverence. On another boat, on ours, on land—sunsets are a time to focus, breathe, and appreciate. One of the things we love about cruising is the focus on small things. Putting down anchor in the Bahamas after an overnight sail across the Gulf Stream. Fresh mahi mahi with friends in the Turks and Caicos. Getting into clean clothes after our evening shower.

There's no doubt in my mind that we're definitely going again, though where we would go is more open. The Caribbean as a whole is awesome. The east coast of the US is not a place we've really seen. Canada? Maine? Bermuda? Western Caribbean? Panama Canal and points west? We love traveling with our own house and our own resources. We love the flexibility and self-sufficiency of sailing as a lifestyle. The focus on nature and adapting to the weather. The ability to live in an area and know the people, both locals and other sailors. If we could take the kids again, we'd have to get a larger boat as they just don't fit in the spaces we have for them. That said, if someone told us tomorrow, "Leave!" we'd shove the kids in and head off. We will go again, once the kids are in college. The countdown is on!

CANADA-TO-FRANCE · LIVES IN FRANCE

The only stressful part was the flight to France. We were all so excited, my daughter could not rest for the entire eight-hour flight. We landed anxious to get there, but we still had an hour train ride to Aix-les-Bains. We got on the train with all our luggage, but we got on the wrong car and had no seats so had to stand the entire trip. We were all beyond exhausted, and my husband and I were frustrated at the mistake and our daughter got upset since she could see the stress on both our faces.

In truth, I feel like every day is amazing. As soon as I leave the house and walk outside it hits me that *we are in France*. I don't take it for granted even for a minute. Yet, I have to say that the best moments are when we travel. In 2016, we were able to travel to nine countries, from Portugal to Italy to Switzerland. Places we never thought were possible. We've been to so many beautiful places, and our daughter is learning so much. For me that is the absolute best.

ELIZABETH · LIVES IN ITALY

When my baby was really sick in the night after we had only been in Italy only a few weeks—that was the worst. I was panic stricken. I couldn't figure out the medical system and didn't know which hospital I should go to or if I even needed to go. I was saved by the WhatsApp Nursery Mums Group and Google Translate. I wanted to throw in the towel, but we got through it.

My highlight was when my son said his first Italian word without being prompted. I asked for a *piccolo gelato* for him, and he ran forward to shout at the waitress, *"No, grande!"*

KRISTIN · LIVED IN COSTA RICA, THE NETHERLANDS, AND ARGENTINA FOR ONE YEAR

In Costa Rica, the five of us were in the middle of the jungle, with lots of spontaneous moments of greatness. For instance, rescuing the tiniest baby gecko from our sink, hiking in the woods and finding a sloth, driving home from the café to find two crocodiles in our driveway.

Two of our good friends lost parents while we were abroad, and that was very hard to watch from afar. Also, the terrorist attacks in Paris were really scary for us. The Netherlands was on the European front line of the immigration issues in 2015, and we felt really out of touch and confused about the fear, anger, and militarization that ticked up after those tragic attacks. We were so scared that we changed our plans and stayed away from airports and train stations for a few weeks.

Also, our initial transition to the Netherlands was tough for me because I get nervous on bikes near cars. I overcame my fear and by the end of our stay, we were biking home in the dark, through a typical drizzle, after canal-side beers and fries with our Dutch friends, as my kids sang Dutch Christmas carols. I was positively joyful.

The school in the Netherlands is part of what made that experience wonderful. As an International School, most of the students were expats. About half of the students were from India, the remaining half were from other less-wealthy European countries whose families were in the Netherlands to take advantage of the high salaries, benefits, and relatively lower tax rates. The Netherlands has a vibrant economy so we met many people chasing professional dreams. We also made friends with Dutch families, making us feel more connected to the Netherlands. The school knows how isolated people can be without a community, so it works extra hard to encourage social circles.

Our stint in Argentina was difficult. Mendoza was unwelcoming, and by that point we had been gone long enough to realize how much we need a sense of community. Mendoza is a mildly economically depressed and isolated area in the country, populated by people who haven't traveled much (unlike the rest of Argentina, which is known to be worldly and well educated). The locals seemed resentful that we had the opportunity to see the world, and assumed that as Americans we prided ourselves on being globally dominant. I understand the anti-American sentiment but didn't enjoy it aimed at me! My husband was better accepted than our children or me, perhaps because he's Cuban.

I have no idea what we would have done if we had been in Argentina longer. We had very limited friend prospects. We were increasingly home-sick and also became annoyed with the culture as a whole because we had so little traction there. I wish I could be more positive but sixteen months out I still feel very disappointed in the way that humans can treat each other!

There were some bright spots. We loved our art classes where we got to know local artists. Our parents visiting was another high.

We will do another sabbatical in five years. Now, we regard those challenging moments as experiences we had to muddle through as part of the tremendous mind-expanding experience our family was lucky enough to have.

NAOMI · LIVED IN INDIA AND SINGAPORE FOR FOUR YEARS

Three days after we arrived in Delhi, my husband left for business. In his mind, I was very capable, and his work was calling. I desperately wanted to go home and felt I'd made the worst decision of my life. Other hard moments include: a terrible experience with a dentist (i.e. no Novacaine for our middle child during a tooth extraction) and a horrifying slaughtering experience at a local market in the heat and swelter of monsoon season. I called my husband and told him he was to immediately book us return tickets to take us home. Thankfully, he talked me out of my panic.

Another awful moment was the night of a terrible earthquake when strong aftershocks shook Delhi. My friends—whose husbands were ALL away on work travel—phoned each other past midnight when the shocks struck to make sure everyone was okay.

Contracting chikungunya was the defining "horrible" moment in our time abroad. It's a mosquito-borne virus that affects me even all these years later. The question "why did we think this was a good idea?" ran through my head on the regular as I berated myself for making a decision that could have jeopardized my life.

What got me through those moments was the power of friendship and the strength of human resilience. We are born for struggle and overcoming chaos and taming the inner critic that tells us we can't possibly manage. I learned a lot about myself during the "horrible" moments and wouldn't exchange them now for the world.

As for the highs: camping on the Ganges River for Thanksgiving one year with all of our friends. Teaching English to the children at the Vivekanand Slum across from the school where my own children were educated. Celebrating Holi with so much laughter and joy. Taking photography lessons with Mr. Singh. Learning how to make olive fried rice with Uncle Louis (a hawker food stall owner in Singapore who came to my kitchen to teach my friends and me how to craft this dish). Some of the best moments are still being lived out, when we gather with friends we made. Those connections mean the world to me.

Our children are now rapidly approaching the final years of their education. If we had ONE more year abroad, I would take the kids out of school and immediately head to New Zealand. The beauty of that country and the extreme kindness that Kiwis show is something I'd like our family to experience.

TANIA · ROAD-TRIPPING THROUGH EUROPE

Thankfully we have experienced no catastrophes. There was one night in France when we couldn't find a hotel. We wound up parking at a gas station and sleeping in the car. It was pretty tight, especially with the dog. Really, the hardest aspect of the trip has been the struggle to maintain our business on the road. We committed to writing a four to five thousand word fiction story every week, recording it, and creating supplemental educational material. There always seems to be a stressful deadline looming.

There are of course moments of awe-inspiring beauty on top of mountains or during sunsets over the water. We've done a lot of hiking, especially in the Alps where a mountain top restaurant can seem unreal. It's easy to miss these moments because life moves pretty fast, and sometimes we get caught up in it all—planning for the next place, trying to find our way around, work and school, even just figuring out where to find the nearest grocery store. It can become overwhelming. We often have to remind ourselves to take a deep breath and look around and soak it all in. Our kids help us remember to be present and enjoy the adventure.

We are considering another trip. We talk about South America and maybe not doing as much traveling, but instead picking a couple places and settling for longer periods of time.

SARA · LIVED IN MOROCCO FOR SEVEN YEARS

I remember feeling really homesick at about the six-month point. I was very thankful for the few friends I had at that time in Morocco. They were great listeners, could empathize, and were able to carry me through that brief period.

We were thankful we never required emergency medicine in Morocco. I always told myself that we couldn't get in a car accident or become seriously ill; we just couldn't risk it. The time that I *did* get sick was in

Bali. This was the situation I feared when I started traveling without my husband. I was so sick that a doctor was called to my guesthouse. I was throwing up nonstop and had the worst headache and neck pain of my life. I was initially told by the doctor it was either dengue or spinal meningitis—I called it Bali roulette. It turned out to be neither. Thankfully, a fellow worldschooler staying next door to me took care of my kids until I recovered. This demonstrates the necessity of making connections with other travelers, rather than staying solitary, which often seems easier.

I also had a challenging moment when I was pulled over by Moroccan police who demanded a bribe. My son was 1-year-old, sitting in his carseat, and the officer took my license from me before crossing the autoroute to the center divider. He spoke very little French and would not explain to me why he had pulled me over, only that he wouldn't return my license without my paying him more money than I had. I had to grab my son, cross the busy autoroute, and try to negotiate. Eventually I called an Arabic-speaking friend who spoke to the officer and convinced him to take a lesser bribe. I remember feeling terrified and so helpless. Again, it's so important to have friends wherever you are.

Those were challenging experiences, but in the almost eight years we lived in Morocco, I mostly just felt grateful. Weekday afternoons we would drive out to the beach, just because we could. We sat on plastic chairs at sundown, watching our fresh seafood be cleaned in the ocean, filleted, then grilled on a portable grill, served accompanied by fresh salads and bread from that day's "pop-up" restaurant. We attended several Moroccan weddings, which were phenomenal. I watched my kids become so comfortable in the *medina* that they would confidently walk through the streets, saying hello in French and Arabic to all they knew. I love that my kids now understand where their food comes from. They've helped slaughter sheep for Eid (the big Muslim holiday), and they've seen beef carcasses hanging in the *medina*. I felt gratitude watching my kids play with their friends from Denmark, England, Portugal, and the Emirates, where language and culture differences were no barrier to friendship. I felt gratitude for the times when I heard the call to prayer and realized it had become part of daily life. Seriously, the list can go on and on. We felt so much gratitude.

In the future, I'd like to explore Polynesia, New Zealand, and parts of Africa. I want to see the Maldives before they are covered with ocean. I'd want to do slow travel and sit in places for at least one to two months, so that we sink deeper into other cultures. I want to see places that are not major tourist destinations. I love the big cities of Europe, but there is something magical about experiencing a place that has not adapted to tourism.

HEATHER · LIVED IN ITALY FOR TWO YEARS

The hardest part was our son's homesickness and depression. It threw him (and us) for a loop and made that first year tough.

The best times were when we ALL felt like Italy was home. I remember once, we had been living in Italy for six months and traveled to Prague at Christmastime. Returning to Milan and being greeted in Italian and being able to read the signs and know where we were going and what to do, it suddenly clicked that home was Italy, and it was comforting to come home after being in a foreign land. Travel was a definitely a highlight. I cried the first time I took the kids to Rome and they loved it deeply. I love Rome so much and we had been traveling with a lot of grumpiness over the previous months. I was thrilled to hear something positive come out of their mouths, and also that we could share this love of the eternal city.

I'll also remember how much fun I had exploring the food of my region. We were surrounded by arborio rice fields, so I had to learn how to prepare a proper risotto. I still make it often. I took as many cooking classes and food adventures as I could and loved shopping for groceries and using local ingredients and Italian brands.

We had several restaurants within a short walk of our home and became regulars at those places. The staff became like family to us. It was those sorts of moments, made of small things, that stick with me. Day trips, food shopping, listening to my kids order their food in Italian, listening to the church bells while walking home from dinner, and wanting to pinch myself and anyone within reach.

26

HOW WE CHANGE

I'm bewildered by people whose greatest aspiration is that nothing ever change. I can understand not wanting to relocate or not wanting to change jobs or even not wanting to travel. My values are different, but I can imagine craving stability and a serene plateau of life events. What I can't understand is being okay with not changing as a person. I look back on who I was at twenty-six and I feel nothing but gratitude for twenty years of stretching. Not changing means not growing. It means stagnating. Don't you just shudder at the thought?

We change whether we want to or not. It's developmentally scripted. So turning a blind eye towards growth just leads to change in undesirable directions. Really, I would rather be clear that there are aspects of myself I like and aspects of myself I'm working on. I am a work in progress, and that is okay by me.

Here's the thing about travel. Travel shines a spotlight—nay, a flood-light—on our limitations and on our areas of potential growth. You might be able to ignore your perfectionism or shyness or stubbornness or inflexibility or defensiveness on home soil, where everything is convenient and everything is easy. But starting over in a foreign location is a recipe for coming to terms with your work.

So how did I change? Oh, so many ways. For one, I learned to love other people's children instead of using them as yardsticks for my own. I didn't *want* to use other children as a yardstick, but in my crazy, pre-Italy life, connection was just less valued than success. Since our year in Italy, I'll sometimes ask clients, "Do you want to be idolized, or do you want to be loved?" That always stops people short. Our American society (would love to hear from you Brits and Aussies) is so intent on winning, we completely neglect that love has far more staying power.

Love is the heartbeat of my most profound changes during our year in Italy. I learned connection was worth awkward moments. I learned that you can love people without knowing anything about their background or beliefs. I learned that loving people who live half a world away from where I once churned my everyday existence means that I now feel tapped into a shared humanity. This forced me to realize that much of what I have and take for granted, I have by the sheer luck of where I was born. Why feel superior? Instead, I cultivate a sense of empathy. The cheesy song is right, *love lifts us up where we belong*. Where we *all* belong.

It's this sure feeling in my bones, that we are all connected and the arcs of our journeys are often a by-product of chance, that has led to my work with local refugees. A year ago, I hosted a fundraiser for International Neighbors, a local nonprofit that assists refugee families with integrating into our community. Believing that there are good people who strive to put light into the universe, I recruited what I called "Soup Divas," who led their own individual army of soup makers. Not wanting anyone to be excluded from the event because of cost, we had a pay-what-you-will structure to attend and eat dinner together. Best of all, refugees attended, made soup and cookies, and took turns telling their stories. We raised almost $20,000 USD for International Neighbors, but more than that, we created connections and conversations between people. Would I have done that if I hadn't been so aware of the impact of a warm welcome? If I hadn't been so heart-wrenched at the thought of these families leaving their homes for safer, but probably very frightening, shores? Probably not.

Another sign that I changed in our year abroad is that there were people I always liked before we left, but our friendship never clicked. Until

I got back. I get it. Pre-Italy, I was one of those people who got sideways if the napkins didn't match the flowers at her *child's birthday party*. Now? I just don't sweat those details. Which leaves me much more room for thinking deeply, loving fiercely, and probably being a more pleasant person to be around.

Since we're being honest, I will admit that sometimes I do still sweat those details. But rather than fixate blindly on not being able to find Nicolas's favorite Italian *chinotto* soda made from bitter oranges, I can acknowledge that I'm probably anxious about him coming home from college, and forgive myself and practice letting go. It's not a light switch, it's growth.

And like all growth, it's kind of a miracle.

Relationships also shift and stretch during an expat adventure. Relationships with your children, relationships between your children, relationships with people back home, relationships with your spouse. It's pretty impossible for all those not to be subject to some amount of transformation. In regards to marriage, I want to point out that while our contributors speak to strengthening unions as a side effect of their adventure, I'm sure they would also all agree that the stress of the transition either did stress their marriage, or would have stressed their marriage had their relationship not been rock solid in advance. Travel can be maddening; full-time immersive travel is monumentally more so. That kind of stress can expose a marriage to cracks and fissures. Much like having a baby won't fix a marriage, neither will travel. I'm saying this because it would behoove you to think about your marriage in advance of leaping across the pond. Think about when you work well together and when you don't. Consider how you each behave when you are under the gun, and in those moments, do you support each other well, or do you explode and/or hide out in separate corners? If there is an ounce of doubt that your union is shatterproof, I suggest seeking out couples counseling. That work will help you see the best in each other, communicate in helpful ways, and support each other when the chips are down. All useful skills as you prepare to feel more vulnerable and exposed than you have ever felt before.

I'll be frank, I do know of marriages that didn't withstand a global adventure. An expat experience is like a pressure cooker: it will be the fire that hones your relationship into an unshakable union, or it will expose the dormant weak spots and press on them until the relationship implodes.

I want this to be an excellent experience for you, so invest now, prepare now. Nourish the garden of your family, so that healthy growth can happen. You'll be glad you did.

How Weathering Storms Shifts Perspective

JENNIFER'S STORY

In 2014 and 2015 I sailed sixteen thousand nautical miles halfway around the world with my husband and 10-year-old son. We anchored off of beautiful beaches, sipped cocktails in the cockpit while watching another sunset, and traveled the world. Jealous? Don't be. That's the Facebook version. That's the romance novel version. The real story is that I was scared most of the time. And the rest of the time I was worried about being scared. I was not cut out for sailing around the world. But I did it. And what I learned is that you learn a lot more from the things you think you can't do than the things you feel confident about.

I didn't grow up sailing. It was not a passion of mine. I dreamed of adventure—but all of it was on dry land. When I met my husband, he told me he wanted to sail around the world. It's not that I didn't believe him, it's just that people say they are going to do a lot of things. When we were in Portofino, Italy, for our honeymoon my husband looked at me romantically and said, "Someday we're going to sail here on our own boat." I thought, "Whatever, buddy."

You know that feeling in the pit of your stomach when you see a siren and lights behind you on the freeway, and it looks like it's coming for you? That's fear. It's your flight or fight response. It's your limbic system overtaking your ability to reason. And that is what I would feel just thinking about sailing around the world.

I was scared of storms, scared of big swells, scared of rough weather, scared of rogue waves, scared of making a stupid mistake that would turn into a life-threatening problem. You name it. I was scared of it.

And nearly all of the things I was scared of happening, happened. We lost our autopilot in forty-knot winds off the coast of California's Point Concepcion. We spent three days in thirty-five-knot winds off of Mexico. We got caught in a thunderstorm off of Cape Fear. We ran aground on the island of Vulcano off the coast of Italy. We spent the night in a severe gale off the coast of Portugal. We got pushed towards the coast overnight in twenty-foot and greater swells and thirty-knot winds off the coast of the Dominican Republic. We lost our engine as we approached shore in Portugal. We lost it again in twenty-five knots of wind at a crowded anchorage in Greece. We lost the ability to raise our main sail crossing the most treacherous gulf in France in the middle of the night. And once we got caught in hurricane force winds in Spain. And that's just the top ten scariest moments.

It doesn't even include all of the times I was scared *anticipating* something. Things like, well, crossing the Atlantic Ocean. And unlike people who confront their fears and overcome them (if there are such people), I faced my fears and was still scared. Towards the very end of the trip we were in difficult conditions crossing the Straits of Messina off of Sicily and I remember thinking, "Shouldn't I not be bothered by this anymore? What is wrong with me?" I remember my husband turning to our son and asking him, "Who's braver? Dad, who isn't that scared right now? Or Mom, who's scared and doing it anyway?" Our son stared quizzically back at him, and my husband said, "Mom. Mom's braver."

I can't tell you how many times I longed to be sitting at a desk, in beautiful stillness, not worried about my own physical safety or the safety of my family. But I learned a thing or two along the way.

I learned that life is always throwing things at you that trigger your flight or fight responses, whether you're at sea or at work. I've come to think of it as an opportunity to expand your circle of comfort, if even just a little bit. The things I could do at the end of our voyage were miles apart from the things I could do at the beginning.

I learned that I will probably never stop feeling scared of some things, but that I don't have to feel bad about it. My amazing captain of a husband would tell me that men were scared out there on the ocean too. But the difference is that they didn't beat themselves up about it.

I learned that what matters most to me is how I deal with a situation and whether I can look back on it with pride. The most rewarding situations of my sailing trip were also the most difficult.

And perhaps the most important thing I learned is that *confronting your fear is what makes you brave*. Not conquering it.

It is simply putting yourself in situations that you do not think you can handle, and then surviving, that makes you realize that you are capable.

Jerry Seinfeld does a routine where he makes an observation about the irrationality of human fear. Jerry begins (I'm slightly paraphrasing), "I saw a study that said speaking in front of a crowd is considered the number one fear of the average person. I found that amazing. Number two was death. Death is number two? This means, to the average person, if you have to be at a funeral, *you would rather be in the casket than doing the eulogy*."

If death is not the end result of whatever you are afraid of, it's a good time to remember that there is a difference between dangerous and uncomfortable. Let's face it, most of our fears really just make us uncomfortable. Truly the only way to expand your circle of comfort is to get outside of it.

I am not going to tell you not to be afraid. I'm not even going to tell you that you will stop feeling afraid after you've faced your fears. But what I am telling you is that if you face your fears, you'll be really proud of yourself. You'll have a sense of accomplishment that you will never get from doing something that doesn't challenge you. You may even gain enough confidence to face another fear or two.

The Journey Changes Us

CONTRIBUTORS' STORIES

MARIE · MICHELLE'S MOTHER, REMEMBERS
LIVING IN PANAMA CITY IN THE 1970S

As our Braniff flight made its final approach into Panama City airport, my throat went dry. I was 21-years-old and married for three days, taking the leap to a new country with a new language. I watched my life—my friends, rock concerts, San Francisco's hippy culture, my beloved Go-Go boots, miniskirts, and the long, long hair that I diligently ironed each morning to get that oh-so-pretty Cher look—fading away.

As I walked down the jetway, the humidity frizzed my hair into an instant afro.

Around me, everyone spoke Spanish, including my Mexican-American husband. I tried frantically to remember even a word of Spanish, but with the humidity so high, I had trouble breathing, let alone speaking. My hair was now a dripping mess.

The days and weeks passed, and I met Americans, Australians, French (like myself) and started to fit in. I cut my hair very, very short (*à la* Mia Farrow), changed my wardrobe, and bought a few cocktail dresses. Slowly, I ventured out on my own, timidly trying to speak Spanish. I discovered the *mercados* with amazing seafood. I learned to drink coffee. My Spanish improved.

Within a few months, I found out I was pregnant. Exciting, but hard to fully wrap my mind around given the horrible nausea and mood swings that plagued me the entire nine months of my pregnancy. As my delivery time neared, Dr. Campana tried to get me to eat more *remolachas*, beets, to get my iron up. But all I could keep down was ice cream. So up went the weight, and down went my oxygenated blood. As challenging as this may sound, and aside from the nausea that was my constant companion, I was quite content with my life. I enjoyed my friends, the culture, having someone to clean and cook, when all I wanted to do was sleep and eat ice cream.

My baby was born in December, and I added becoming a mother to the changes in my life.

We had been in Panama a year at that point, and Spanish began tripping easily off my tongue. I mastered entertaining and having parties (inviting the Panamanian friends to arrive an hour before the Americans, so that everyone came at the same time). I loved the adventure of flying to Taboga for the weekend and visiting Las Perlas Islands.

Year one rolled into four. My little girl and her friends used dramatic mannerisms to emphasize their words. I found myself doing the same. Every trip back "stateside" made clear that I wasn't the same person as the new bride who had left. As anxious as I had once been to resume my life in the United States, I was now eager to return home, to Panama.

Then Sears decided to move us to Belgium.

Our beloved Latin furniture disappeared, destined to reappear in grey, grey Brussels in a few weeks. I wondered how our little Costa Rican cart and Brazilian table would fit in. I wondered how I would fit in.

Honestly, I didn't want to fit in. I tried to be excited, but I felt so Latina, it was anguish to have to once again reinvent myself. I didn't want to shop for "European" clothing—sweaters, jackets, and heavy shoes to replace my sandals. I didn't want to say goodbye to my golden tan and hello to pasty white skin. Worst of all was saying goodbye to our friends who had become family—my daughter's godparents, my godchild, the friend who donated blood to me after my daughter was born. This was my family. I had been in Panama four years...a lifetime. I just wasn't the same person who stepped off the plane four years before, trying desperately to pat down her humidity-forced afro.

AMANDA · LIVES IN MOROCCO

We're still changing as our journey continues. We see the world as much smaller and have a global outlook. Our move has brought us closer to our children, and opened up a different way of communicating. In a lot of ways we have become more reliant on each other. It also strengthened our marriage. My husband came to the US and went through the challenge of being an immigrant; then we moved to Morocco and I did the same. In both cases, we had to rely on each other to help pave the way and be our support system. I realize this could drive people from each other, but for us it showed us how to better empathize and communicate.

NICA · SAILED THE CARIBBEAN

My husband and I are more sure of our future. Cutting the docklines once is hard. Cutting them a second time means we can do it again and again and again. Our focus on heading off "permanently" as soon as the kids are in college has become more intense. We're more aware of how short life is, how precious each moment is (how cliché does THAT sound) and how much more there is to life than jockeying for position on the highway.

Personally, the return shook me enough that I've changed a lot about my life. My wellness has become paramount, and my life has changed to accommodate that realization.

My children learned the importance of self-reliance. Our daughter still loves her social life but is also fiercely solitary and in need of alone time. Our son has decided to change the world by running for political office while still in high school. These are not paths I'd have guessed for them, nor can you point to them and say, "Oh, yeah, that's because of the sailing thing." But there has to be some kernel of our trip that impacted their determination to create their own learning, and not what everyone says you should do.

CHERYL · RV-ING THROUGH EUROPE

Our daily rhythm is totally different now. I'm sure anyone with three kids under three would agree, the only way to survive it is to have a solid routine. Our kids were up early, non-stop all day, we had the nursery run first thing in the morning, then playdates, activities or appointments in the afternoon, and bedtime was a strict 6:30. Now that we are traveling, we have a much more relaxed approach to routine. To everything really. We go to bed later, and as a result we sleep in later. There's no rush to be somewhere, no time schedules, so we live a relaxed and natural flowing lifestyle day-to-day. Because of this, we enjoy each other more. Before, we felt we needed to always be *doing* something, or going *somewhere* on Jason's days off. Now, there's no pressure to cram quality time into weekends, because we have nowhere to be and no time constraints. We can genuinely just enjoy each day and go or do what we want, as a family.

Jason and the kids have always been active. On the other hand, I was a stay-at-home mum and though I felt like I never stopped moving, I didn't really do much in the way of exercise. I always made sure the kids ate healthily, but my own diet was pretty poor. I still had the home-cooked meals I made for them, but being housebound in cold Scotland, it's so easy to have three or four cups of tea a day. And of course, it's compulsory to have a biscuit with each cup. I always joked that I eat the same as everyone else in my family, yet I'm the only one who is overweight.

Motorhome traveling has completely changed that. Because of limited space, we need to prioritize what foods we can have. Sweets, biscuits, and crisps now take last priority. We simply don't have the room. I now tend to eat more fruit along with the kids, and we are active every day. I've never walked so much since before having kids. So in short, living this type of life has made me much healthier. I do however still manage to find storage space for a bottle of wine or two!

NAOMI · LIVED IN INDIA AND SINGAPORE FOR FOUR YEARS

We became a close-knit nucleus. We now know that we can depend on each other for every single thing that we need, and even when the world around us feels as though it's caving in on us, we have each other.

Our children are open minded, and I attribute that 100% to their time abroad. They are not conservative like the extended families they descend from, and it's fascinating to watch them create their own narrative and how they view the world they live in.

I'm asked all the time how my husband and I created a strong marriage, even though we vote opposite parties and feel differently about many mainstream topics. I feel it's because we said yes to the adventure of living outside of our comfort zone. We worked through the many issues presented to us, and emerged on the other side—seeing each other differently, with new lenses and with a different perspective on who our partner is. We talk openly about our thoughts, dreams, and desires, something that we only began doing after living abroad.

ANDREA · LIVES IN ITALY

When we lived in the UK, we had almost no family time and our lives were exhausting. So fifteen years ago, we decided to move to Italy. We sold our house and bought a town house in a small village. Tony found work, while I became a stay-at-home mum. Now we spend quality time together, we even eat all three meals together. Tony and I have time to consider and agree on parenting techniques. Because of this, our twin daughters are well-rounded girls, who understand their boundaries, what is expected of them, and feel secure and comfortable in our company. If we hadn't moved, I don't think our relationship with each other or with our daughters would be this close.

I do feel Mia and Cara have missed out on some important experiences, like seeing immediate family, and participating in activities that are common in the UK. But they agree that they wouldn't want it any different. When we visit the UK, they don't really like some of the kids' attitudes and how parents overcompensate for not being home to spend time as a family. They're not impressed with materialistic people. Cara and Mia are very level-headed, polite, caring young ladies. They only have a handful of friends, but they're happy with that.

Would I do this again? Hell, yes. Could anyone do it? Hell, no. It's challenging, scary, and if you don't have a strong marriage or relationship, it's tough.

TANIA · ROAD-TRIPPING THROUGH EUROPE

This wasn't just a trip for us, it was the result of years of dreaming about what it would be like to spend a whole year on an adventure together. We've shared so much in this time, and all those experiences have bonded us in a special way. We've learned how much we can do, how much we want to do, and how everyone needs to follow their own path.

It's also been an adventure for Matt and me as we launched a business together, and therefore have developed a new appreciation for each other's talents. People sometimes assume we're on some kind of extended vacation, but honestly we've worked harder on this trip than we ever have before. There have been many sleepless nights to meet deadlines or fix problems or answer customer emails. We've recorded stories in parked cars and occasionally had to use McDonald's or an ATM booth as an office to access the Internet. But we're so proud of what we do and what we've built.

Over the year, our three girls have grown closer. They genuinely love spending time together, creating memories. Our middle girl has developed a love for writing stories and is constantly creating new ones. Our youngest has shown us how fast she can soak everything in, and can make us all laugh no matter the situation. Our oldest daughter, for better or for worse, has developed a taste for extreme sports—rock climbing, skydiving, surfing, paragliding. She's also shown us how brave she is in other ways, trying new things and meeting new people.

SARA · LIVED IN MOROCCO FOR SEVEN YEARS

We are no longer as caught up in keeping to society's framework of what's "normal." Instead, we do what's best for our family. We educate how we want, we eat how we want, we approach life how we want. We understand that every family is different and there are a thousand right ways to parent. We understand the importance for our family to sit down together for meals and to have days where we have nothing planned. We've also seen that with a little effort of thinking outside the box, just about anything is possible.

SUSAN · REMEMBERING MOVING TO SINGAPORE AS A CHILD

While childhood experiences before and since those three years have become quite vague, our time in Singapore stands out like a color photo amongst black and white.

HEATHER · LIVED IN ITALY FOR TWO YEARS

When we arrived in Italy, my husband had his work, but I was lost. The rose-colored glasses I'd worn while planning the move were gone. It's hard to know how things will affect you until you are right there standing in the thick of it. Plus, I made the mistake of trying to shield my husband from the craziness at first. It was better once he was diving into the mess of parenting/household stuff with me.

In retrospect, it was interesting to see how the four of us banded together during those two years. I've never felt closer to my family than the time we lived there, except maybe when we returned to the US, because no one else could understand the huge range of emotions we were feeling.

I'm sure we would have taken our kids to Europe by now if we hadn't moved there, but visiting and living are not the same. Both are good, but living there is filled with so many tiny challenges that some days you think your head will explode, and so much beauty in the everyday moments that you think your heart might explode.

27

REVERSE CULTURE SHOCK
(IT'S REAL)

When I opened my eyes on our first morning back in the United States, I wondered if I'd hallucinated our entire Italian year. It wasn't just that we arrived late the night before, with only enough energy to let the cats out of their carriers before collapsing into our beds. No, it was certainly more than sleep deprivation. It was shock.

Which shouldn't have been surprising. It's called *reverse culture shock* for a reason. Not *reverse culture gradual acclimation*. Ever the researcher, I had prepared myself to be stymied by too many choices and astonished by jumbo sizes on my return to the States. I just hadn't anticipated that the previous year would feel like it never happened.

Over the course of that first week, I shoved down my creeping panic at the blaring stimulation all around me—Five Guys felt like a circus and I was overwhelmed by the movie theater's textured walls and multi-media menu. All the while, I vacillated between feeling like I was walking through a dream and feeling like my Spello life was a fantasy concocted by my fevered-for-Europe brain. It was unsettling, and packed in with that swinging sense of reality came a creeping darkness. I felt empty. Flat. And like a spoiled brat for feeling that way. I berated myself, "Really? You had a year in paradise and now feel pouty to be back? *Really?*" But the more I tried to deny those feelings of regret and grief, the more intolerable the joint feeling of suffocation and lowness became. It was my friend Lisa who reminded me that trying to talk myself out of emotions very rarely changed them. Why not allow myself to feel my truth?

I tried that instead.

I cried and I railed and I vented and I complained to people who could hear me without judgment, and then I felt much better. Only once I gave myself permission to live the 2-year-old within did I begin to get my feet back underneath me.

A month later, my mind finally caught up. I was there then. I am here now. It was like that shift was so huge, my brain couldn't process. But eventually I was able to wrap my head around what seems obvious. What I found harder to resolve was this feeling of being shoved against the grain. It's almost like I was three sizes larger in Italy, and being back forced me to squeeze into my normal clothes again. I was different there, by necessity, by intention, and with gratitude. That "Italian me" no longer fit in my old American life. The rat race bored me, the culture of bests only served to make me anxious until I realized I had swung onto that merry-go-round and was fully capable of stepping off. Then it just made me tired. The constant bifurcation of time, the cultural demand to answer "How are you?" with "Busy! So busy!"—all of it chafed.

Also, a year is too much to sum up in the school pick-up line. When someone asked me "How was Italy?" I was stumped. There was so much. *There was so much.* The language mistakes that taught me to be comfortable making a fool of myself, the friendships that I never expected, the joy of living a life based on my leadings rather than others' expectations, the challenges of watching my children suffer the pain of being outsiders and being powerless to do anything other than trust them to heal themselves, the upswell of gratitude when people embraced us without reason, the gratification of hearing my children effortlessly speak a language I still have to work to understand, the meals that fairly sang, the thrill of skiing in the pink-topped Italian Alps and the relief of plunging hot toes into impossibly blue Sicilian waters, the burgeoning acceptance of my own vulnerability, the love and humility that comes from looking people in the eye when you clink glasses in celebration of anything and everything.

Frankly, when people ask how my year was, I'm not sure if they even want to hear anything other than "Great!" Few people asked more than a passing superficial query. I'm still astonished when I receive a thoughtful, in-depth question about our experience and our reentry, and befuddled when it's followed by an apology for being nosy. This is not nosy. This is caring. But I do understand why so few people ask me what it feels like to no longer write every day, what has surprised me about my old life now that I'm back, how I plan to keep my Italian self present, whom I miss from this year that changed me in ways small and profound. I get it. It's a lot to wonder about another person's experience. It's not like I went to Disney for a long weekend, I went across the Atlantic for a year. My experience is out of the mainstream and hard to grapple with enough to connect around. Kind of like I steer away from IT workers at parties because I just don't understand what they do, so I can only ask broad questions, and stare vacantly while they answer. So it makes sense. It does. But I have to come to terms with the fact that there is a part of me that most people in my life, people I love dearly, will never know. Partly because they don't ask, and partly because I feel muted. Sometimes I can feel alone, even when I'm surrounded by others.

Travel changes us. Fitting back in our old routines is complicated in a way I never imagined. I was asked during an interview a year after our return, "How long did it take to reacclimate?" My answer was, "Any day now." For the most part, five years later, I have gotten used to being back. It helped to return to Spello two years after our departure and feel so instantly at home. Spello doesn't seem as far away when I know I can slide back in. I also know that this Charlottesville phase is just that. A phase. So I can appreciate what I do love about my hometown. It's not forever, it's for now. I glory in the blooming of the dogwoods and my children playing bluegrass music and the fried chicken available at just about any gas station. Charlottesville has become a bit of a hashtag lately what with it being where Nazis choose to parade. That's a lot to process. But we respond with real thought about issues of systemic racism, and that reminds me that this town is vibrant, thoughtful, intellectual, and heartfelt. I'm enjoying that while I'm here.

Meanwhile, the jar is back on the shelf. You know the one. You may have one yourself. It has a big label on it, "AROUND THE WORLD." Not going out to dinner and instead sticking $80 in the jar, soothes the reverse culture shock that can still rattle me from time to time.

So what's the answer? I wish I knew. I'm not sure I even understand the specifics of the question. All I can do is hang onto the Italian phrase that became part of our DNA during our Italy year—*"piano, piano."*

One step at a time. It will unfold.

Way will open.

Piano, piano.

Repatriation

NITSA'S STORY

I am often asked what was the most memorable part of our family journey. Perhaps it was my children's faces when we finally found the Eiffel Tower lit up in the night sky after weaving through tiny streets, or how we forgot to breathe for a moment the first time we saw Venice. It could also be one of the times (because there were a few) when I thought it might be the end for us. When we chartered a boat in the choppy, black waters off the coast of Ibiza, the same waters Odysseus sailed, past the rock where the sirens lived. What were we thinking? A dead, purple octopus floating against the rocky black canvas; an image I will never shake, along with the memory of my hand hovering over a door that said "*salvavidas*" ready to grab my children's life jackets first.

I have so many incredible memories, most of which I have not even gotten a chance to thoroughly reflect on, ten months into repatriation. When someone asks what I miss most about those three years in Europe, I usually mention how much I miss the travel, having our own family-of-four adventures, seeing my children absorb many cultures and languages, feeling like a citizen of the world.

Settling and relaxing back into your old/new life can really catch you by surprise, and there is something that always seems to sneak into the conversation, because your old life is ever-present. Although some of the intensity has waned, we still are reaping the good and bad parts of reverse culture shock. Perhaps it stems from our own mindsets. Since we moved back home, life should immediately go back to normal, right? This is where we are so very wrong.

When you move back to your home country, repatriation is like the grand finale. You are still coming down from the exhilaration of your experiences. It is a little bit like watching fireworks on the Fourth of July. Chaos and noise as the ground shakes beneath you. Suddenly, as fast as it had started, it abruptly ends. A scurry to pick up chairs, snacks, and picnic blankets as everyone makes their way home. There is nothing more to see. Life goes on, just like that. You are no longer an exciting visitor once you have moved home, and the stardom fades.

But in repatriation, we don't just get to pick up our things, throw them in an overseas container and keep our feelings shrink-wrapped with them. There is so much sorting to do. Not only with the objects we bring or housing situations, but with the cultural adjustments every family member encounters in their own, unique way.

Finding your niche among the changes that happened in your absence is not an easy task. As you leave, you are the same old person you always were, but when you come home, you may have become someone entirely different. Even though we are taught to anticipate the reacclimatization, it can still catch us off guard, in our most vulnerable moments. It can make us burst into tears in the cereal aisle because there are too many choices, or it gets you when you eat a really bad soft pretzel that is nothing like it was in Germany. It stalks you, and it can find you anywhere.

Perhaps repatriation feels like the most salient part of my journey because we are living it daily. One day, it might blend in along with all of the other stories. But for now, it is the strongest, most dramatic take away from our family's three years. Would I have changed anything about our decision to move a 4- and 7-year-old across the ocean with no idea how it would all work? Absolutely not. Although, if I could go back, I would force myself to do an intensive language course and I would rent a fully furnished apartment (instead of living on blow-up mattresses and out of our suitcases for weeks while our container was stuck in Northern Germany). But perhaps, I would not opt to do these things over. I would not have had such hilarious communication debacles, and my kids would not still smile about eating macaroni and cheese on a beach towel on the balcony as we waited for our furniture. They still talk about how cool it was to watch the one DVD we had over and over on my laptop, which we propped up on the one folding chair we had.

After all, there may be nothing I would change.

To all who migrate, my greatest compassion and respect. To those who do move home, embrace the laughter, tears, and confusion. As with everything else, it shall pass.

Returning Home

CONTRIBUTORS' STORIES

NICA · SAILED THE CARIBBEAN

Reentry is rough. The pace of life ashore is so fast. Nobody cares what you've done on the ocean, or maybe it's more that nobody can understand and it's too weird to try. All anyone asked when we got back was whether we'd encountered any pirates or hurricanes. How do you really ask questions about an experience you can't even begin to visualize?

Life on shore is a radical shift. The weather no longer affects you in a life-or-death way. You turn on any light you want. You don't watch the sunset every night; you can't see it the same way. There are not really any unexplored places to check out.

Our daughter slept on the floor in our room for two months after we got back. The house felt huge. The choices available to us as Americans are mind-boggling. About a week after we got home, I was standing in the grocery store with "canned tomatoes" on my list. For nine months I had lived in a world where you were lucky to FIND any can of tomatoes in the store, and you bought it if you saw it. All of a sudden there were six shelves, ten-feet long, two-feet deep in front of me with all manner of tomatoes to choose from.

I cried.

Not because it was a thing of beauty. Because it was impossible. Who can choose? Why should grocery shopping be so hard?

I remember a couple of months later helping a woman in a hijab. She was looking at the shampoos with bewilderment. I asked if I could help reach something (I have no shame in climbing shelves), and she just looked at me, "There are so many."

I knew exactly how she felt.

HEATHER · LIVED IN ITALY FOR TWO YEARS

Moving back to the States was emotionally exhausting. Everything seemed crazy. How huge things were, how ridiculous people were, and—my husband's favorite—how horrible the drivers are here compared to Italy. When we got home, every time I left the house I noticed about thirty things that were weird. Eventually that lessened, but for a good nine months we were freaking out about all those little details. We missed the beauty and the language, the people and the food. We found ourselves shocked when a restaurant was open at 5 PM.

We were excited to reunite with our friends, but because of our struggle with reentry, we weren't sure how much we had in common with them anymore. I hoped this was a temporary feeling (which it was), but at the time it was hard to know.

Feeling both elated and overwhelmed was a daily occurrence. Making a "reappearance" to anyone who was not the closest of friends required a great deal of energy because we felt disconnected, like we had to put on a show of some sort. We smiled and told cheerful stories of our years in Italy, knowing that people had no idea what struggles and stress come with daily life abroad. It's not what people wanted to hear, and I found myself guarding my time, energy, and interactions very carefully those first few months.

SUSAN · REMEMBERING SETTLING IN SINGAPORE AS A CHILD

I hated returning to the UK. I missed my friends back in Singapore. The return to English weather was a huge challenge. We returned in December when it was cold and raining or snowing, and I can remember my mother keeping her mink coat on in the house all day. Changing schools again was hard. Everything was colorless and dull. The single good point I can remember was English milk. Singapore milk was sterilized and had a very strange taste.

ESTELLE · CROSS-GENERATIONAL LIVING IN ITALY

People will rarely be as curious as you would hope they will be. They will listen politely, but it is a special listener who is more interested than that.

NELL · LIVED IN FRANCE FOR ONE YEAR

Well, not to whitewash it—the return was terrible. My whole family was in mourning for our life in France. I loved feeling like a fish out of water in France, but when we got back, I felt like a fish out of water in the US and that did not feel good at all. I felt out of step, irritated with things I hadn't noticed before, and very lonely.

I can imagine spending a year in a terrific place and being ready to come home, experiencing some culture shock but nothing dramatic. But France for me is more than a wonderful place to visit—it feels like home in a profound way. That I belong there somehow. I don't fit here, and so ever since we got back, I've been plotting my return.

KIRSTY · ROAD-TRIPPED THROUGH NORTHERN AFRICA AND CENTRAL ASIA FROM HER ADOPTED HOME IN ABU DHABI

Our trip cemented for us how important a simple life is. Once home, we tried to avoid the busyness that life in a capital city entails, but eventually got sucked back in. Which makes me think we'll be hitting the road again someday.

One of my daughters fit back into her old life easily, but my other daughter found her friends had moved on. Even though she was back in the same class, friendships had evolved during our year away. Kids made disparaging remarks about our trip, though I suspect that filtered from the attitudes of some of the parents, who didn't understand or thought it was irresponsible. At least our kids were academically ahead, despite not being in school for a year.

NAOMI · LIVED IN INDIA AND SINGAPORE FOR FOUR YEARS

Oh, boy! Repatriation was so intense for me, I created an entire online community around the inherent challenges. Here's what I have learned through years of reflection.

I over-researched our move to Delhi but under-researched our move back to the United States. I underestimated the need to prepare for repatriation.

I "went dark" when we repatriated. I went from wearing very colorful clothes, jingly jewelry and loads of sass, to black tank tops, yoga pants, and flip flops.

It was extremely hard to fit in or feel as though I belonged when we returned. Even the act of speaking and having a conversation felt foreign.

I remember going to the grocery store and being completely frozen in the toothpaste aisle. So many choices! Why so much excess? Who needs all of this? In the end, I left the store with nothing.

It took me a solid year before I started feeling myself again. I wrote a blog post and created the "I am a Triangle" community in 2014, and it's been fascinating to see the vast number of individuals who struggle with repatriation.

LEWIS FAMILY · LIVED IN MALAYSIA FOR TWO YEARS

We were ready when we returned to the UK in 2009. Richard had completed his education and returned to the UK to attend university. Both girls were now working and no longer able to come out for long holidays. Our mothers were then 94 and 89 years of age and both needed more and more support. Many friends we had made in Kuala Lumpur had already left. All these factors made our returning home feel right.

It was relatively straightforward to slip back into UK life. We met up with old friends and were able to be more involved with our families again. We also maintained a network of friends we had met in Kuala Lumpur who had also returned to the UK.

I returned to my freelance training work on a part-time basis, taking up several projects that meant I traveled through the country. It felt very positive to be using those skills again.

SARA · LIVED IN MOROCCO FOR SEVEN YEARS

Our children were so young when we moved to Morocco that it was all they knew until we moved back to the States three months ago. Therefore, they've had a harder time adapting to the US than they did to Morocco. They don't always understand why kids say or do certain things in the States, and they definitely don't understand any of the cultural references. We're also shocked by how caught up everyone is in their electronic devices. One nice aspect of returning is that my kids never understood the physicality of Moroccan kids. Being back in a country where it's uncommon to fight makes the reentry easier.

The pace of life is a bit jarring right now. We're still finding our way. Right now, as my son said, "It feels like we're just in another Airbnb and we'll be going home soon."

SARAH · LIVES IN THE NETHERLANDS AFTER YEARS OF WORLDSCHOOLING

I knew I would love living abroad, and I did. I dreaded going back "home," and reentry was even worse than I expected. I had changed. I had become more myself. I felt at home outside my homeland in a way I never had inside of it. So I guess you could say our move abroad ruined me forever for living a normal existence in my home country. It was hard to fit back into a place where my experiences had been so different from other people's. When the entire last year (or more) of your life has been lived elsewhere, especially if you've taken the opportunity to do some regional traveling wherever you are, very few things you say will be relatable in a normal conversation. I found myself constantly vacillating between blurting out what I was really thinking (an experience, insight, or observation from my recent life abroad), and keeping my mouth shut to avoid sounding out-of-touch or like a show-off. I just didn't have a lot of normal things to talk about.

It helped to find people who also had international experiences. But it helped a lot more to move back abroad, this time permanently.

Be prepared for the fact that moving abroad may change you forever, and leave you discontented with your former life. Be prepared for the possibility that you might be happier living elsewhere. And don't be afraid to consider moving permanently, even to somewhere "weird" or "exotic." In our age of modern, transient workforces, digital commuting, and entrepreneurialism, there are lot of ways to accomplish that dream.

28

FINAL THOUGHTS

Here's the occupational hazard of writing about traveling families—they rarely end up where they were when you began the book. Often their journeys change from what the writers even conceived when they first offered you their stories. I love that. It speaks to the flexibility of these families, how they are tuned into who they are and what they want or need. Sometimes what they want or need is to abandon the plan that once made so much sense. Rarely with bitterness, almost always with gratitude for the journey. Remember what I said about expats: They trend toward optimism, and so rather than wait for the universe to make things well for them, they take their lessons, fold that journey into their pocket, and move where they feel led.

Nica and her husband, who you may remember sailed the Caribbean with their two children, are now in countdown mode for their next sail, this time as empty-nesters. She and Jeremy plan to cruise "as long as it's fun." The Galapagos and New Zealand are in their sights.

Elizabeth, who moved to southern Italy from her home in Scotland has decided to close the book on their Italian journey. She and her husband love the friends they've made and the beauty around every corner of their lives, but as a stay-at-home mom of two young ones, she would like the accessibility of more activities, like museums and mom groups. Also, having children has underscored for her the importance of family, so she'd like to be just one flight from Scotland. With one more year before their eldest starts school, they are considering another venture, perhaps to Prague. She adds, "I've fallen in love with Italy and I know that when the boys have flown the nest, we will return. This was a brave time to choose to have our adventure, but it was a case of now or never. I've loved the time with my boys and feel so lucky to have had that. The journey has had its bumps, but we have no regrets. I can't wait to see what the next chapter of family life brings."

When last we left Cheryl and her family, they were RVing around Europe. Since then, she and her husband decided that they were interested in house-sitting for a bit. They posted to Facebook groups asking for advice on how to find a situation willing to accept their three children and two dogs and no references, and were told to not hold their breath. While they were mulling the suggestions to post their inquiries on smaller sites that would be less competitive, they received a private message from a couple living on a truffle farm in northern Italy. Years before, the couple had RVed with their kids and dog through Canada, and in that process they had met with nothing but kindness. They wanted to pass that on, and invited Cheryl and Jason to house-sit for them for two months. If you ever meet Cheryl, ask about their very boozy handover. Two months turned to three, and now Cheryl and her family are slated to live on the truffle farm for a year, while the owners take up residence in the UK. They plan to make this a permanent partnership. Cheryl says, "We are now somewhere we never imagined would be within our reach, with an opportunity that could change our lives forever."

Julie, who was in Mexico when she responded to my call for contributors, on the first leg of her year-long family global adventure, is now in Malaysia. They've sped up their travels, which means they are seeing more, but it's tiring, and she misses the slower pace. They are now considering not returning to Texas and instead keeping this traveling gig going. She says, "Living in and experiencing several places around the world has changed us in so many positive ways, it's hard to imagine going back."

When I was coordinating with Kirsty about using her breathtaking photographs for the cover of *The Road Taken*, she casually apologized for the lapse in communication, but her family was preparing for a move to India. They loved their lives in the UAE, but India had always exerted a pull on their family. With the girls getting closer to the demands of senior school, exams, and university, the family decided it was now or never.

A cool crew, you must admit. They eschew the static, and move toward the unknown with not a little alacrity. I hope their willingness to embrace their dreams and allow for transformation inspires their children to do the same.

As for us, we're still settled here in Charlottesville, five years post-Italy. Nicolas is at a university in Texas (which he says is like a foreign country), Siena is wrapping up her second year of high school, and Gabe is gearing up to start middle school. As you know by now, our plan is to leave during Gabe's eighth grade year and travel around the world. Part of the purpose of the trip is to get an idea of where we might want to settle once the parenting gig is winding down. Yes, it's probably going to be Italy, but we're happy to entertain other possibilities, especially when that means spending a month in an Irish farmhouse overlooking the rustling ocean (with goats, if I'm lucky), or maybe discovering Silk Road cuisine and architecture in Uzbekistan, or trying to decipher Serbian menus. We have a running list of possible destinations, mostly added by Gabe who spends an obscene amount of time flipping through atlases and gazing at the giant map we've hung in his room (with pins for where he's been and where he wants to go). Cuba is almost definite, as is South Africa. Istanbul, maybe? Talking about India with friends last weekend suddenly put that in the hopper of possibilities. Gabe keeps sending me images of some island in the South Pacific, and after putting this manuscript together I'm suddenly seized with a desire to learn to sail, so I can watch the sunset with that deep appreciation. I also have a leading to enroll Gabe in an International School to experience for ourselves the international connections our contributors spoke of. Funny that

I embarked on writing this book with the hope of inspiring readers to reach beyond what they thought was possible, and I wound up inspiring myself and my family. Our dinner conversation is peppered with the exciting tales these contributors shared, and the ideas they spark. I hope yours will be, too.

Certainly, if you have suggestions for our global year, send them my way! Join our Facebook group ("The Road Taken") to connect with our contributors, ask questions, and share your dream. It's a supportive group, and we'd love to have you join us.

Siena will just have graduated high school when we are slated to leave, and we're hoping the lure of a global adventure convinces her to travel with us for a gap year before starting college. She's been studying Mandarin, so if she joins us, Xi'an is a definite on our itinerary. Nicolas will have just graduated from college, so he's tapped to take care of the cats, and visit us for Christmas in the Italian Alps. Keith will likely keep working as we travel, and after reading about our contributors who have become life coaches, I'm considering doing the same. It seems a logical outgrowth of the strength-based therapeutic style I already gravitate toward. Plus, I'd love to help more people realize their dreams. In addition, I plan to write about our year abroad again, around some hook or common thread that I have yet to fathom. I'm not worried, there's time.

After that, we'll return to Charlottesville so Gabe can have the high school experience he craves. I suspect Keith and I will use those four years to plan our next and final move. Or maybe not so final. After all, remember Estelle, who moved with her family during her retirement to a place that suited her better. The pull of children and grandchildren will likely mean no place will be home for all four seasons of the year. We're open to whichever turns become illuminated as we travel life's glorious road, eyes and hearts open.

And I just can't wait to find out, so don't leave me in too much suspense—

What will your journey be?

CONTRIBUTORS

 **JOHN AHERN** has traveled through 85 countries and been shot at, poisoned, tear-gassed, robbed at gunpoint, and locked in an African jail. He has also stowed away in a Colombian cargo plane, ridden across countries on the roofs of buses, and flown in an ultralight over the Zambezi. Yet the scariest adventure of all was his year in a motorhome with his wife and two small kids. Winner of the Queensland People's Choice, *On The Road...With Kids* tells their story from the Arctic Circle to Africa's highest peaks, as they got mugged by monkeys, charmed by snake handlers, and challenged to live a life less ordinary. Find John at *www.johnahern.co*.

ELIZABETH ANCELL is a mother of two boys who fol-lowed her husband's job to Bari, Italy. As a lover of travel, languages, and culture she couldn't wait to see how her family would adapt and enjoy their new life. It came with huge highs, and many lows, but with no regrets at all.

 **SARAH BRINGHURST FAMILIA** has lived on five continents, but she's still not sure where (or if!) she wants to settle down. Her adventures include a year in Italy getting citizenship, eight months in Tunisia just after the revolution, and now Amsterdam, where the cosmopolitan village vibe is the right mixture of home and away. She serves on the editorial board of *HiraethMagazine.com*, a digital magazine and podcast that explores migration and homecoming via the literary, visual, and performing arts. Sarah blogs at *Casteluzzo.com: In Search of a Dream to Call Home*.

ANDREA CAMEROTA is 46-years-old and has been with her husband Tony for 29 years. They have twin daughters, Mia and Cara, who will be 18-years-old in April 2018. They moved to Italy in 2002. They have no immediate plans while their daughters finish off college and maybe university. They manage properties in Umbria; some are available to rent for a vacation. Check at *www.restassuredrentals.com*.

Follow Our Journey!
CanadaToFrance.com

CANADA-TO-FRANCE is a Canadian family following their dream of adventure and culture by starting over in France. Exploring the world one country at a time, they are discovering how Europe is enriching and full of history. Excited to trade-in the fast paced life in North American for a calmer, more fulfilling lifestyle through the eyes of mom, dad and daughter. Follow their adventures at *www.canadatofrance.com*.

HEATHER CARLSON is an avid Italophile, cheese enthusiast, and recovering expat. She is the creator of *Smitten Italy*, a website filled with travel resources and inspiration for Italy bound travelers. When she's not planning her next trip, you'll find her cooking for her teenagers, playing with her pups, and sipping some red wine (Italian, of course!). You can find her at *www.smittenitaly.co*. Also look for Smitten Italy on Pinterest and Instagram.

KRISTIN CLARENS is the mom of three young children who struck out for a year-plus overseas when they were just 1-, 4-, and 6-years old. Their adventures were beyond compare and she and her family now spend their spare time back at home in the States planning long summer journeys and looking forward to the next extended adventure abroad.

LISA COLE is the mother of four teenage girls who recently returned to Australia from a year-long backpacking adventure. You can follow them at *www.sixbackpacks.com*, where their motto is "Let's go!" They value raw and authentic cultural experiences, exploring the world's diversity, and connecting with people. Since

2012, the family has visited Asia, Europe, and Africa. They plan travel to more countries and hope you'll come along, enjoy the ride, and get inspired.

KATE COLLIER and **ERIC GERTNER** with their son Oscar make their home base in Charlottesville, where they own the specialty food store, coffee shop, and lunch cafe, *feast!* (*www.feastvirginia.com*). In 2015, the family downsized their house, sold their stuff, started homeschooling, and began their intermittent travel adventures. From three-month excursions to South America to impulsive three week jaunts to Barbados, the family is figuring out how to balance business responsibilities with the joys and freedom of family wanderlust.

NICOLAS DAMIANI is an Economics and Political Science student at Rice University. According to Michelle Damiani's bestselling *Il Bel Centro*, he spent a truly formative year in Spello, Italy, where he discovered a love of language, cats, and dessert. He enjoys drawing, fashion, and piano, and never forgets his keys.

ESTELLE DAVIDSON DEL PORTO majored in French, and met her French husband at the Thunderbird Graduate School of International Management. Estelle and Charles raised three multilingual children who live on three continents. They recently moved to Italy with their daughter Marjorie and son-in-law Chris, who are the new owners of a wine and olive producing property, Tenuta Marino di Monterado. Find out more at *www.tenutamarino.com*.

JULIE and **JODEE DESPAIN** are traveling the world and homeschooling their four kids, ages six to sixteen. After driving through Mexico for six months, they are traveling through Southeast Asia for a few months before ending their year-long trip in Eastern Europe. You can see their adventures on Instagram *@ifyougiveakidapassport* and *ifyougiveakidapassport.blogspot.com*.

CHERYL and **JASON FALCONER** are self-proclaimed novice travelers who are learning as they go. Tired of living a "normal" life of work, bills, and routine they sold their house and all their belongings to take their three young children and two dogs on a year-long travel adventure. Follow their journey on their Facebook page *@FamilyWorldTravelAdventure*.

MARIE FOX-EDGAR was born in Paris, France, and immigrated to the USA with her parents when she was 10-years-old. She currently resides in Northern Arizona on a fifty-acre ranch, with her three horses, four boxer dogs, and an assortment of cats. She is a fine art artist, exhibiting her work in local galleries as well as painting commissioned art.

RACHEL GERSON is a mother of three and a radiologist specializing in musculoskeletal radiology/women's imaging. She is based in Seattle but also works with Telemedicine Clinic in Barcelona, providing teleradiology to clients in the UK. Thirty years ago she was an exchange student in France (before gap years were called gap years, and people thought she was crazy). She believes the world is a big place and that life is too short not to get out there and live the variety.

As a child, **NELL GODDIN** rode in the back of a station wagon (no seatbelts!) from Virginia to Montreal, and has loved traveling ever since. She grew up in Richmond, a much less hip place in those days, and always dreamed of moving somewhere else. Nell graduated from Dartmouth College and has an MFA from Columbia. She writes the *Molly Sutton* cozy mystery series, among other books you can find at *www.nellgoddin.com*. She's constantly eyeing her suitcase, ready to take off.

SUE HARWOOD was born in the UK and spent three childhood years in Singapore. After working in UK local government, she and her then-husband moved to the US in 1989. They wanted to give their 6-year-old daughter the opportunity to see more of the world as Sue had. Their stay extended into permanent residence. Sue has re-married and works as a manager of a small company that imports and distributes British grocery items. Her favorite hobby is travel, instilled in her by her stay in Singapore.

NAOMI HATTAWAY is the founder of *I Am A Triangle* (*www.iamatriangle.com*), a community with thousands of global members who have lived away from their passport countries. Offering in-person gatherings in over eighty cities around the globe, I Am A Triangle offers resources for those pondering a move abroad, currently on their adventure, or are repatriating back "home." She also owns 8th & Home Real

Estate and Relocation (*www.8thandhome.com*), a US-based referral network matching families with real estate professionals who chase communities and not commissions.

JERRY JONES is a cross-cultural trainer and coach who lives with his wife and two children in Qingdao, China. He works as a Transition Specialist with Leadership Development International, serving the staff of seven International Schools in China and the United Arab Emirates. He loves exploring the joys and challenges of crossing cultures and helping people start, stay, and leave their international assignments well. He writes about transition and life abroad at *www.thecultureblend.com*.

After years of late-night big-dream conversations, **MATT** and **TANIA LANDIN** quit their jobs, sold their posses-sions, and left their US home with their three daughters and sweet labradoodle to adventure abroad together. In June 2016 while traveling around Europe, they began *www.aroundtheworldstories.com* creating audio stories for kids about countries and cultures around the world. Now,

they are full-time traveling storytellers and world-schoolers and are currently traveling through the UK and plotting their next global storytelling adventure.

KIRSTY LARMOUR, her husband, and two children were born in four different countries. They have been nomadic for many years, sometimes settling and oftentimes traveling. There was that one time when they jumped in the family car and set off on a 60,000 km road trip from the Middle East and across three continents, or that other time when they took the train from Hong Kong to England for fun! Kirsty documents their travels on Instagram at *www.instagram.com/kirstylarmour* and her blog *www.kirstylarmourblog.com*.

The **LEWIS FAMILY** originates from South Wales. The children were twenty-one, nineteen, and sixteen when the family set off for Malaysia in 2006 (only Richard moved to live in Kuala Lumpur, the girls were studying at UK universities but both

came out to stay for frequent long holidays). All five family members have very fond memories of the stay in Malaysia and view this as one of the best opportunities the family had.

GABRIELLA and **VERNON LINDSAY** left their jobs to move to Mexico with their three children in 2016, hoping to live more with less. As a lifestyle strategist, Gabriella manages *La Vida Lindsay*, helping others become location independent. Vernon is a personal development coach, consultant, writer, and speaker. Together they have been featured on HGTV, Thrive Global, The Good Men Project, The Black Expat, and Naturally Curly. You can find them at *www.lavidalindsay.com*.

JENNIFER MASSARO can be found working as a public relations professional at Nutanix when she's not out sailing. She holds an MBA from Santa Clara University and an undergraduate degree in Urban Planning from the University of California, San Diego. Jennifer presents to groups of sailors and non-sailors alike about life lessons learned from sailing around the world. Follow their sailing journey and get her social media links at *www.easethemain.com*.

AMANDA MOUTTAKI is a mom of two tween boys. They moved to Morocco, her husband's home country, in 2013 with the plan to stay for one year. It's now year five and they have no plans to leave! Amanda is a blogger and freelance writer and she and her husband own a food tour company in Marrakech. They love traveling whenever and wherever possible. You can find Amanda at *www.marocmama.com* and their business at *www.marrakechfoodtours.com*.

NITSA OLIVADOTI chronicles thoughts from her life abroad on her Facebook blog *Bridge the Divide*. The stories will be compiled in her upcoming book with the same title. Nitsa is fascinated with voices of growth and migration and is the author of the *Cicada Series* (available on Amazon), books based on the life of her Greek grandmother. Nitsa also writes for *I am A Triangle*, an online community for those living overseas, moving home, or considering life in a new country.

ALLYSON SHAMES is a mother and writer who lived abroad three separate times many years ago, in Brussels, London, and Cossonay-Ville, Switzerland. She currently lives with her husband, three children, two dogs and a cat in Charlottesville, Virginia. Her short stories and essays have appeared in *Brain, Child*, *Literary Mama*, and *The Jewish Literary Journal*.

ALLISON SHERMAN, her husband, and two girls were living in Arizona before they set off for a two-year trip to Panama in 2014. After a few months, they instead decided on an open-ended exploration of the world. They now travel where their interests take them, attempting to follow spring-like weather. Sometimes they dig roots into a community, and other times they travel like their hair is on fire, checking all the tourist boxes. They plan to travel until 2020. Follow along on their adventures at *www.letsjusttravel.com*.

ALISHA STAMP, her husband, and three children live in Kyrgyzstan, in the heart of Central Asia. Before that they lived in Tanzania, and have many "homes" in the United States. They have traveled through East Africa, Europe, and now Asia...and they aren't finished yet. In their free time they read, craft, hike, ski, and homeschool. Their website encourages travelers to explore their corner of the world and can be found at *www.taiganexpeditions.com*.

M'KENZIE TILLOTSON is the founder/editor of the travel blog *Five Take Flight*. She sold her house to travel the world with her husband and three little kids. She specializes in writing about how to successfully travel with young children, giving real world tips and honest personal travel stories. Her aim is to inspire families to travel so that in a shrinking world the next generation can have broader minds. You can find her work at *www.fivetakeflight.com*.

ASTRID VINJE is a mom of three, and an avid traveler. She has visited over thirty countries, and writes about her family travel adventures on her blog *The Wandering Daughter*. She loves experiencing new things with her family, and is currently preparing to embark on a multi-year, multi-country adventure around the world with her husband and two kids. You can find her blog at *www.thewanderingdaughter.com*.

SARA WARDEN, a former musical theatre dancer performed on the stage in New York and nationally, as well as for TV and film. Always drawn to traveling, she taught dance in Beijing and made Morocco her home for over seven years. There she taught dance and homeschooled her kids, going wherever the learning led them. The family has moved back to the States, where they've committed to staying for the next few years...but the dreaming has already begun of where to move next.

HEIDI and **ALAN WAGONER** are passionate about travel (more than fifty countries) and authors of the travel blog *wagonersabroad.com*. In 2012 they quit the "perfect American life" and moved to Southern Spain with their two kids, and spent a year as nomads exploring Southeast Asia. Spain is their home base, and they help families move to Spain through their consulting and ebooks. The Wagoners are proof you can make your dreams come true.

NICA WATERS is a teacher and entrepreneur who spends much of her time trying to convince people that they can do more than they think they can. She lives with her husband and rapidly-growing teenagers in Charlottesville, Virginia, working and planning for the next adventure, which will be on board the same twenty-eight foot boat that has already carried them across miles of ocean. You can learn about Nica's work at *www.nicawaters.com*.

MELISSA WIRINGI is a mother of three children in a blended family, and a survivor of domestic violence. She has been paying off debt and saving for travel since 2015, with a launch date in 2018. Melissa authored a book detailing her journey through violence and depression to happiness and success, titled *Domestic Violence on Ice*. She is a business coach, helping women develop location-independent businesses. Find out more *www.melissawiringi.com*.

STEPHANIE YODER is a girl who can't sit still! Since 2009 she has been traveling the world and writing about her adventures on her website *Why Wait to See the World* (*www.whywaittoseetheworld.com*). In 2017, she moved from Seattle to Bologna, Italy, with her husband, toddler, and her little mutt Leo.

RESOURCES

MAKING MONEY ABROAD

Jobbatical · *www.Jobbatical.com*

Res Artis (residency program for artists and writers, some allow families)
www.resartis.org

Transitions Abroad · *www.transitionsabroad.com*

Workaway · *www.workaway.com*

The Working Traveler · *www.the-working-traveller.com*

Upwork (global freelancing platform) · *www.upwork.com*

TEACHING ENGLISH

DaDa (based in China) · *www.dadaabc.com/teacher/job*

Dave's ESL cafe (teach ESL online) · *www.eslcafe.com*

Higher Ed Jobs (if you have an advanced degree) · *www.higheredjobs.com*

TAL Education (teach ESL online)
teacheslonlineanywhere.com/tal-education-teach-esl-online

VIPKID (2017 Forbes pick as #1 "Work from Home" company)
www.vipkidteachers.com

Also, join and query in family travel oriented Facebook groups for more ideas,
particularly specific to where you want to land

VOLUNTEERING

Helpx.net (more diverse than WWOOF, you pay for access to global listings)
www.helpx.net

Numundo (eco-villages, intentional communities, volunteer opportunities)
www.numundo.org

Transitions Abroad (work and volunteer opportunities) · *www.transitionsabroad.com*

Workaway (build, work on a property, teach English, again for bed and board.
This one will take some digging for families) · *www.workaway.info*

Volunteer South America · *volunteersouthamerica.net*

World Wide Opportunities on Organic Farms (work on a farm in exchange for
bed and board, you need to pay for access to listings by country) · *www.wwoof.net*

Also, post in Facebook groups for communities you are interested in to find out
about local opportunities

FINDING AIRFARE DEALS

The Flight Deal · *www.theflightdeal.com*

Hopper (app for finding cheap fares, including the best time to buy) · *www.hopper.com*

Kayak · *www.kayak.com*

Next Vacay · *www.nextvacay.com*

Skyscanner · *www.skyscanner.com*

Research small carrier airlines in the region you'll be. RyanAir is a budget airline in Europe,
there are many in Asia such as Air Asia, Bangkok Airways, Vietnam Airlines. Find out which
are the lowest cost airlines in the region you'll be going, and then try to plan your travel
around airports that airline serves.

FOR RV-ERS AND ROAD-TRIPPERS

iOverlander app · For finding places to park up

Park4Night app · Llists every type of parking available, wherever you are in Europe so
you can choose between campsites, free parking, aires and much more.

FINDING A BED OR RENTING YOUR HOME

Academic Homes · *www.academichomes.com*

Airbnb · *www.airbnb.com*

Couch Surfing · *www.couchsurfing.com*

Home Exchange · *www.homeexchange.com*

Housesitting, check out Hecktik Travels (they have figured out how to travel by housesitting) · *www.hecktictravels.com*

House Trip, vacation rentals connected to TripAdvisor · *www.housetrip.com*

Love Home Swap · *www.lovehomeswap.com*

Sabbatical Homes · *www.sabbaticalhomes.com*

Tripping, compares and filters other booking sites · *www.tripping.com*

Vacation Rental By Owner · *www.vrbo.com*

Vida Rustica, limited to home rentals in Andalusia · *www.vidarustica.com*

World Schooler Exchange (also useful for finding rentals, pet-sitting, and work exchanges) · *www.worldschoolerexchange.com*

Also, post inquiries in Facebook groups for your destination for more leads

BUDGETING

Calculating costs of living in other countries · *www.numbeo.com*

YNAB ("You Need a Budget", budgeting tools) · *www.youneedabudget.com*

GETTING YOUR BUSINESS READY FOR YOU TO LEAVE

Emyth · *www.emyth.com/business-coaching*

WHAT TO DO WITH YOUR MAIL

Virtual Post Mail · *www.Virtualpostmail.com*

PHONES

Project Fi · *fi.google.com*

GLOBAL HEALTH INSURANCE

IMG · *www.imglobal.com*

MOVING YOUR PET

Air Animal · *www.airanimal.com*

LANGUAGE LEARNING

CD's/videos can often be found on eBay

Duolingo App for any platform

Italki · *www.italki.com*

Memrise · *www.memrise.com*

Muzzy videos

Michel Thomas CD's · *www.michelthomas.com*

Pimsleur CD's · *www.pimsleur.com*

Rosetta Stone (often a discount on *www.stacksocial.com*) · *www.rosettastone.com*

Udemy · *www.udemy.com/courses/language*

Watch movies/TV shows in your target language, listen to the radio (many foreign ratio stations are accessible on-line)

FOR HISTORY BUFFS
(YOURSELF OR AS PART OF HOMESCHOOLING)

History of Europe by Rick Steves

The Story of the World by Margaret Wise Brown

WORLD-SCHOOLING RESOURCES

Acellus (an accredited online school, also offers tutoring)
www.acellusacademy.com

Brain Chase Academy (adventure oriented courses) · *www.brainchase.com*

Calvert Education (curriculum and lesson plans to help parents educate children)
www.calverteducation.com

Christa McAuliffe Academy School of Arts and Sciences
(accredited, personalized courses) · *www.cmasas.org*

Classes by Beth (live and recorded classes) · *www.classesbybeth.com*

Coursera (offers courses and degrees) · *www.coursera.org*

Crash Course (supplemental videos) · *www.youtube.com/user/crashcourse*

High schools and universities often offer courses or degree programs;
Google is your friend here

IXL (comprehensive, personalized K-12 curriculum) · *www.ixl.com*

K12 (an online school) · *www.k12.com*

Khan Academy (supplemental videos) · *www.khanacademy.com*

Open Tent Academy (classes for grades 3-12) · *www.opententacademy.com*

Outschool (small, online classes) · *www.outschool.com*

Time 4 Learning (classes and lesson plans for grades K-5) · *www.time4learning.com*

FURNISHING YOUR ADOPTED HOME

Craigslist for your country

Facebook Marketplace

Google will lead you to local marketplaces

LONG-TERM CAR RENTAL

In some places you can buy a used car locally, some it's more difficult (in Italy, for instance, it's complicated for a foreigner to own a car, so leasing is a better option)

Mechanics in some places will lease affordable cars

Peugot has a long-term lease program

Rental car companies often have long-term rental plans

BLOGGERS TO FOLLOW FOR DETAILS ON THE WORLD TRAVEL EXPERIENCE

Lisa Cole · *www.sixbackpacks.com*

Julie Despain · *ifyougiveakidapassport.blogspot.com*

Jerry Jones · *www.thecultureblend.com*

Jennifer Massaro · *www.easethemain.com*

M'Kenzie Tillotson · *www.fivetakeflight.com*

Wagoners Abroad · *www.wagonersabroad.com*

World Travel Family (outlines how to make money via blogging) · *www.worldtravelfamily.com*

Stephanie Yoder · *www.whywaittoseetheworld.com*

CONNECTING WITH EXPATS

Facebook groups in your intended community

Mum Abroad (Europe's leading online resource for English-speaking families living in, relocating to, and holidaying in Spain, Italy, France and Germany) *www.mumabroad.com*

WhatsApp

REPATRIATION

I am a Triangle · *www.iamatriangle.com*

Leaving Well or Leaving Happy, Jerry Jones *www.alifeoverseas.com/leaving-happy-or-leaving-well*

This is Where You Belong, Melody Warnick · *www.melodywarnick.com*

FURTHER INSPIRATION

Check out podcasts like *The Expat Chat* · *www.theexpatchat.com*

ADDITIONAL RESOURCES

Information for expats · *www.expatfocus.com*

Information for expats · *www.expatexchange.com*

Information for expats · *www.internations.com*

Exploring issues of relocation with children · *www.expatchild.com*

SOMETHING MISSING?

If you have a question, please hop onto our "The Road Taken" Facebook page and ask us anything.

AFTERWORD

I'm so glad that you stayed until the closing credits!

Would you consider leaving a short review of *The Road Taken* wherever you purchase books? I would be ever so grateful. You can also contact me directly to let me know what you thought of *The Road Taken* at *www.michelledamiani.com*, where you can find links to my contact information as well as my social media outlets.

If you enjoyed *The Road Taken* and want to read more about how we created a home in the green heart of Italy, I encourage you to pick up my first book, *Il Bel Centro: A Year in the Beautiful Center*.

Want information about upcoming book giveaways and releases? Sign up for my newsletter *Contorni* (*A Little Something Extra on the Side*) for updates. Once every couple of months I'll contact you with that information, as well as travel gems only locals know, tantalizing recipes, and Italian inspirations. You can sign up at *bit.ly/ContorniSignUp*.

I hope you enjoyed your time with us. We're so happy you stopped by.

ACKNOWLEDGMENTS

I want to take a moment to thank our contributors. They opened their hearts to this project and were patient with my (many) nosy follow-up questions. Special thanks to Kirsty Larmour for the gift of her photography. It is fair to say that without you all, this book would have been a spare novella. You added the heft and the spice, and I am so grateful.

As usual, I handed Emily Morrison a jumbled mess and she methodically told me how to untangle the knots to create a cohesive manuscript. And then she read it again. A writer couldn't ask for a better editor and friend. Kristine Bean assiduously researched foreign words and pointed out my punctuation errors; I'm so lucky to have her eagle eyes on my team. Dora Joffroy de Piña lent the gift of her sharp vision to the final manuscript, cleaning up typographical errors that others would miss.

My husband, Keith, dipped his toe back into the world of design to create the cover and book styling. A thousand thanks for his creativity and patience. Plus, for all those times he listened while I waxed rhapsodic about this book as I fell headlong in love.

Nell Goddin not only took time from her writing to contribute to this book, but also continues to make herself available whenever I have a question about the industry. Even without the promise of a keto cocktail.

It's easy for independently-published authors to drift alone. All of you kept me afloat, and my thanks know no bounds.

ABOUT THE AUTHOR

MICHELLE DAMIANI is a freelance writer and clinical psychologist currently living in Charlottesville, Virginia. Her heart, however, is in Spello, Italy, where she and her family spent a year growing accustomed to being fish out of water, grappling with the hardships of parenting on foreign soil, and ultimately cleaving into the soul of Italian village life. While in Italy, Michelle used the time that her children were in Italian public schools to write a blog about their experiences. Once back in Charlottesville, she transformed the blog into a book, *Il Bel Centro: A Year in the Beautiful Center*. Her daily life in Umbria later inspired her novel, *Santa Lucia*. Written in sweeping telenovela style, and packed with drama, *Santa Lucia* is nonetheless grounded in the green heart of Italy. When not writing, doing therapy, or relaxing with her family, she can be found experimenting in the kitchen or tucked away with a travel memoir, dreaming of once again hitting the open road. You can find out more at *www.michelledamiani.com*.

CPSIA information can be obtained
at www.ICGtesting.com
Printed in the USA
FSHW01n0754071018
52814FS